Generous-Minded Women

THE WINSOR LAMP

GRADUATION 1920

Generous-Minded Women

A HISTORY OF THE WINSOR SCHOOL

Dianne Haley

MEMOIRS UNLIMITED
Beverly, Massachusetts

To all Winsor teachers, past and present

The Winsor School is grateful to the extraordinary Class of 1957, who have generously underwritten the publication of this book.

Library of Congress Cataloguing-in-Publication Data
Haley, Dianne.
Generous-minded women : a history of the Winsor School /
Dianne Haley.
pages cm
Includes bibliographical references and index.
ISBN 978-0-9830988-1-2 (alk. paper)
1. Winsor School (Boston, Mass.)—History. I. Title.
LD7501.B7H35 2012
373.22'20974461—dc23   2012002279

Except for the aerial view on page 38, all illustrations
are from the Winsor Archives.

Design by Joyce C. Weston
Manufactured in the United States of America

Contents

❦

Introduction

※❦❀❦※

HOW DIFFICULT IT IS to put oneself into an earlier time period! This is the frustration of examining history: we think we can know the past, but the baggage of our contemporary lives clouds our best attempts to understand.

Girls and young women in the twenty-first century have such a clouded awareness of the lives of the females of the 1800s in Boston. They may even be accused of taking for granted their freedom to learn, to speak, to play, and even to dress as they please. It was a desire to teach my Winsor students about the earlier days of their school that motivated me to embark on this book and to spend over seven years exploring The Winsor School archives.

The story of The Winsor School is fascinating—or, rather, the stories. There are the plucky students, the indefatigable teachers, the ambitious and groundbreaking graduates, the generous parents: there are stories galore. Books and authors I had never heard of sprang to life thanks to the modern miracle, the Internet. There were myths to uncover and sometimes to debunk. There were grave editorials, funny poems, and clever fables in the *Winsor Lamp*.

I dedicate this book to every teacher who has taught in a Winsor classroom in the hope that those who are still alive will forgive my sentence structure and comma use and acknowledge the difficulty of choosing what to include and what not to include.

To one magnificent person I give as much thanks as it is possible to give: I could not have written this book without Jane Hoeffel Otte 1957. Her knowledge of the archives, her keen editorial eye, her expertise as a writer herself, and her cheerful encouragement have made this history what it is. More than anything else, she supported my vision and blessed my sometimes quirky decisions.

Two former Directors read my drafts and made invaluable and courteous suggestions. Virginia Wing (who hired me in 1977) and Carolyn McClintock Peter (who let me grow as I stayed) represent for me and for many others the essence of excellent leadership. Two of Winsor's finest teachers,

Jennifer Slingerland Skeele 1971 and Dorian Bowman, also read the manuscript and helped me keep moving forward. Both Kathy Cole and Rachel Stettler helped by reading the final manuscript. Thanks to all.

Most of the work I did on my own with my good friend Google. I wish there had been time to talk to and request help from the many individuals whose knowledge of Winsor could have made this a better book, but—alas—time ran out and I had never realized how long the book would take. It is mostly my own personal research and interpretation, and the omissions and errors are mine alone. Perhaps some other lucky person can pick up from here and make the history fuller and more even.

As a classicist, I have always loved history. The older I grow, the more I realize how wonderful it is that we have the words, deeds, and images of the past. We are privileged to be able to look at the people who came before us and to be able to turn aside from the noisy and glittering present to learn valuable lessons from our predecessors. Following their stories helps us to create our own.

I considered calling the book *The Privilege of Knowledge.* The phrase occurs in a graduation speech by Ruth Graves 1917 called "Knowledge in Women's Work" (*Winsor Lamp*, Graduation Issue, 1917). Her speech acknowledges the gifts of disciplined thinking and the blessings of a Winsor graduate's schooling, which will "make her time, her talents, her energies, worthily useful to mankind. For the flower of knowledge is service." Ruth Graves defines the future duties of her classmates as the traditional ones of the "women's sphere," but she exhorts her listener to go beyond the home and family to use her education to be "the housekeeper of the nation" who cares about healthful food and housing for all, who beautifies her town, who is concerned about "the social evils confronting the commonweal." I think she would be proud to see what the Winsor graduates of the twenty-first century are giving to the world. I know she would be proud of the many ways in which the School has reached out to extend to so many, many girls the privilege of having a Winsor education.

I hope that readers will read the book with an open spirit and a curiosity to explore further the aspects of the School or of education in general that intrigue them.

Generous-Minded Women

.

Chapter 1

It was either the next year or very soon after, that the school moved out of its back door, across the alley, into the back door of a house on Newbury Street. A great step in advance! A quiet street and more refinement and dignity in its surroundings.

—Dorothy Appleton Weld 1895

For us to reach school daily at 9 A.M. meant breakfast at 7:30, walk or run ½ mile to catch the 8:04 train to Boston . . . up over Beacon Hill to our destination in the Back Bay, picking up various classmates enroute.

—Susan M. Hallowell 1901

Mary Pickard Winsor in 1885.

The Historical Setting

✦✦✦

"To reach the land beyond the strife"

*I*N 1886, WHEN WINSOR'S STORY BEGINS, Americans were living in one of the most vibrant and productive periods in the history of the country, a time of scientific advances as groundbreaking and startling as those in the late twentieth century. That extraordinary period of American innovation and ingenuity in the late nineteenth century, which brought us, among other things, the telephone and the phonograph, was so full of creativity and discovery that it in many ways resembles the end of the twentieth century, when the technology of communication and music reproduction made those earlier inventions almost unnecessary, especially for young people.

The School's earliest history is part of the larger story of other histories: the city of Boston after the tumult of the Civil War, the interest in the education for girls fostered by the women's rights movement, the country's beginning the second century of its astonishing democracy, and the world's entering the twentieth century in the midst of radical social, religious, and scientific changes. As one follows the historical record into the twenty-first century, one perceives the story of how the School reflected and reacted to its environment, both locally and globally.

The story of The Winsor School contains within it innumerable less well-known stories. These tales tell of determined parents who have supported the School, of intelligent, lively girls who matured into strong young women within its walls, and of the erecting and widening of those walls.

Not everyone's story can be told, for there are literally thousands of individuals who have taught and learned and built and paid for and cleaned and protected and nurtured the School. Some stories, however, illuminate what is special about the School and illustrate the larger history of an educational institution that began without fanfare and grew to impressive size and importance through the efforts and energy of many tireless individuals.

In the decades after the Civil War, the country was also in the midst of a flourishing of civic pride, urban expansion, and cultural blooming that—especially in Boston—would lay the foundations for what American cities would be a century later. Our iPhones and Blackberries and TiVos, the diversity and excellence of Boston's culture, the architectural landmarks that are still being created—all of these advances grew from seeds planted a century before. Winsor itself—I will often use the name "Winsor" as a shortcut: the early Back Bay school was Miss Winsor's School, and the name was changed in 1910 to The Winsor School—was a part of the social and educational flowering that was beginning to give young women new ways to contribute to the world. Their opportunity to receive an education equivalent to that of their brothers was hastened because girls' roles in the household were rapidly changing. Winsor maintained its commitment to the idea that girls and young women should be specially prepared to develop themselves for the unexpected possibilities.

From a woman's perspective, the turn of the century brought the inventions that would gradually diminish the drudgery of housekeeping: the electric washing machine (1900), the electric stove (1906), and the electric vacuum cleaner (1907). As homes were transformed by electricity, upper-middle-class wives and mothers no longer needed so much household help from servants.

It is likely that no other invention has changed more radically in the last century than the telephone. Alexander Graham Bell, a teacher of the deaf and teachers of the deaf, was a professor of vocal physiology at Boston University. He first patented his telephone in 1876, and although there is no record of such a device in Miss Winsor's early schools, we know that she requested one in the new building at Longwood: "Miss Winsor writes me that there should be provision made for a public telephone somewhere in the building. I suppose she means a slot machine in addition to the one in her private office."[1]

Mary Winsor could not have imagined that her twentieth-century counterpart would carry around with her a tiny cell phone that worked without wires and would even let her see who was calling before she answered—something a school head might find valuable both then and now. Nor could she have foreseen nearly every student in the School carrying such a device.

In 1886, the year Mary Pickard Winsor started her school, two experimenters, Chichester Bell, Alexander's cousin, and Charles Sumner Tainter, building on Thomas Edison's earlier efforts, patented the first gramophone—a machine that reproduced music exactly as it had been played. In 1887 Emile Berliner patented his version of the gramophone and began commercial production of disks with etched sound grooves. His earliest gramophone records were disks only slightly bigger (12.7 cm) than the modern CD disc (11.5 cm), recorded on one side only. When records and phonographs became available later on in the century, a gift of musical recordings from the Carnegie

Corporation would thrill Mary Winsor, who played them for students at some of the Monday morning assemblies. Teachers would have to wait until 1962 to have easy access to cassette tapes in their classrooms, although magnetic tape recording had been invented in 1928. No one could have predicted that weekly assemblies would someday feature video recordings produced by students themselves.

In 1880 Thomas Edison and J. W. Swan, independently of each other, had created usable electric lights, and two years later Boston's Bijou Theatre became the first American playhouse lit exclusively by electricity rather than by limelight, which was created by burning quicklime (calcium oxide). The first performance was Gilbert and Sullivan's *Iolanthe*. And in the year before Mary Winsor began teaching in her first little school for eight girls at 334 Boylston Street, Karl Benz of Germany built a single-cylinder engine for a motorcar. The automobile would significantly contribute to the success of the Fenway site of The Winsor School.

Other improvements and innovations in transportation would be factors in Winsor's growth. Most significantly for The Winsor School, the first railroad line would run from downtown Boston to Brookline. Boston was the first city to build electric traction for a large-scale rapid-transit system. Its development corresponded to and accelerated the city's geographical expansion to its west, which was spurred on by a need for more open space and by the development of the Emerald Necklace park system. In addition, the neighborhoods of the city were changing as the second generation of immigrant families was able to purchase houses.

Boston was also growing intellectually and developing a rich artistic, architectural, and educational life. The impressive Boston Public Library building was begun in 1887 in the newly formed Copley Square at what had been the intersection of Huntington Avenue and Boylston Street. Across the square from the library was the dramatic new edifice of Trinity Church, which had been completed in 1877. Trinity's congregation had lost its original building on Summer Street in downtown Boston in the catastrophic fire of 1872. No fire in Boston was larger or more costly than that conflagration, which began on the evening of November 9, 1872, and burned until late afternoon on the following day. Nearly a thousand financial firms and businesses were burned out, as were warehouses, dry goods stores, and public buildings. At least twenty people are known to have died in the fire. The rebuilding of the downtown area paralleled the growth of the city westward into the Back Bay area, stretching the boundaries of the city to Massachusetts Avenue and its intersection with Huntington Avenue, where Symphony Hall was built in 1900. The city grew to include the Fenway area, and there were plans for an art museum just six blocks from the site on the Riverway where the new building for The Winsor School was constructed in 1909.

In his history of the Roxbury Latin School, *Schola Illustris*, F. Washington

Jarvis tracks the rapid population growth in Boston during the eighteenth and nineteenth centuries: from 1700 to the date of Boston's officially becoming a city in January 1822, the population grew from 6,700 to 43,000.[2] Because of this, the city's various sections were continually being redefined, as those who could afford to eagerly built new residences in the newly filled-in Back Bay, by 1870 essentially abandoning the South End, which until then had been an upper-class neighborhood of houses built around elegant squares and small parks. As European immigration to Boston increased and the city's center shifted, single-family homes in the South End were transformed into boardinghouses, and some wealthy families were building large houses in the nearly rural areas that today are called suburbs. By 1875 further immigration had increased the population of Boston to 341,000.[3] William Dean Howells's novel *The Rise of Silas Lapham* is an enlightening picture of the social and economic changes in Boston during this period.

As the population grew, Boston began to look different and feel different. The demands of more people living in the city and the rapidly burgeoning land development stimulated civic efforts to improve the city. The changes also created stress: Boston was no longer a homogeneous small city of Anglo-Protestants who shared common values even across class lines. The diversity of the population as a result of immigration challenged the culture and the assumptions of the oldest families in Boston. The established citizenry throughout the country in the mid-1800s believed in educating all children for democracy, improving living conditions for the worker classes, setting aside public parkland, and protecting the health of citizens. Many of these concerns took on new urgency as large numbers of immigrants and newly freed southern blacks came to the cities. Cities and institutions everywhere were trying to adapt to the needs and possibilities of a nation newly defined after the War between the States. Boston continued to be an intellectual and forward-thinking hub of activity—a consistently powerful center for the abolitionist movement as well as a source of leadership for the female suffrage movement—and the city's cultural life flowered. Boston's long tradition of excellence in higher education and the flourishing of its arts found expression during the 1880s in the works of writers, philosophers, and painters. Henry James published *The Bostonians* in 1886, and Mary Baker Eddy's Mother Church was built just beyond Copley Square in 1894. John Singer Sargent in 1888 painted the striking full-length portrait of Isabella Stewart Gardner that now hangs in the museum she opened to the public on New Year's Day in 1903. Several Winsor-related women sat for Sargent, including one of Winsor's incorporators, Harriett Lawrence Hemenway (Mrs. Augustus Jr.), who with her friend Minna Hall founded the Massachusetts Audubon Society in 1896.

The enthusiasm about new possibilities and fresh beginnings was enhanced by "premillennialism" fervor at the end of the nineteenth century, not unlike the excitement and wariness that prevailed on the eve of the year 2000.[4] In Massachusetts there were at least two strands to the idealism and promise that underlay the new social concern. Always a religious town, Boston continued to be a place where people took their churchgoing seriously. There had from early years been an Episcopalian-Unitarian dichotomy in the city, but after the Civil War the picture was fractured by the tensions of abolition, suffrage rights for blacks and women, and a new generation of activist preachers who could not easily be categorized under the old labels. The Anglican heritage was strong, and the Episcopalians founded several schools, mostly to educate boys. The Congregationalists (sometimes called Trinitarians), whose roots were in the Puritan beginnings, championed public schools, as did the more liberal Unitarians. This commitment to social justice had grown from the values and beliefs of the city's founders.

The founders of The Winsor School designated the School "unsectarian" in their bylaws.[5] There was never a policy of excluding any religious or ethnic group from the School. Winsor, however, developed as it did because of the social stratification of Boston neighborhoods at the time and, as such, grew out of the School's white, Protestant clientele who lived near its original location. If the School had any bias, it was toward the educated and intellectuals of the city, without regard for religion. The earliest class rosters contain the names of girls from both Jewish and Catholic families.

The Civil War and the assassination of President Lincoln deeply affected the educated families of Boston. Some of their brightest young men had died; Charles Russell Lowell and Robert Gould Shaw, both with connections to Winsor's founders, were bitterly mourned. The patriotism and abolitionism of the war years had been particularly fervent throughout Massachusetts. The combined struggles to end slavery and to expand women's rights had a long history in Boston. The New England Anti-Slavery Society, founded in 1831 by a Bostonian, William Lloyd Garrison, donated to the national organization more than $10,000, a sum "larger than that contributed even by the Empire State; more than five times as much as was given by Ohio, though there are more anti-slavery societies in that State than in this Commonwealth; more than was contributed by Maine, New Hampshire, Vermont, Rhode-Island, Connecticut, and Penn., though the number of their societies, jointly, is nearly twice as large as exists in our own State."[6]

The girls in a small school on Boylston Street in Boston's Back Bay began to feel the effects of these striking social and political shifts, little knowing that they were to be part of remarkable educational advances. The new ideas affected girls in nearly all kinds of schools; some of their mothers and grandmothers were disgruntled that their demands for rights and suffrage had been relegated to second place after the survival of the Union and the emancipation of the slaves. Families that routinely sent their sons to Harvard or Princeton had decided that they wished their daughters to have the same quality education and the opportunity to attend college. Eventually they were demanding girls' schools that were comparable to the highly regarded boys' schools such as Andover, St. Paul's, Groton, and the Roxbury Latin School.

The education of young children grew organically out of the principal nineteenth-century view that the home was the basis of all training, moral and otherwise, and that the family was the source of information on how to live. At the end of the nineteenth century in Boston, most girls were still being educated at home and in small, neighborhood schools like Miss Winsor's. At the time Boston did have one very good educational option for girls: Girls' Latin School, a sister school to the all-boys Boston Latin School, had been established in 1877 to provide the same European-based classical education that had been available to boys since 1635. Both of these schools were, of course, public and open to all who met the admission requirements.

Boston was renowned for providing free education to all, and in the centuries following the Latin School's founding, Boston public schools acquired a reputation for excellence. There was a place for everyone, and for everyone there was opportunity for a good education. (The system, however, had maintained separate "caste schools" for blacks until 1855.)[7] Children of every social class were educated, but the children of newer immigrants probably reaped the most precious benefits of Boston's fine school system. Mary Antin, in her stirring book *The Promised Land*, describes the thrill of coming to Boston from eastern Europe and being allowed to learn freely and happily under supportive and gifted women teachers at the Girls' Latin School.[8] That school, like Winsor, was small at the beginning, enrolling only thirty-seven students in 1878 and only six in the first graduating class in 1880.

The public schools in Boston grew out of the Puritan conviction that education was a necessary part of training citizens. In the beginning, however, because the brightest boys were also being groomed for the ministry, the curriculum had a Protestant and Episcopal slant. Newcomers from countries like Ireland and Italy realized that their children were losing a sense of their Catholic heritage, and they sought to live near each other and near their parish church. As early as 1829 the Provincial Council of Bishops had urged Catholic communities to establish their own schools,[9] and in 1852 the First Plenary Council in Baltimore decreed that next to every Catholic parish church there should be established a Catholic school.[10]

The many small "dame schools" (like Miss Winsor's) scattered throughout the city in 1886 were not part of the public school system. Nor did they offer a rigorous high school curriculum. Furthermore, parents preferred to keep their daughters close to home. Most of the families who sent their girls to Miss Winsor's lived on Beacon Hill and in the Back Bay; it was, in other words, the neighborhood school, one of many in the city. At the beginning, the Brooks daughters commuted about five miles from Medford on a daily commuter line run by the Boston & Maine Railroad.

The town house at 21 Marlborough Street was the fifth location of Miss Winsor's School in the Back Bay and is the only building in which the School operated before moving to the Riverway that is still in existence.

When Mary Pickard Winsor took her first steps in teaching young women at her own school in the Back Bay, she was taking her place in a traditional yet already outmoded method of educating girls. She had some untraditional ideas, however, about the goal of women's education. In addition to the usual courses in the arts, French, literature, and history, she added more challenging work as the original class moved forward each year, soon offering the Latin, mathematics, and science courses that would prepare a girl to take entrance examinations for Radcliffe or Bryn Mawr. In 1893 the first graduate went to college; by 1895 there were "seven well-established classes [that is, grade levels]." This seriousness of purpose attracted the attention of more and more parents whose families were settling the Back Bay. Records show that girls came to Winsor from no fewer than eighty-eight dame schools, but Miss Winsor's had become one of the most respected and forward-thinking; it had attracted educated teachers, developed a progressive and ever-widening curriculum, and continually sent young women on to graduate from excellent colleges. Miss Winsor's was also fortunate in being in a Back Bay neighborhood where the well-to-do and educated resided. In 1908, when the student body had grown to more than two hundred girls, Mary Winsor found herself being asked by a group of parents to take a giant leap from the Back Bay out to a virtually unsettled area on the edge of Boston proper, where a group of pioneering Bostonians was planning to establish a new school for their daughters.

It was probably a larger leap for forty-nine-year-old Mary Winsor than we can imagine, and we know that at the start she refused the headship of the proposed new school in the Fenway. "I blush to say that fear of huge, unknown expense of running such an establishment, coupled with fear of an old dog's inability to learn new tricks—for I was almost fifty years old—moved me to refuse their magnificent offer."[11] The founders had at first asked Mary Winsor to rent the new building they were planning, and it was only when they removed the responsibility of handling the finances of the school that she took what she called "a risk."[12] Mary Winsor, however, did ask for complete freedom to choose both pupils and teachers, and, having attained that assurance, she accepted the offer to be the Director (she had eschewed the titles "headmistress" and "head") of what would become a modern school in a carefully designed building in a new area of the city. It would be a major step forward for girls' education in Boston.

> So we moved out to Longwood, as this region was then called, and became an incorporated school, with our name only slightly altered, since the Graduate Club had begged that the old name should not be completely given up, or replaced by that of St. Botolph, as I had suggested. The lamp and the banner came with us, presented by the last class to graduate from Beacon Street. . . . All those who came out to Pilgrim Road with me, in 1910, will remember how far from a bed of roses our new Paradise proved, for the first few months. But finally the carpenters departed. We cleaned up and quieted down. Peace descended and joy arrived.[13]

A century after this move to Longwood, Winsor's setting continues to be significant. The Longwood area is the vibrant home of numerous schools, colleges, graduate schools, hospitals, and research laboratories; Winsor is the only nonsectarian, independent high school for girls in the city of Boston, and its roster of student names reflects the diversity of a metropolitan area that attracts a global community. It is one of the most highly acclaimed schools for girls in the country. By the time The Winsor School was celebrating its 125th year, both the students and the faculty were using technology that could not have been dreamed of in 1886: telephones without wires, typewriters replaced by tiny keyboards and screens, cameras as small as a deck of cards, and personal music systems that could play every song ever written. The School had four fully equipped computer labs, each teacher had a laptop computer for personal teaching use, the annunciator* (long gone) came back in the form of an updated public address and telephone system to meet the security needs of the treacherous modern world, and the public telephone

---

*An annunciator was a wooden call box wired to send signals from one location to several others. They were used in early elevators, for example, so that the operator could see where he was to go next, and in hotels to signal guests about messages. Some were merely light connections; more advanced ones had speakers included. The term is still used for the elaborate fire alarm boxes in large buildings.

This photograph of the new school building appeared in the architectural magazine Brickbuilder *in 1910.*

booth had no phone—it was simply a place where girls could legally use their cell phones. Every girl went to college; girls were participating in "boys' sports" such as crew, ice hockey, and squash, and girls were winning top prizes as speakers and debaters in local, national, and international contests. They could hardly appreciate that when Harriett Hemenway established a public speaking prize for a senior in 1910, it was still almost unheard of (and even unseemly) for a woman to speak in public. Winsor students can now boast dozens of local, national, and world awards in debate, public speaking, and involvement in the Model United Nations and Massachusetts Bar Mock Trial programs.

There are, however, things that have not changed: books and libraries, classrooms and desks, playing fields and art studios, handwritten test responses, paper report cards, and, of course, a human teacher who engages, face to face, with each student. The School has continued to be just for girls, and the majority of its teachers and administrators are women.

Winsor's story is one that has its origins in almost all of the changes in post–Civil War Boston: new schools for specific kinds of students, a new character for certain sections of the city because of immigration, new outreach in philanthropy that included settlement houses and immigration services, new transportation locally and globally, and new churches and religious ideas. More significant than any of these was the flourishing of women's education and the new sense of a woman's place in the world.

Although surely raised with the Victorian expectation of being an unobtrusive, obedient, and diligent young woman, Mary Winsor grew to adulthood in the living context of her School, where educating the intellect, taking a moral stand when necessary, and striving for the best use of one's time on earth parallel so closely the idealism of twenty-first-century young people that one cannot help being in awe of her prescience.

Chapter 2

In this special province of hers, the home, she needs an understanding of the arts to make it a place of beauty. Few of us can do great work in the world, but we all can have influence in making the home a center of high ideals of beauty and truth.

—*Eleanor Childs Dodge 1920*

Girls, do not let yourselves drift. Have a purpose in your lives, form your own opinions and have the moral courage to live them. What you dare to dream of, dare to do.

—*Sarah W. Hallowell*

Miss Winsor is surrounded by the Class of 1905 in this first class portrait.
The girls are not wearing white dresses because the photograph
was not taken on Graduation Day.

The Early Mothers, Teachers, and Daughters

"COMPETENT, RESPONSIBLE WOMEN"

THE WINSOR ARCHIVES contain hundreds of pictures that document the School's history. Some of the most interesting ones illustrate the differences and similarities of the lives of girls and women over time. The formal photograph of each graduating class has been framed and hung in the School. The earliest was taken in 1905. Unlike the later pictures, it shows the twenty-eight seniors not in the traditional all-white graduation dresses, but rather in the constricting blouses and long skirts of young women whose mothers had been born in the middle of the Victorian era. Each of the more than one hundred graduation pictures on display reflects the hairstyles and dress fashions of the time, but the young faces reflect a combination of seriousness and vitality that is timeless. There is no class picture for 1935, when, because of the Depression, the girls decided that a picture would be an unnecessary expense.

The 1904 portrait of the extended family of Mary Winsor's parents, Frederick and Ann, includes Mary's six siblings and their spouses and more than a dozen grandchildren. This was a large family even by Victorian standards, for between 1800 and 1900 the number of children per family had declined from 7 to 3.5 in the United States.[1] When this picture was taken, it was forbidden for females to vote, serve on juries, or hold public office. Although upper-class women of this period rarely worked for pay, the women of the Winsor family had to work to support the household, especially when their father, a physician, was serving in the Civil War.

And yet seven years later, in 1911, Mary Pickard Winsor was sitting for a portrait of herself as the founder and first Director of a school named for her. Her erect posture and faint smile are fitting for a teacher, mentor, and educator who left an ineradicable imprint on what would become one of the finest girls' schools in the country.

Mary Winsor is standing to the left of her mother (who is wearing a small white shawl) in this early twentieth-century portrait of the family of Frederick and Ann Ware Winsor.

Although teaching young children was a common and well-accepted choice before marriage (or if marriage never came), most girls of upper-class Boston married immediately after high school and thereafter were helpmates for their husbands, who were for the most part clergymen, physicians, financiers, and lawyers. Some of the fathers, future husbands, and brothers of these women were members of the Massachusetts Association Opposed to the Further Extension of Suffrage to Women, men who believed in a "women's sphere," the nurturing of children and husband in the home, and there were also many women who felt that their cherished status of mother and wife would be sullied by the changes that "getting the vote" might bring.

Some of these married women volunteered in hospitals, settlement houses, schools for new immigrants, and even prisons, but the role in society and the future of an upper-class female in the late 1800s were limited and circumscribed. Women functioned as part of a tight community of extended family and neighbors who were linked through Boston's colleges and universities and churches and hospitals. By 1900 new connections for young women were emerging through their schools and colleges; the young Winsor women in the class picture at the beginning of this chapter started to forge a new bond that would soon affect not only their families but also the very School itself.

The Winsor Graduate Club commissioned this portrait of Mary Winsor in 1910
by the prominent Boston artist Cecilia Beaux. It hangs with the portraits
of the other Directors of the School in the library.

They would be among the first American women to pursue advanced degrees in law, medicine, college teaching, and other male-dominated professions.

As far as Mary Winsor was concerned, it was not she, but her cousin Louise Winsor Brooks who deserved to be called the founder of the school.[2] These two first cousins began a rather small "dame school" that would become The

Winsor School chiefly because Louise (Mrs. Francis Brooks) of Medford desired a small school for her daughter Louise in downtown Boston that would run from November to May. Her family and others like them lived in their cooler, rustic summer homes from June through October.* A third woman who should receive founding credit is Ann Ware Winsor, Mary's mother, who educated not just one but four future school founders: Mary, Annie, Frederick, and Elizabeth.† Harvard President Charles Eliot told Mary Winsor at one point that the School should have been named Ware-Winsor.[3]

Ann Bent Ware was the daughter of a scholarly Unitarian minister, Henry Ware Jr., who served as president of Harvard (though without the actual title) in 1810 and again in 1828–29. Members of the Ware family were generous supporters of Harvard, endowing honorary chairs and buildings and donating to the college the famous glass flower collection at the Harvard Museum of Natural History. As a minister in his North End Unitarian Church and as a professor at the Harvard Divinity School, Henry Ware was an influential antislavery advocate. He died when Ann was twelve. When Henry Ware's widow, Mary Lovell Pickard Ware, also died early, their daughter Ann was already supporting her family by teaching in a public school. After studying teaching techniques with Nicholas Tillinghast, principal of the Bridgewater Normal School, Ann set up her first school on Somerset Street in Boston, and her philosophy there and later at her Winchester school was "progressive," in the argot of the day. The Winsor School referred to itself as progressive throughout its early years.

Ann Ware married Dr. Frederick Winsor in 1857. After several moves to accommodate Dr. Winsor's growing medical practice, the family settled in a large, comfortable house in Winchester, behind which Ann built a small schoolhouse so that she could continue her teaching. During the Civil War, Ann managed the household without the help of her husband, who was serving as a surgeon to the Union Army. Doctors in those days were not wealthy, and Ann was very much on her own, one of many independent and capable young wives maintaining a family in the absence of a husband and father. Ann was an example for her daughters of what a determined young woman could accomplish in those days. She helped put her brothers through college, educated all seven of her own children, and added to her classes the children of numerous neighborhood families as well, charging them tuition to help support the Winsor family. Two of her sons were the ninth generation of her family to graduate from Harvard, and a third son graduated from the Massachusetts Institute of Technology. Frederick Winsor (1829–89), the

---

* Two lovely books of memories of such summers are Lydia Rotch 1928, *Hilltop Farm* (1929), and Mary Coolidge Perkins 1899, *Once I Was Very Young* (1960; repr., Portsmouth, N.H.: Peter E. Randall, 2000).

† Ann Ware Winsor's children would found The Winsor School, the Roger Ascham School in Scarsdale, New York, the Middlesex School, and the Eliot-Pearson School.

youngest of twelve children, had been raised virtually single-handedly by his mother; his father, a merchant and member of a shipbuilding firm, had died when Frederick was only two. His life before his marriage followed a path traditional for young men of his era.

> Frederick attended prep school at Boston Latin School and entered Harvard in 1847. Although he had been reared in Orthodox* faith, he departed from it in college. He was known as a great athlete at Harvard, and would have been a better student if not for eye trouble, which forced him to leave school in his senior year. Although he was forced to give up his books, he persevered, and had his lessons read to him. He still managed to graduate with his class in 1851. He then attended Harvard Medical School, graduating in 1855. That same year he was established as a physician at Salem, Massachusetts.[4]

Robert and Mary Pickard, the first two children of Ann and Frederick, were born in Salem; the next child, Paul, was born in Milton. The rest of the children, Annie, Jane, Elizabeth, and Frederick Jr., were born after the family moved to Winchester following the Civil War.

In eulogizing Ann Winsor, Theodore C. Williams described the Winsors as living "in a generation of unique intellectual activity. It was the period of the Civil War, of New England Transcendentalism, of boldly advancing science; the age of Lincoln, of Emerson, of Agassiz and Darwin.... The Winsors knew the best books, the world-problems, the spiritual movements of their generation."[5] June Gale, a niece of Mary Winsor, says in her reminiscences: "Their grief for Lincoln's death remained a living pain which they carried through life. They were vitally interested in public affairs. [Massachusetts government] mattered deeply to them, and Grover Cleveland's plain honesty and courage were a joy and pride. They founded their home in a roomy, comfortable house adequately furnished with wedding gifts and some heirlooms. They had only the essentials but these included a piano, some land and flowers and privacy, a view and many books and several open fireplaces."[6]

In this lively home of learned and civic-minded people the seven Winsor children were educated; the boys went on to college, but Mary spent only one year at Smith College, "under the reign of its first president, who, in those early days of higher education . . . was fearful lest we should know too much and actually urged our Zoology professor from Amherst to teach us 'as little as possible.'"[7] She was already in charge of her own small school for children ages five to fifteen in Winchester when her cousin asked her to establish a new school in Boston. Louise, who would quickly turn the complete running of the school over to Mary, was the daughter of Mary's uncle Henry

---

* The Winsors were Congregationalists, a denomination that eventually split into Trinitarians and Unitarians. Bostonians seem to have been able to slide flexibly among various denominations.

Winsor. She had married Francis Boott Brooks of Medford, a descendant of the successful Boston merchant Kirk Boott. Francis Brooks was a significant landowner in the town of Medford, which was incorporated as a city in 1892. The Brooks family, like the Wares and Winsors, were civic-minded and philanthropic, and Miss Winsor's School was not their only educational involvement. In 1888 the Brookses helped establish the Sarah Fuller Home for Little Children Who Cannot Hear, one of the first schools in the nation promoting Fuller's revolutionary methods of teaching deaf nursery school children.[8] Sarah Fuller was one of Helen Keller's earliest teachers.

Mary Pickard Winsor was just twenty-six when she started the school near the Boston Public Garden. At the end of the second year, she recalled later, "Mrs. Brooks took a gloomy view of future registration," and Mary stepped forward, "to take over the school—rent, enrollment and all. From that time there was no future trouble, for as soon as the school was no longer a personal affair, under the aegis of a patroness, applications poured in, and from that time to this—although we soon became a nine-months school—there has always been a waiting list—a sight dear to the heart of a treasurer."[9]

When the little dame school first opened in the late fall of 1886, seven other ten-year-olds had joined Mrs. Brooks's daughter Louise: Helen Brooks (Louise's cousin), Elizabeth Cheney, Eleanor Bacon Emmons, Susan Emmons, Isabel Perkins, Hetty Appleton Sargent, and Clara Bowdoin Winthrop. Most of these family names echo throughout an account of the School's history as well as through the history of the city of Boston. It is not easy, however, to find the names of girls and women in the historical record, and for the most part it is only through painstaking and close reading of the lives of their male descendants and ancestors that one finds any brief reference to their wives or daughters, most of which are included purely for genealogical clarification. As Claude M. Fuess said, in a 1961 article for the *Winsor Bulletin*, "The preponderance of men in the *Dictionary of American Biography* is distressingly overwhelming."[10] Most public records and genealogical annals of the time are about men and are of course catalogued in their names.

Helen Brooks, shown here when she was in Class II, was one of the eight original little girls at Miss Winsor's School in 1886. After graduating in 1895, she married a stockbroker and had two children.

Mary Winsor set up an enrollment book in which the School secretary, Sarah E. Darling, recorded each year's new girls and the class in

The whole School gathered in 1903 in the Public Garden for a picture in the space they used at recess for walking and playing. At that time the School was located at 95–96 Beacon Street. The structure in the background is the Ether Monument, which commemorates the first use of ether as an anesthetic at the Massachusetts General Hospital in 1846.

which they entered.[11] The student's home address and years of attendance were given, and the lists were amended to record married names and new addresses. The handwriting and the inconsistent types of information present a challenge to the historian, but the mere existence of such records is priceless. Fortunately, as the girls left the School, they continued to stay in contact with each other, and in 1907 they established the Graduate Club, which published two *Graduate Club Register*s—in 1910 and 1915—to record its activities with and for the School as well as brief entries from fellow Winsor graduates. Although not every former student is represented, the records that we have are rich with details about travel, marriage, college, husband's and children's names, and work, paid as well as volunteer.

The young women who graduated from Miss Winsor's small establishment in the 1890s and early 1900s represented not only the culture of educated Bostonians at the time but also the subtle changes in young women's lives as they began to earn college degrees, have fewer children, and engage in social activities outside the family circle. The post–high school activities of Winsor students from the beginning of the new millennium until the First World War show how the Victorian ideal of the "women's sphere" broadened and then began to disintegrate. With their involvement in the Great War overseas, women's lives acquired a global perspective.

The 1910 *Graduate Club Register* has preserved miniature portraits of the first graduates' lives. Ethel Davies Abbott from the class of 1893 married

Fritz Hermann Jordan, "a merchant," on August 22, 1905, and was living in Portland, Maine. Her date and place of birth are given, as well as the schools she attended ("Miss Staple's, Gilman, Cambridge; Miss Winsor's, 1891–93") and her travel ("Europe").* Theodora Knight's husband, George Wade, was a "bond broker"; but Rosamund Smith Hall, who did not marry, listed no occupation other than "travel" and "partly supports herself by needlework." Hetty Sargent married Francis L. Higginson Jr., a scion of the impressive Higginson family that included Henry Higginson, the founder of the Boston Symphony Orchestra in 1881, and Thomas Wentworth Higginson, the intrepid Civil War hero, abolitionist, and mentor of Emily Dickinson.

In 1894 twenty-three girls graduated from Miss Winsor's School, and most of them were soon married. Seven girls eventually married "bankers or brokers," four of them married lawyers, and Susan Emmons married Irwin McDowell Garfield, the younger son of President James A. Garfield. Two 1894 graduates married men in business ("merchants") and two became wives of physicians; two married clergymen and another, a farmer. All but two of these first graduates reported traveling abroad; thirteen of them took some postgraduate courses. Only five listed "coming out in society" in their brief vitae; eleven listed their children. A few mentioned further study of drawing and painting, often at the School of the Museum of Fine Arts, after graduation.† Several women reported studying at the Garland Training School for kindergarten teachers, the Boston Art School, and even the Massachusetts Institute of Technology.†† It was a time when requirements for bachelor's and master's degrees were just beginning to be codified for both men and women.

Pauline Wright Brigham 1894 finished Radcliffe in 1898 and, after studying in Paris, went on to teach briefly at Bryn Mawr, the Cambridge Country Day School for Girls, and Wellesley College. She did not marry and died at the age of twenty-eight. Henrietta Faxon 1894 graduated from Radcliffe in 1901 and eight years later married Arthur Pease, a professor of classics.

Another member of the 1894 class, Isabelle Perkins, reported in her modest biographical update in 1910: "Studied for several years with French and German governesses; took courses at Boston University. Has written short stories and articles for magazines and newspapers." Isabelle's wedding to Larz Anderson, the son of the secretary of the American Embassy in Rome, had been a prominent news item, partly because she was the heir to a $17 million dollar fortune from her grandfather William Fletcher Weld. Her en-

---

* Names and birthdates of children are also given. These details may in some instances be the only genealogical record for these women.

† The Museum of Fine Arts in Boston established its school in 1876 at its original site in Copley Square and moved to its Fenway location in 1909.

†† MIT was founded in Boston in 1865. The first woman to attend, Ellen Swallow Richards, was given special permission to study chemistry in 1873.

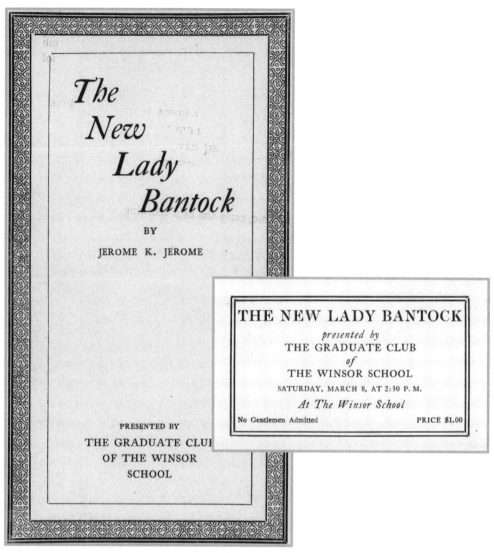

*The program and ticket for one of the Graduate Club's fund-raising plays, 1913.
Nota bene: "No gentlemen admitted."*

try in the *Journal of the New England Historic Genealogical Society Memoirs* (an entry unusually long for a woman of that period) reveals a woman who continued to develop a rich and useful life after marriage, earning honorary doctorates, transporting supplies to the army in the Spanish-American War, and serving as a nurse on the Belgian and French fronts during World War I. Isabel Perkins Anderson also wrote at least fifty books, and on her estate in Brookline (now Larz Anderson Park), she supported the American Drama Society by setting up a theater.[12]

The social lives of many upper-class girls were captured in newspaper items in what until recently were called the society pages. A majority of early

Winsor students came of age in a social milieu that required debutante teas, balls, elaborate engagement announcements, and fairy-tale nuptials. The newspaper articles listed party and wedding guests both male and female, and the length of some of these articles conveys a message that coming out and being married were important goals for the daughters of the well-to-do whom Winsor educated. Many, however, attended Miss Garland's Training School after graduation and planned to teach until they were married.*

At the end of the 1800s and increasingly in the new century, Boston women with only high school educations volunteered their time and energy in social action work at hospitals, libraries, and settlement houses, following the example of many of their mothers. Some went into teaching to support themselves, and some even came back to teach at Winsor. Educated young women had few options, but greater opportunities were coming, and the stated mission of The Winsor School was to prepare women for that future.

On the other hand, there were girls in Miss Winsor's School who would enter professions at a time when, frankly, the males did not want them there. Greta Coleman came to Miss Winsor's in 1906 and after graduation in 1911 went to Radcliffe, where she teamed with a classmate and began to lobby the college to add legal studies. The Cambridge Law School for Women opened in 1915, and Greta Coleman studied there before transferring to the University of Chicago Law School.[13] After working for the law firm of Dunbar, Nutter and McClennan for four years, she opened her own legal practice in 1922. Greta also taught law, worked for the Boston Legal Aid Society, was the first female member of the Council of the Boston Bar Association, and with the League of Women Voters challenged the Supreme Judicial Court in Massachusetts on the issue of women serving on juries.†

The stories of women involved in the early growth of the School must include the first teachers, and although the legion of faculty has its own chapter in this history, those very first teachers deserve mention as early career women. (Throughout the book, years of a teacher's tenure are given in brackets after their names using the connective *to*.) The original staff was small, consisting of "Miss Mary P. Winsor and a little French maid named Eugénie Martin."[14] New teachers were gradually added: for drawing, Miss May Hallowell [1886 to 1900]; for French, Mme. McLaren [1887 to ?]; for German, Fräulein von Blomberg [1890 to 1918]; and for mathematics, Miss Paine [1891 to 1902].[15]

Maria ("May") Hallowell trained at the Boston Museum School, at the Académie Julian under Tony Robert-Fleury and others in Paris, and at Cowles Art School in Boston. Evidently her main work was in portraits, but she was

---

* Mary Garland established her school for kindergarten teachers in 1872. It became Garland Junior College and graduated its last class in 1976, when it became part of Simmons College.

† This right was not granted until July 1950. The play *Twelve Angry Men* was rewritten as *Twelve Angry Women* in 1955 and performed by the Winsor Drama Club in 1962.

~ GENEROUS-MINDED WOMEN ~

also known as an art educator. She was a member of the Boston Watercolor Club, the Copley Society, and the Society of Arts and Crafts. "She made a specialty of portraits in pastel of children." She married Joseph P. Loud, who was a founding trustee of the Calhoun Colored School in Alabama.[16]

Eva von Blomberg was described by Mary Winsor in her Fiftieth Anniversary Address as "a delightful lady from Weimar, who remained for thirty years, till her retirement during the war." The concern about the teaching of German is preserved in a set of letters revealing the attitudes of the Board and of Mary Winsor (see chapter 7).

Harriet Paine was just one of many Winsor women, teachers and alumnae, who wrote and published books; one of her works was *Girls and Women,* a nonfiction book whose first chapter, "An Aim in Life," expresses a sentiment appropriate for a teacher in a school begun by women for women and sustained by idealistic teachers: "For the sake of girls who are just beginning life, let me tell the stories of some other girls who are now middle-aged women. Some of them have succeeded and some have failed in their purposes, and often in a surprising way."[17] Having "an aim in life" beyond the women's sphere required examples of women who had themselves gone beyond the sphere. Mary Winsor was able to hire such women; the first faculty members were strong, independent, and motivated.

Leslie White Hopkinson [1895 to 1918] published in 1918 *Greek Leaders,* a book intended to supplement ancient history textbooks. She reveals her teacherly qualities in her provocative opening sentence: "They say that Solon, coming to Croesus at his request, was in the same condition as an inland man when first he goes to see the sea."[18] In his introduction to Hopkinson's book, William Scott Ferguson, a professor of ancient history at Harvard, commends the stories as being "written by an accomplished teacher, and for that very reason, perhaps, are not written down to the assumed level of children."[19]

Ella Lyman Cabot [1902 to 1911] taught ethics at Winsor to Upper School (grades 9–12; the Lower School comprises grades 5–8) girls and "special students" after taking logic courses at Radcliffe and metaphysics classes at Harvard. Both her family background and her educational involvement were notable. Her ancestor, the English settler Richard Lyman, had come to New England in 1631, and his descendents included fur merchants, China tradesmen, clergymen, cotton manufacturers, and Harvard graduates.[20] She married into an equally distinguished New England family: her husband, Richard Clarke Cabot, was a noted physician and professor of social ethics at Harvard. Mrs. Cabot taught at the Garland School of Homemaking, Pine Manor Junior College, and the University of California, and from 1905 until her death was a member of the Massachusetts State Board of Education. In 1906 she published her first book, *Everyday Ethics.*[21] Ella Lyman Cabot was the quintessential female volunteer of the early 1900s, serving on multiple boards and committees for Radcliffe, the National Religious Educational Association, the Massachusetts Civic League, the Boston Women's Municipal League, the Permanent Charity Fund of Boston, the College Club of Boston, and the King's Chapel Children's School of Religion. She worked for causes such as the American Peace League, civil service reform, farm schools, the Museum of Fine Arts, and the Red Cross. Lacking a college degree and having decided (with her husband) not to have children, Ella Lyman Cabot nonetheless was a woman who made a difference in her world.

She was typical of educated upper-class women of her time, women who were likely to be the Winsor mothers, teachers, and graduates whose social commitment and intellect would help the young Winsor School flourish at the very time when society needed richer possibilities for women. These exceptional women were models for Winsor students. Many of them were pioneers who were among the first to challenge the assumptions about what a woman could and could not do. As the historian Nancy Cott has noted: "The women who filled their lives with public activity from 1890 to 1920 were in a minority. The vast, and mostly silent, majority of American women did not seek changes in gender roles or the existing social order."[22]

Cabot's writings reveal a wonderful mind thinking in detail and in depth about what it is to be a responsible human being. She must have been a treasure to have on the Winsor faculty. Her pages are full of examples of the real world, and her book includes a teacher's guide with suggestions for teaching that are as modern as a microchip. In *Ethics for Children: A Guide for Teachers and Parents,* she suggests hands-on activities such as building a brick kiln in connection with reading Booker T. Washington's *Up from Slavery.* Some of the prompts for ethical discussions reflect the breadth of her perspective:

> Would you be willing to be so made that you could not help doing right always, as a clock is wound up and made to strike at the right time? In what ways should you not like it? Should you be glad if your lessons were all learned every day just as soon as you glanced at them? Why or why not?

> Confucius said: "I do not know how a man without truthfulness is to get on. How can a large carriage be made to go without the cross bar for yoking the oxen to?" What do you think he meant? Can any nation succeed in which there is great dishonesty and distrust?[23]

The stories in this chapter have been about some of the early women—parents, students, and teachers—who played important roles in creating an atmosphere of feminine achievement in Miss Winsor's School. Their names are not as famous as their husbands' or brothers', and their work in the world has not been sufficiently valued. But these first women are not mere footnotes in Winsor's historical record; what they did shaped the way the story unfolded.

In the century to follow, Winsor women continued to make break-throughs into "male" careers. They have been among the first female symphony conductors and museum curators, and they have founded dance and theater groups. They have led the YWCA, the American branch of UNICEF, the Massachusetts Audubon Society, and been pioneers in birth control, pediatric psychiatry, and midwifery in Appalachia. They have defied stereotyping in the clergy, have composed symphonies performed by the Boston Symphony Orchestra, and have authored studies on immunology and nuclear power plants.

Many of their stories will be told in this book.

Chapter 3

*I am sometimes asked what does the Corporation of the School do? . . . You sup-
port the School, like the flying buttresses of a Gothic building give it support from
without.*

—Frances Dugan

*I am most grateful to those of you [corporation members] whom I have pursued
for suggestions, to the officers . . . whom I consult often, to those . . . who have
appeared at 8:50 assemblies and chilly afternoon games, and to all who have
undertaken special tasks—be they judging Hemenway speeches or coping with
alumnae projects or fundraising problems.*

—Virginia Wing

*Huybertie Pruyn Hamlin wrote a detailed and personal description of the building of
The Winsor School, relating the early efforts to start the "new" School on the Riverway.
Her daughter, Anna, attended Winsor from 1910 to 1913, before the family
moved to Washington, D.C.*

Founders and Sustainers

❦

"TOO MUCH PRAISE CANNOT BE GIVEN"

THE 1907 LISTING OF ORIGINAL INCORPORATORS of The Winsor School included names of the area's most prominent families, respected educators from Harvard and Radcliffe, and influential financiers and businessmen in Boston. The Winsor Archives contain handwritten letters to and from these individuals and minutes from group meetings held in private homes. Although the men often communicated via typed or handwritten letters on their business letterhead, the women used the still-viable custom of afternoon tea and the existing social action network that had allowed them to participate outside the home in clubs and escape the women's sphere.

The lives of these men and women represent a facet of life in Boston at the time and a connection to the families who founded the city. There are three broad categories to consider—women, educators, and financiers. There were a few women educators, but fewer women financiers. The majority of women on the list had no profession, but neither were they idle.

The committee included eighteen women and fourteen men; considering the time period, the preponderance of females is impressive. Only recently had Massachusetts given women the right to own property. The right to vote as full citizens was a decade in the future, but many of the women on the committee were already finding ways to contribute to the world beyond their homes, not content to "stay in their place" until they achieved their full status as citizens.

From a modern perspective, it is dismaying and somewhat surprising to see how long the struggle for equal voting rights lasted. Women had made their initial formal request for the right to vote at the first women's rights convention in Seneca Falls, New York, in 1848. Twenty years after that, when the Fourteenth Amendment identified citizens as "male" and the Fifteenth Amendment gave the vote to black men, the disappointed women were facing a backlash among men and even among some of their own sex. Ironically, between 1776 and 1807, some states that had permitted women to vote passed new laws that stripped women of their voting rights. It would take 113 years to regain that right.

The suffrage movement progressed by increments until Tennessee's deciding vote on August 20, 1920, assured the ratification of the Nineteenth Amendment. One of those incremental steps—in Massachusetts, at least—was the right to run for and serve on school committees. This responsibility may have been one the men were willing to give to women because of the tradition (going back to antiquity) of mothers or their surrogates—governesses and spinster aunts—teaching the younger children at home and eventually sending the boys off to study with a local clergyman, master philosopher, or famous don. Teaching had also started to be considered a female role, one of the few ways in which a woman could earn money.

Women's status as "noncitizens" (the suffragists' cry) did not, however, prevent them from working actively for social causes such as abolition, prison reform, and, especially, education. When the Boston School Board opened its membership to women in 1872—but withheld the right of women to vote for members—it merely acknowledged what women were already doing in the areas of establishing kindergartens, training immigrants in English and job skills, and fund-raising for a number of social action initiatives.

As their activity in community causes expanded, however, so did a strident antisuffrage movement made up of men as well as women of all classes. The antisuffragists' impassioned arguments against a woman's right to vote can hardly be read with a sober face in the twenty-first century, but their voices were loud and persuasive at the time, especially in Massachusetts.

The women who took part in the incorporating of a groundbreaking new girls' school in Boston included many who were active in community causes, but nearly all of them were upper-class Bostonians married to influential husbands. Although intelligent and talented, there is no record of any of them having been to college, yet they already had hopes for their daughters, several of whom had attended or graduated from Miss Winsor's School in the Back Bay or would attend in the future. By 1908 a college education was a part of the new frontier for women, brought to consciousness by, among other things, the women's rights struggle.

Wesleyan College in Macon, Georgia, was in 1836 the first all-women college, Mount Holyoke began as a "female seminary" in 1837, and Mills College in California in 1852 became the first women's college west of the Rockies. In 1900 only 2.8 percent of the women in this country went to college, and this number had risen only to 7.6 percent by 1920.[1] As secondary school education improved and expanded for American girls, they were increasingly eager to continue their intellectual development, and many were also becoming aware of the possibility of having to support themselves. John Simmons in 1899 said, "It is my will to found and endow an institution to be called Simmons Female College, for the purpose of teaching medicine, music, drawing, designing, telegraphy, and other branches of art, science, and industry best calculated to enable the scholars to acquire an independent livelihood."[2] Then, as now, being admitted to college depended on passing rigorous entrance examinations, and Boston parents wanted to establish a school that would prepare their daughters for these examinations. Intelligent and socially active mothers were particularly motivated to seek higher education for their daughters, and it was from this group of women that Winsor's female Incorporators came.

Harriett Lawrence Hemenway was one of the most spirited members of the group; archival records and letters show that she contributed time and money (and gifts such as plantings and a mahogany bench) to the School for many years. A stunning portrait of Harriett at the age of thirty-two by John Singer Sargent shows an intelligent, captivating woman with whom afternoon tea would be a delight.* When Harriett Dexter Lawrence married Augustus Hemenway Jr. in 1881, two of New England's most illustrious and generous families were united. Harriett's grandfather, the philanthropist Amos Lawrence, beneficently funded colleges, libraries, churches, and hos-

* Harriett's portrait by Sargent can be seen online at http://jssgallery.org/Paintings/20044.html.

pitals; her father, Amos Adams Lawrence, founded Lawrence, Kansas, and Lawrence College in Appleton, Wisconsin.

Harriett Hemenway invited her cousin Minna Hall to join her for tea one afternoon in 1896. No one else was invited (so the story goes) because Harriett had an agenda: she wanted to discuss the rather unladylike subject of "the bloody hunts at the egret rookeries"[3] and the then-current fashion of decorating ladies' bonnets with birds' feathers and sometimes even wings and heads and (occasionally) a whole bird. She was thinking about organizing her friends into some sort of group to spread the word about the horrible ways birds were being bred for the sole purpose of adorning hats.

Going to tea and organizing clubs were, as we have seen, highly suitable activities for women, and Harriett and Minna resolved to form a club to save the birds. Their model may have been the New England Women's Club, which was founded in 1868 to provide a weekly forum where women could discuss topics of cultural or social interest. In her history of that club, Julia Sprague speaks of the inspiration women had drawn from the antislavery cause and of their realization that patriotic fervor during and after the Civil War had stimulated immense contributions to humanity: "The most observant and thoughtful women … had become aware that this power which they had had opportunity to exercise for the good of the nation, could have been tenfold greater in the beginning, had they been united by an intellectual, as well as by a social, bond."[4] The two women planned another tea for selected Boston women, many of whom pledged to boycott hats containing feathers. From that tea party arose the Massachusetts Audubon Society.[5] More than a century later, in 1999, a Winsor graduate, Laura Johnson 1972, became the society's president. She served as a Winsor Trustee from 1990 to 1996 and returned to speak to the assembled student body in 1999.

Clearly ahead of their time as environmentalists, the women had as their goal the education of people about the destruction of birds and their habitats and the protection of all wildlife. The bird protection movement expanded rapidly under women's leadership.

Harriett and Augustus Hemenway sent four daughters to Miss Winsor's School, and all went on to graduate.[6] Many families sent more than one daughter to Winsor, and the enrollment lists contained sisters and cousins galore.

Amy Aldis Bradley (Mrs. Richards M.) also had a large family of six children, four of whom attended The Winsor School.[7] Tea with Amy Bradley at her home on Brimmer Street might have included serious conversations about the Women's Municipal League of Boston, which she had founded. Her article "Market Inspection Work Carried on by the Women's Municipal League in 1912" describes the inspection process done by the league's Market Committee. The full article is well worth reading as an example of the foresightedness and political savvy of these women doing what we might dismiss as "volunteer work."[8] Although the report gives a bleak picture of shops in "poorer parts of town" that were "very dirty and sometimes disgustingly so," it mentions that the committee had met with the Board of Health, which appointed one of the committeewomen a market inspector whose three-month salary would be paid by the league and the South End House. The Board of Health later extended the position to run for a full year. The women also organized consumers who did their own independent inspections of over 450 shops in the neighborhoods. In their subtle way, this group of Boston women was creating the infrastructure for social services by forming committees that took on the task of inspecting nurseries, settlement houses, restaurants, prisons, hospitals, and housing for the poor. Their daughters in the 1930s would be going to college and taking higher-level jobs and responsibilities in these areas, and their granddaughters would obtain graduate degrees and become doctors, professors, researchers, and lawyers.

Amy Bradley's article shows her sociological insight: "It is not surprising that these shops are sometimes exceedingly dirty, when one considers the small profits made. . . . The great hindrance to sanitary conditions is that the small shops are so numerous and competition is so keen that the owners barely make a living and really cannot afford to keep clean."[9] This was not the only example of women forming social action committees that were eventually taken over and made state agencies. Women wanted very much to widen their sphere, and they were intelligent enough to see what needed to be done, sometimes before their husbands did. Husbands, as we shall see, also served on multiple boards and civic committees at the time: running a growing city required volunteerism from everyone in the community. And so the afternoon tea gathering evolved into a committee meeting where tea was served, and the sewing circle, where debutantes did indeed sew bandages for Union soldiers, had by 1906 become the Junior League, whose purpose was organizing and serving in social service agencies.

Amy Bradley as tea party hostess might have invited guests to see her studio at the top of her Beacon Street home. She was an accomplished sculptor who studied sculpture in Paris before her marriage and later sent several of her daughters to do the same. She displayed two plaster busts at the 1893 World's Fair in Chicago[10] and made a bust of Father Jacques Marquette for the Marquette Building in that city, which her husband was involved in building.[11] She passed her civic-mindedness to her daughter Sarah Merry 1916, who with her husband, Clarence Gamble, founded the Pathfinder Fund, a nonpolitical, nonprofit organization that still today "promotes and supports population and family planning activities in less developed countries."[12]

Three other Winsor mothers on the incorporating committee illustrate women's increasing involvement in the world outside the home at the beginning of the twentieth century. Mary Hamilton Hill Coolidge (Mrs. J. Randolph Jr.) assisted in the creation of the League of Arts and Crafts in

Sarah Wharton Hallowell

New Hampshire, established during the Depression and still a flourishing business in that state. "Governor Winant [of New Hampshire] anticipated the WPA's Federal Art Project with a state program. In 1931, in response to a proposal from Mrs. J. Randolph Coolidge and A. Cooper Ballantine, the governor established and funded the League of Arts and Crafts, making New Hampshire the first state in the nation to publicly support arts and crafts as tools for economic development. The league organized cottage industries, such as rug hooking, blacksmithing, and woodcarving, into a cooperative to produce and market high quality crafts more effectively and to teach hand-crafts to others."[13]

Sarah Wharton Hallowell (Mrs. Norwood P.) was one of Mary Winsor's closest friends and maintained an ongoing, supportive relationship with Mary's school. Her daughters, Anna, Esther, and Susan, all attended the School during the years 1888 to 1901. Early records of the School refer to Sarah Hallowell as the "mother of the School," and many of her speeches to the graduates at "Last Day" exercises are in the Archives. A staunch Quaker related to the Wharton family in Philadelphia, she married the Civil War hero Norwood Penrose Hallowell, who became lieutenant colonel for the state's first black regiment, the Massachusetts 54th, after its leader, Robert Gould Shaw, was killed in battle.* The Hallowells often traveled from their home in West Medford to the Cambridge Friends Meeting, where Sarah became one of their most respected leaders. From 1914 until 1920 she was the president of Winsor's Executive Committee, becoming not only the first woman to hold that position but also one of a few women members of the Board for many years.† Her daughter Susan 1901 describes Sarah Hallowell's joy in being part of the very first Monday morning assembly at the new Winsor School: "From then on until the end of her life she would be seated at 9 A.M. in the same seat in the front row of the balcony of the Assembly Hall, dressed always in Quaker gray, including a small gray bonnet, to share the Assembly with all the students and to enjoy many short chats with individual students afterwards."[14]

Eleanor Brooks Saltonstall (Mrs. Richard M.) was the mother of Eleanor ("Nora") 1911 and Muriel 1913. The Saltonstalls were well known throughout the Commonwealth of Massachusetts, not just in Boston. Their oldest son, Leverett, began his lengthy political service to the state in 1923 in the Massachusetts House of Representatives, going on to become Speaker, governor, and then a United States senator from 1945 to 1967. Nora Saltonstall, in whose name and memory Winsor's scholarship for study in France was established in 1920, wrote a gripping personal account of her work with the Red Cross in France during World War I. *"Out Here at the Front"*[15] reveals a feisty, capable, intrepid young woman, one of fifty-four Winsor alumnae who contributed to the war effort even before the United States was involved.[16]

One of the prominent educators among the Winsor Incorporators was another scholarly woman, Agnes Irwin (1841–1914), the dean of Radcliffe College from 1894 until 1909 and a great-great-granddaughter of Benjamin

---

* A biographical note by J. E. Wright in the *Harvard Graduates' Magazine* 22 (September 1911) describes Norwood Hallowell as a man who was "physically, born to command." Hallowell spoke to the Winsor student body on more than one occasion. The movie *Glory* tells the moving story of the Massachusetts 54th.

† The second female president was Elizabeth Partridge Heald 1957, who served from 1988 until 1995.

Franklin. "I should really like to help in such a work and I thank you for giving me the opportunity," she responded when asked to be on the committee.[17] She was an especially fine choice because of her experience as principal of a young ladies' seminary in Philadelphia from 1869 to 1894. That school was eventually renamed for her and is one of the few girls' schools in the country (including Winsor) that has not become coeducational. Agnes Irwin was snubbed when, in 1899, a man was selected to replace Radcliffe's first president, Elizabeth Agassiz, with whom Agnes had worked as the college's first dean. LeBaron Briggs, dean of faculty at Harvard, was appointed in spite of Irwin's extraordinary achievements in behalf of the Radcliffe women: she had set up the first doctoral degree program for women with Harvard and raised money for the library, dormitories, and a gymnasium on the campus. The last sentence of her obituary in the *New York Times* reads: "She was not a college graduate, but possessed a reputation for learning."[18] Agnes Irwin did, however, receive an honorary doctoral degree from St. Andrews University in Scotland as her progenitor Benjamin Franklin had in 1759. She was the only unmarried woman on the Committee of Incorporators.

Charles William Eliot, president of Harvard University from 1869 until 1909, served with Agnes Irwin on the committee. He had not trusted the Radcliffe presidency to her, and although he did not have daughters who would attend Winsor, his granddaughters Rosamund 1913 and Elizabeth 1915 began their education at Miss Winsor's School. Ellen 1911, Carola 1915, and Frances 1918, who became a writer and illustrator of children's books, were students at the new school on the Riverway. His credentials as an educator were impressive. His reforms and innovations at Harvard marked the beginning of Harvard's becoming a wealthy and nationally recognized university. President Eliot was not so enthusiastic about higher education for women as one might suppose, revealing his bias in his speech at the inauguration of Wellesley's president, Caroline Hazard, in 1899: "Women's colleges should concentrate on an education that will not injure women's bodily powers and functions."[19]

Eliot married Ellen Derby Peabody and thereby created another powerful coalition of Boston first families. He had no daughters, but his two sons, Charles and Samuel, had significant careers in the Boston area, Charles as a landscape architect who worked with Frederick Law Olmsted, Samuel as a minister and church leader who was instrumental in barring women from the Unitarian ministry.

It is hard to believe that Charles Eliot had time to commit to the literally dozens of committees and foundations on which he served, let alone have afternoon tea. Eliot is credited with expanding the professional schools at Harvard. During his tenure he served as head of an influential national committee, the Committee of Ten, formed to standardize the high school curriculum in this country.

The Incorporator Joseph Lee was known for his activism and support of social legislation, in particular for promoting the development of public playgrounds. His book *Constructive and Preventive Philanthropy,* first published in 1902, was reprinted three times. He stated, "Play is the intensest part of the life of a child, and it is therefore in his play hours that his most abiding lessons are learned, that his most central and determining growth takes place."[20] His approach to play as a basis for educating children was one the new Winsor School appeared to adopt in its planning for both indoor and outdoor play space. Like Maria Montessori and Friedrich Fröbel, Lee promoted a philosophy that influenced later educators, especially in its emphasis on the whole child: "Lee's view of play was idealistic and purposeful. . . . He believed that play forms had to be taught and that the process required capable leadership. Lee did not make a sharp distinction between work and play, but saw them as closely related expressions of the impulses to achieve, to explore, to excel, and to master."[21]

Lee and his wife, Elizabeth Perkins Cabot Lee, sent three daughters to Winsor: Margaret Lee Woodbury Southard 1915, Susan Mary Lee 1917, and Amy Lee Colt 1921, who wrote the book *A Few Memories.*

The Incorporators included several businessmen and civic leaders whose expertise was an essential component of the work of the founding committee. Their wives were members of Boston's cultured elite, and many of their daughters would attend Winsor and go on to college and careers and leadership roles. These men were the first of many fathers and relatives who donated their time and wisdom to the School.

The lawyer Charles Sumner Hamlin was the first chairman of the Federal Reserve Board, serving from 1914 to 1916. Between his two terms as assistant secretary of the Treasury, Hamlin lived in Boston and was one of the most politically active members of the committee. He ran several times for the Massachusetts Senate and twice for governor, but he was unsuccessful and turned his attention to civic responsibilities and supporting Democratic candidates for national office. His wife, Huybertie Pruyn Hamlin, and his only daughter, Anna, kept memoirs, scrapbooks, and diaries that exist, unpublished, in the Library of Congress.[22] Huybertie Hamlin's firsthand account of the many meetings held in their home as early as 1905 contains details about the incorporation of the School found nowhere else. The daughter of a prominent Albany, New York, family, she also wrote a widely admired account of her early years.[23]

Charles Wells Hubbard, a hands-on philanthropist whose gifts of land to the town of Weston led to the preservation of more than one hundred acres along the Charles River, used his wealth not only to create public access to the meadows and woodlands along the river but also to inspire other citizens to do likewise.[24] In a letter to Mrs. R. M. Saltonstall in 1935, Mary Winsor praised Charles Hubbard, the School's treasurer, as "the most hard-working and long-headed of them all."[25] Hubbard's civic vision was evident in his leadership of the Ludlow Manufacturing Company, started by his father in 1868. At one time the company, a mill that made industrial fibers, employed five thousand people. Hubbard "worked to make Ludlow a 'model village' for workers, building a library, hospital, textile school and recreation center and swimming pool."[26] His two daughters, Elizabeth 1912 and Anna 1913, went to Winsor, as did his granddaughter Nathalie Hubbard Bramson 1959.

Mary Winsor's older brother Robert provided crucial support for the committee. A highly respected and powerful investment banker, Robert Winsor had joined the firm Kidder, Peabody & Company after graduating from Harvard in 1880 and rose quickly to partner and then senior partner. Robert was a key player in creating a unified public transit system (which eventually became the Massachusetts Transportation Authority) for the city of Boston.[27] He also played a major role in a controversial merger of nine Boston commercial banks to form the National Shawmut Bank, the city's largest bank at the time. Robert Winsor's expertise and connections were vital not only to the development of his sister's school but also to that of the Middlesex School in Concord, founded in 1901 by his brother Frederick Winsor Jr. Robert Winsor shared the prevailing upper-class values about philanthropy, land use, and city beautification. On his estate in Weston he sought to create for his four children the atmosphere of an active farm that could supply fresh food for the family.[28] As he acquired additional land in the area, he asked Frederick Law Olmsted Jr., the son of the well-known landscape architect, and his firm, Olmsted Brothers, to lay out roads on his property following the "naturalistic design principles" of his father. He foresaw the eventual subdivision of the land when he set up the Weston Real Estate Trust to develop the property. Although the aim was to build modest, affordable houses, "land cost $3,000 an acre. The trust has been described as 'choosy' about who was allowed to purchase lots. Prospective buyers had to be of the accepted socioeconomic and religious background."[29]

In a 1919 letter from Robert to his sister with the salutation "My dear Pickard," the financier replied to her questions about a scholarship fund circular and the possibility of starting an endowment fund for her new school. While admitting that "an endowment fund is a very useful thing to have about the house,"[30] he said he did not think the time was right to establish an endowment for Winsor; he felt private schools should "pay their own way," even though it would be challenging to set fees at a rate high enough to cover costs while not barring "people of limited means."* Robert himself had graduated from the highly endowed Phillips Exeter Academy in New Hampshire.

Since a large number of the Incorporators would be sending their daugh-

---

* The letter closes with the ominous observation: "I believe that Mr. Eliot is quite right in being apprehensive about a general industrial catastrophe in this country."

ters to the new school on the Riverway, their interest in its success, both financial and educational, was obvious and ongoing. Many of them continued to be closely involved with the School and truly deserve to be called founders. These Incorporators helped set the tone and maintain the standards that Mary Winsor hoped for, and she was no doubt grateful for such a strong showing from the larger community.

The Board of Trustees continued to be devoted sustainers of Winsor's excellence and success throughout the next century, and every Director expressed gratitude for their dedication. In 1996 Carolyn McClintock Peter, the School's sixth Director,* praised them: "I particularly want to thank the Board of Trustees for its unfailing willingness to work with me and others on the increasingly complex institutional issues which face a small independent school with large ambitions. Most importantly Marlyn Lewis, Richard Lubin, and Jay Westcott provide extraordinary guidance with uncommon kindness and generosity."[31] The involvement of the parents who serve as Trustees is another of Winsor's strengths. Alumnae too become Board members whose knowledge of the School and dedication to its ongoing success provide both perspective and leadership.

---

* Carolyn Peter was Winsor's Director from 1988 to 2004.

Chapter 4

The mayor of Boston was most helpful. It was something that had never been done before in the history of the city. Our Committee was afraid it was a forlorn hope, but Mayor Fitzgerald became interested and the matter went through!

—Mrs. Charles S. Hamlin

We walked to the Museum across the Fenway on a narrow path through shoulder-high reeds. No buildings at all were there until we got to the main one of Simmons College.

—Elizabeth Saltonstall 1918

The building at 95–96 Beacon Street was the last Back Bay location of Miss Winsor's School before the move to Pilgrim Road.

The Schoolhouse

❦

ON FENWAY'S "GREEN AND PLEASANT LAND"

SEVENTH-GRADERS AT Winsor in the early twenty-first century studied the geologic origins of Boston as part of their science course and learned that the section of Boston land known as the Back Bay is not actually a body of water but a landmass created by filling in the original salty tide marshes. This area to the west of Boston proper (at high tide it appeared to be a bay) was a "receiving basin"—that is, it received incoming tidal flow from the ocean.

These students' counterparts in the early days of Miss Winsor's School on Beacon Street knew a Boston topography not much different from today's. The streets west of the Public Garden, however, would have been only recently paved for the first time, and the trees along the Commonwealth Avenue Mall were still very small, but grand new houses along Beacon, Marlborough, and Newbury Streets and Commonwealth Avenue were already built and occupied. Winsor girls attended school from 1886 to 1910 in original structures on the one square mile of landfill that is still called the Back Bay, despite the absence of water.

After only a month in a "dreary"[1] house at 334 Boylston Street, Miss Winsor's hardy scholars moved into Mrs. Francis Brooks's own home at 97 Beacon Street. The following year the growing school population moved to larger quarters at 415 Boylston Street, where it stayed for five years; from that location the School sent forth its first three graduates. From 1892 until 1896 Miss Winsor's "seven well-established classes" occupied 36 Newbury Street, a building no longer in existence. The next move—to 21 Marlborough Street—was an exciting one, for there the school had its first science laboratory, "way at the top of the house, a real laboratory . . . for physics and chemistry."[2]

At the beginning of the school's eleventh year Miss Winsor moved for the last time within the Back Bay, this time to 95–96 Beacon Street, next door to Mrs. Brooks's house, where everything had started.

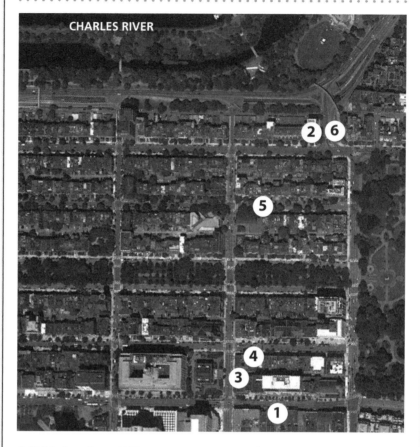

Locations of Miss Winsor's School in Back Bay, 1886–1910

CHARLES RIVER

1. 334 Boylston Street, 1886

2. 97 Beacon Street, 1886

3. 415 Boylston Street, 1887–92

4. 36 Newbury Street, 1892–96

5. 21 Marlborough Street, 1896–99

6. 95–96 Beacon Street, 1899–1910

The Beacon Street houses . . . were so charming, so airy, with their high, old-fashioned ceilings, so light and sunny . . . even though they could not meet the requirements of a model schoolhouse. Number 95 was lovely, with white marble fireplaces, and stuccoed walls and ceilings, but 96 was grand! Colonel Henry Lee had built it for his own home, and in it he had incorporated a beautiful French Louis Quinze ballroom, taken from the Deacon House on Boston Neck, when it was pulled down in the '70s. This room, with its delicate gray and gilt paneling, its great mirrors and chandeliers, made a highly picturesque Assembly Hall, but a school of over two hundred girls could be squeezed into it only by removing all the chairs and packing the children on the floor as close as in a box.[3]

Frances Parkinson Keyes 1903, who entered the School in the fall of 1899, recalled that "Miss Winsor's was already regarded as the leading institution of its kind in Boston . . . and was located in two large chilly houses, on the water side of Beacon Street, which had been thrown together and more or less adapted to their current usage."[4] Mary Winsor loved the fact that there was a real ballroom in this building. Only one of the early buildings—the one on Marlborough Street—still stands, and it has long since been converted to apartments. To create an exit from Storrow Drive onto Beacon and Arlington Streets, 97 Beacon was sacrificed. The present site on the Riverway, to which the School moved in the fall of 1910, was on a rise of land connected to the Back Bay salt marshes via the Muddy River, which, with a stream nearby called Stony Brook, rose and fell with the tides. The Muddy River was never a glorious sight, and as Mary Winsor herself remarked when the land for the new school building had been bought and a name for the new school was being discussed, "The less mention made of Muddy Brook, the better."[5]

The Museum of Fine Arts (1909), the Opera House (1909; now gone), the Isabella Stewart Gardner Museum (1903), and The Winsor School were among the first structures in the Fenway area. Simmons College moved from its location on St. Botolph Street into the property adjacent to the Gardner Museum in 1904, the Harvard Medical School opened on Longwood Avenue in 1906, and Beth Israel Hospital was founded in 1916. Fenway Park was built in 1912.

The filling in of the Back Bay had led to the stabilization and development of the areas around the Muddy River, most significantly because of the public park system created by Frederick Law Olmsted. Boston's "Emerald Necklace" stretches from the Public Garden past Winsor's very doorstep to Jamaica Pond and Franklin Park. (Olmsted's original plan was to connect the "necklace" all the way to Castle Island in South Boston.) The geologist Selby Cull writes in her article "Below Boston's Hills": "The Wisconsin Ice Sheet, the last glacier to blanket New England, retreated about 16,000 years ago, leaving in its wake boulders and gravel it had carried down from the North, and forming Cape Cod and the islands of Martha's Vineyard and Nantucket. Around Boston, the glacier left dozens of drumlins and "kettles" (bowl-shaped hollows created when glaciers melt), which form most of the ponds of the city's "Emerald Necklace," one of the oldest series of parks and parkways in the United States."[6]

The historian Brendan Donovan, a Brookline resident, has researched this area through careful study of old maps and land records. He has suggested that the land along Pilgrim Road (which originally ran from the eastern

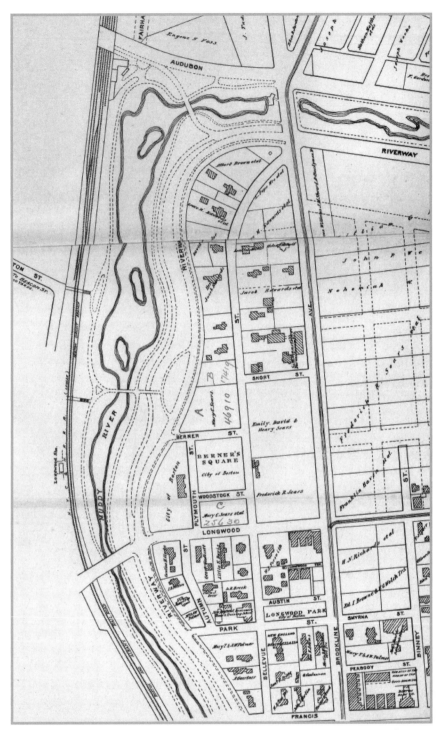

The areas in the middle of the map labeled A and C (in Charles Hamlin's hand) are
the original plots purchased from the Sears family. Lot B was acquired later.
The map shows the Simmons College buildings along Short Street and Brookline
Avenue, but there were as yet no hospitals on Brookline Avenue.
The Longwood Station is to the left of center at the top of the map.

end of Brookline Avenue to Francis Street) followed a ridge of land higher than the unsettled and somewhat marshy land around it.*

The Riverway site did not appeal to the founders at first. In an April 1906 letter from the real estate firm of Edward H. Eldredge & Company, Russell G. Fessenden had described some lots that might be available in the Back Bay but said that there was little available in the desired quadrangle bounded by Beacon Street, Massachusetts Avenue, and Boylston and Arlington Streets. "If we had a little more time we could undoubtedly find four houses for you on Newbury Street between Gloucester and Hereford Streets." Fessenden adds, "There is plenty of land that would suit your purpose to the southward of Boylston Street, lying between Mass Ave and the Fenway, but I understood that this would not suit you."[7]

A number of subscribers who had made a commitment even before the land had been bought immediately began a drive to raise additional funds. Huybertie Hamlin's firsthand account conveys the excitement of the group at their first meeting in 1905. Six families "got together . . . for dinner one night and had a thorough talk as to our ideas, ideals, and possible plans."[8] The Hamlins and the other assembled families lamented the lack of private school options for girls when the sons of the well-to-do had several Boston-area choices. Primary among their concerns was the need for "a playground, a gymnasium, and plenty of light and air." These amenities could not be provided in any of the Back Bay houses where the dame schools were operating, and to build a new school seemed the only solution.

This was the era of school building throughout the United States, but the concept of a larger and perhaps more structured secondary school was hard for some to grasp.[†] After sending their daughters down the street to Miss Winsor's intimate establishment for so many years, the parents were initially wary of a huge, purpose-built school like those being built for public school systems. Hearing of the possibility of situating the school in the Fenway, some parents deplored the idea of a school that was not in the immediate Back Bay area. They were also concerned about the size of the new school, fearing that a larger faculty and student body would lead to tighter regimentation and a less nurturing environment than the cozy dame schools the girls were accustomed to. Some were under the impression that all the existing Back Bay dame schools were to be put under one roof. Huybertie Hamlin spoke of one

---

* Some old maps indicate lands on a highland between two rivers (Stony and Muddy), a location near Rev. Eliot's Meeting House on a road called Mapleton in the early days of Roxbury, Massachusetts. Wheelock College is adjacent. Donovan believes that early settlers operated a cooperage, box-making firm, blacksmith shop, icehouse, fish-drying stages, salt-works, herring weirs, ropewalks, and a toll road at and around this site.

† In 1910 only about 9 percent of adults had a high school diploma, but by 1940 the rate was around 50 percent. See Jurgen Herbst, *The Once and Future School: Three Hundred and Fifty Years of American Secondary Education* (New York: Routledge, 1996).

mother who said "that she would withdraw her child if she had to stick out her tongue and have her temperature taken before school each day." There was also suspicion about a plan for an indoor swimming pool, which was, at the time, an unusual facility for any school. Was it true that girls would be required to have a swim every morning? "One excited mother wrote Mr. Hamlin that such an idea was insulting—that her daughter always had a bath every morning at home."[9]

As the word spread, numerous meetings were held during the following months in the Hamlin home at 2 Raleigh Street, and as many as thirty different families were eventually involved in the discussions. In 1907 the group formally appointed a board; Charles S. Hamlin was president, Charles P. Curtis was clerk, and Charles W. Hubbard was treasurer. The Incorporators did not at first assume that Mary Winsor would head the new school, although they did realize that working with someone who had an established educational enterprise in the Back Bay area could provide a nucleus for a student body. A letter written to Hamlin in 1906 verifies that they considered Mary Winsor's reputation to be strong enough to be of help in attracting parents. In fact, they eventually came around to the idea that it was quite important to get her.

When the parent group first approached her, Mary Winsor wrote in reply, "I will say it [taking the position as head of a new school] does not attract." She added, "I should never be willing to give up my own school, and I know besides that I am unfitted to fill a semi-public position."[10] The Board then approached Miss May (whose school would eventually join with Miss Brimmer's), but she too declined.

The committee kept in touch with Mary Winsor, however, and a few months later she acknowledged that Boston should have "at least one properly equipped school house for girls."[11] Although she went on to express concerns about her deafness, she seemed to have caught the excitement of the families as they went forward with plans for the new building, and she contributed ideas, caveats, and (eventually) requirements when she finally accepted their offer.

The Fenway site had much to offer, especially unencumbered land, but some of the parents continued to be worried about placing the school so far from the heart of the city. Huybertie Hamlin noted that although some parents declared they would never send their daughters so far, "in the end only two girls were withdrawn on account of the distance." Transportation was an understandable concern for parents who had been accustomed to a neighborhood school. Many of the original thirty Incorporators lived on Beacon Hill or in the Back Bay, and eight had addresses in or near Brookline. The Hamlin residence, where the early organizational meetings were held, was on Raleigh Street, west of Massachusetts Avenue and crossing Bay State

Road, where five of the Incorporators lived, an address that today is in the same zip code as The Winsor School.

The correspondence about the location for the new school contains repeated references to the need for fresh air and hygiene. In the Building Committee's report to Charles Hamlin on April 29, 1908, Charles Hubbard quotes at length from "a member of the committee" who was eloquent on the need for sufficient light and ventilation, noting that "children are under discipline and . . . if the air is bad and the light is poor, they are not at liberty to go home or to change their seats, but must . . . suffer what detriment comes."[12]

The filling of the salt marshes of the Back Bay had come about in part because of the unhealthful pollution of those waters. As the city grew, the environment was a growing concern, and plans for sewers, safe water, and clean air were as much a part of the civic improvements as new buildings. In addition, both city and state leaders were trying to halt the exodus of upper-class families from the city, many of whom were beginning to build substantial estates in the suburban areas. There appears to have been consensus that only high-end houses and institutions would be allowed to be built in the new Back Bay.[13] The rapidly growing immigrant population in the city had heightened a concern that what we today call low-income housing would attract the sort of people who might sully the cultural tone of the city. In a detailed and readable book on nearly every aspect of the newly formed land in the Back Bay, the authors state: "The design of the area, with Commonwealth Avenue as its focal point and rectangular blocks, served the Protestant elite's dual purposes of setting themselves off from the commercial city that had a tangle of curved streets, with the Common and the Public Garden acting as an effective barrier, while they remained close enough to downtown to exercise control."[14]

The extension of the city limits beyond Massachusetts Avenue and Charlesgate was already a reality, and that area began to seem a more viable location to the founders when they acknowledged the lack of suitable sites for a large new school in the Back Bay itself, especially at the price they were able to pay. The overriding positives of the Fenway site continued to be the open healthfulness of the exurban area, the convenience of transportation by electric trolley cars, train, or private cars and carriages, and the extremely low price of the land.

In March 1907 the committee had finally narrowed the search to three locations: one was "on Massachusetts Avenue past Newbury Street" and a second was on Audubon Road (now known as Park Drive). The third site, near the Longwood Cricket Club and Berners Park on the Riverway, was owned by one of the largest landowners in the area, David Sears. It was within one block of the Ipswich Street electric cars and walking distance of the Chapel Station, the present Longwood stop on the MBTA Green Line.

The architect's rendering shows a wing on the right that was never built.

David Sears's land, originally inhabited by the Algonquian Indians and settled by Europeans in the 1600s, was marshy and uneven, and it was essentially undeveloped, except for the area used by the Longwood Cricket Club, which had created some grass courts (and a none-too-glamorous clubhouse) near the intersection of Longwood and Brookline Avenues. But Sears still owned this property as well as an adjacent parcel of land he had donated, "free and unencumbered forever," for a public park that the city designated as Berners Park. The Winsor Executive Committee negotiated with both the Sears family and the City of Boston to rearrange two plots of land along the Riverway so that the school's land would not be split by Berners Park. Exchanging a Sears property along Longwood Avenue with the Berners Park land was accomplished with minimum fuss. There would still be a Berners Park, and in fact Winsor would use the former parkland as a playground, fulfilling Sears's original intention for the land.

Streets in the area were also rearranged; some disappeared, others were moved, and names were adjusted as part of the agreement with the city. In the mid-1980s another deal would be struck with the city so that the portion of Pilgrim Road that ran from Short Street to Longwood Avenue could be closed and the courtyard and playing fields unified. This action meant that Pilgrim Road was interrupted at the front of the School and picked up again at Longwood, curving to the Riverway, adding to an already bewildering street plan in the area.

On June 16, 1908, the deeds for the two Sears lots were delivered to be held in escrow, final payment being due September 16 of that year. The committee asked the Boston architect R. Clipston Sturgis to estimate the cost and to design the structure, and he began at once to figure out the number, size, and type of classrooms required.

In the original plans for the 1910 building, Sturgis had designed a second wing of classroom space on the southeast to correspond with the classroom wing on the Riverway. The two wings would border the courtyard on two sides, but the inner one was never built. All initial drawings for the School include this extension, and the brick facade on the rather blank, windowless wall on the southwest end of the main building still shows where this wing would have joined the main building. Money, of course, was the problem, and there was consternation on Sturgis's part when he realized his entire vision for the new building was not to be carried out. This unbuilt section would have housed a primary school open to both girls and boys, but there had been uncertainty from the beginning about whether a kindergarten-through-grade-twelve school was really feasible. The idea was finally abandoned because of the concern for transporting younger children so far out of the city. None of the later additions that enlarged the School, however, was built onto this unfinished wall, nor was the 1923 gymnasium, a freestanding building along Short Street.

Like most of the individuals involved in planning the new school, Sturgis was active in the life of the city of Boston: he served as president of the Society of Arts and Crafts; he was chairman of the Boston School Committee and had already designed schools as well as libraries and private homes. Sturgis took seriously the special requirements of an academic building, even weighing in on the issue of class size (an educational issue still debated in the twenty-first century): "While a larger class could be taught more economically, individual scholars would not receive the attention; and a smaller class would lose the interest and enthusiasm which is given by numbers." Both teachers and students in the School today can attest to which philosophy he adhered: the small classrooms on the Riverway side of the main building are still used but are frequently deemed inadequate because there is little room to move about, vary the seating plan, or handle a class larger than twelve girls.

Sturgis envisioned two sizes of classrooms, one of 572 square feet and one of only 286 square feet. Modern classrooms are based on the number of students, size of desks, and lighting and teaching needs; a class of twelve needs a minimum of 637 square feet. From the time the new school opened, teachers lamented the small size of the classrooms. Sturgis suggested that twelve smaller rooms would be sufficient for a total population of 300 students, and he proposed ten larger rooms to accommodate sixteen students each. (There is no indication of the research behind these numbers.) Then he broke down the classrooms as follows: eight "recitation" rooms, two or three labs, two music rooms, and an art room. There would also be a library, a gym, an assembly hall, an office, and teachers' library or "parlor."[15]

In 1908 there was special pride that Miss Winsor's School was offering

A Class VIII chemistry class in 1922.

three science courses, and Mary Winsor herself insisted that there be laboratory facilities in the new building for science as well as special rooms for art and music, "whatever the cost to the school," as well as room for plenty of exercise, both indoors and outdoors. Members of the committee visited Boston-area schools and even went to New York to observe the Brearley School. Financing was the overriding concern as the plans for the school progressed, and the donations of money as well as the support and advice of Mary Winsor's older brother Robert proved crucial. Huybertie Hamlin wrote, "At a most crucial moment Miss Winsor's brother, Mr. Robert Winsor, gave $15,000 to the school fund, and his firm of Kidder, Peabody & Company gave $10,000."[16] The Board also had to establish bylaws and explore the legal aspects of their incorporation. For the latter they were aided by the experience of men who had helped incorporate the Groton School. The plan to design, finance, and construct one large, independent school building was an unusual enterprise at the time. The Dana Hall School in Wellesley, for example, started in one small building in 1881 and added separate, purpose-built facilities as the student body grew and the need arose, and this was the pattern most local private schools followed.

"The greatest agitation of all was over the name for the new school, as

Miss Winsor did not want it to be named for her," Huybertie Hamlin noted.[17] Since the name "Winsor" (which seems so obvious in retrospect) did finally prevail, her account of these deliberations is typical of enterprises where the outcome is important and yet may not be deserving of so much energy. One can almost hear the various voices offering ideas: "I can only remember a few—Shawmut, Blackstone, St. Botolph, Parkway, Longwood, Boston Girls' School, Fenway, Nonantum, and much regret that Chilton had already been used for the new Club." (The Chilton Club, a private club for upper-class women founded in 1910, was named for Mary Chilton, the first woman to step off the *Mayflower*.) When they had settled on St. Botolph, someone wisely asked who this saint was and what he had done. Consulting *Drake's Walks about Boston*,[18] they found that the man who gave his name to the original Boston in England was connected to a lighthouse on the coast of England. "So immediately someone said it was very appropriate—that he would symbolize the light of learning in the new school!"[19]

After debating whether the name would suggest a denominational school, the "St." was dropped and "Botolph" was approved, only to be objected to by Miss Winsor's alumnae, students, and teachers who vehemently campaigned for "Winsor." Mary Winsor, who had her own suggestions (Lowell, Hallowell, Standish, Suffolk, Bay State, Hubbam, and Owl's Head, among others),* finally agreed, and another hurdle in founding a new school was overcome.

The new building opened in September 1910, and the entire community celebrated the formal dedication ceremony on Wednesday, November 9, in the gymnasium/assembly hall: "The Incorporators sat on the stage with Miss Winsor. Mr. Hubbard presented the keys to Mr. Hamlin and he presented them to Miss Winsor—he made her a short speech and after that to the graduates—another to the Faculty and one to the pupils. Each group stood up as he addressed them and there was a great deal of clapping." In response there were short speeches from representatives of the faculty, the pupils, and the graduates, and then Harvard's President Eliot, although not on the program, "made a very short but able address." Huybertie Hamlin wrote, "There was great enthusiasm and the lamp of learning burned on a pedestal at the front of the stage. A banner with a motto was hung up with evergreens at the front of the stage."[20]

The earliest motto had been "Lux Veritatis," chosen after consideration of various combinations of "light" and "truth." At the suggestion of Charles Eliot, the Incorporators approved a new motto, "Sound Mind in Sound Body" in 1907, and it has appeared in both its English translation and the original Latin (*Mens sana in corpore sano*), from the poet Juvenal, over the years.

---

* Another obvious choice was "Longwood," but Mary Winsor firmly said she in no way wanted that name. Longwood was the name David Sears chose for part of his land in the area; he took the name from Napoleon's residence during exile, Longwood House, on the island St. Helena.

A committee from the Incorporators (mostly the women) had planned a gala reception and tea in the dining room for the afternoon, and Huybertie Hamlin reported (thanks to "a maid with a stopwatch at the door to punch each arrival") an unexpectedly large attendance of 1,150 people. Members of Classes VII and VIII, dressed in white with red ribbons, conducted tours through the new school, and teachers were in their classrooms to "show their particular set-up." The outdoor playground, the gymnasium and the swimming pool ("people almost fell into it in their eagerness to see this much talked of innovation") attracted attention on that day, and there was particular praise for the "playrooms on the top floor to be used on stormy days." (Recently one of the maintenance men found a fragile antique shuttlecock made of leather with real feathers in the rafters.) The Planning Committee, expressing the spirit of a time that put great emphasis on improving the environment of the city and the health of its citizens, had brought about a facility with "light, air, and quiet surroundings."[21]

The founders of the School had been ahead of their time in making physical fitness part of the academic regimen for girls. To encourage "a sound body" through outdoor play and exercise, Mary Winsor from the beginning scheduled the day so that the afternoons would be free for the younger girls to be out on the fields. This was meant to be a required part of the day, but it

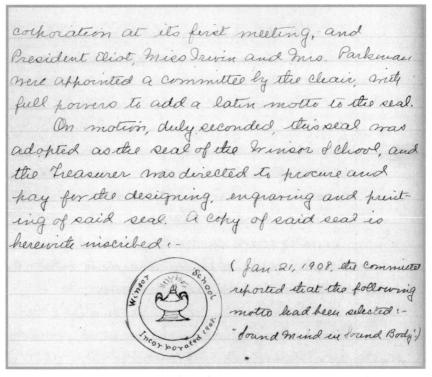

A section from the early Board's minutes contains a rough sketch of the future seal of the School and a note on the motto selected.

Precision drills and Swedish rhythmic gymnastics were popular athletic activities for girls, as illustrated by this picture taken in 1922, from an album presented to Mary Winsor upon her retirement.

took a while for the voluntary "Afternoon Session" to develop. The activity time was an innovation that parents were hesitant to endorse, in part because they were not quite ready to have their daughters in a longer school day. But Mary Winsor's carefully kept records on the number of girls participating in various sports activities show a gradual increase in attendance that led, inevitably, to regular outdoor play and organized team sports being a required part of the curriculum.

The gymnasium/assembly hall of the new school building (one can still see the hooks in the ceiling from which the exercise ropes hung) was a space that could hold the entire school for large gatherings, but it and the third-floor space gradually outgrew their usefulness as an afternoon play space when weather did not permit outdoor activities. The open land around the Longwood site had been part of its attraction, but a decade after opening, Mary Winsor and her successor, Katharine Lord, asked the Trustees to consider buying more land for playing fields and building a dedicated gymnasium.*

In her 1921 Report to the Corporation, Katharine Lord, the second Director of the School, spoke of the success of the Afternoon Session required for the lower four grades three afternoons a week: "The space is not enough to give the girls opportunity for long enough periods of exercise and if we are

---

* Katharine Lord came to the School in 1914 as assistant director and was Director from 1922 until 1939. Her portrait was painted by Charles S. Hopkinson, the renowned portrait artist, whose five daughters graduated from Winsor: Harriet 1922, Mary 1923, Isabella 1925, Elinor 1928, and Joan 1930.

When the Longwood Cricket Club moved to Chestnut Hill in 1922 and the School acquired the club's Longwood Avenue land, Winsor already had a thriving tennis program. Shown here are the four team members and the coach in 1925 (left to right): Elizabeth Palfrey 1927, Fanny Curtis 1925, Frances Jennings, Celia Sachs 1926, and Marjorie Morrill 1926.

adequately to provide for their afternoon needs we must have more space and a bigger gymnasium. Even if a new wing were built, Miss Winsor thought as I do that it would have to be endowed." The care of the building and grounds was a perennial challenge, and Katharine Lord was not the only Director to lament the amount of money spent on repairs rather than on a more important need—faculty salaries. In the same report she noted that owing to a new filter and vacuum cleaner for the swimming pool, "the water is now reported to be better than in any pool which the examiner from the State Board of Health has tested this year."[22]

As more and more parents took advantage of having their daughters spend a longer time at school, the girls began to take an interest in activities other than sports and doing their homework. Katharine Lord remarked, "I expected to find them reading enormously, and I have found nothing of the kind, they want to work with their hands. And we have not sufficient facilities for them, nor sufficient time from our trained people to help them. We need pottery and other crafts."[23] She went on to suggest fitting out the space under the eaves (where in fact the Art Department now resides) in order to add sewing and weaving, and to give more time to art teachers. Her further observation on the need for more teaching space was to be echoed throughout the coming years as the school population grew: "With the increase in classes due to more elective work and with the increase in work with individuals more class-rooms are necessary. Now little groups wander about for a vacant spot; they sit on benches in the hall or crowd into the terrace room three groups at a time or carry on a recitation in the handicraft room with typewriters clattering in the corner."[24] She went on to say that the younger girls needed more room to move about in the classrooms and that some rooms were not suited to the Lower School age group. The population of the school at this point was 264, two above Mary Winsor's "ideal" number.

To add any new structure, the School needed more land, and it was at this point that the Board was able to acquire from the Sears family the land the Longwood Cricket Club had used since 1877. The first Davis Cup tournament was held on those grass lawns in 1900, and a Winsor woman, Helen Homans 1902, won the U.S. Lawn Tennis Women's Singles title there in 1906; Margaret Curtis 1902 was one-half of the winning women's doubles team in 1908.* The timing was fortunate: the Longwood Cricket Club was moving out to Chestnut Hill but preserving some history by keeping the name Longwood. The *Boston Globe* printed a lengthy article about the event and noted: "Old Longwood has been sold. The Sears Estate, which owned it, has transferred the property to the Winsor School for the further development of that institution."[25]

The gymnasium and the additional outdoor space for playing fields were the only modifications to the School until after Mary Winsor's death in 1950. In fact, for fifty years after the School's opening in 1910, the main building was used more or less as originally planned and designed. The classical appearance of the front entrance has hardly changed: stately Doric columns support a portico that shades a brick walk, and double doors open into the wide vestibule, where Winsor girls for decades have sat with books, backpacks, and hockey sticks waiting for their carpool or for the bus to an away game.

The inside stairways, up in the middle and down on either side, are also unchanged except for the periodic cosmetic improvements of paint and wall decorations. Mary Winsor and her successors in their reports to the Corporation mentioned from time to time their attempts to find extra space here and there, adapting rooms to unforeseen uses, and adjusting to demands of

---

* The tournament is now called the U.S. Open Tennis Championship. Other Winsor winners: Sarah Palfrey Cooke 1930 won in 1941 and 1945, and Hazel Hotchkiss Wightman, a faculty member and parent, won three times.

A view of the School taken in 1922. The School had acquired the land in the foreground in 1911.

an increasing student body and new curriculum. Until 1963 the dining room was in the space now known as the Junior Assembly, the kitchen was behind it in the area now inhabited by the Modern Language Department. An infirmary was located on the Lower School corridor next to the Fountain Room, the present Upper School homerooms were the science labs, the present senior homeroom was originally the handicraft room, and the library was only one floor (now the upper library).

One little-known feature of the building that was completely refashioned in 1998 was the apartment for a resident custodian. A self-contained living unit of two floors existed at the front of the building near the Riverway until the School began to modernize security arrangements and replaced it with a suite of offices.

As the school population grew, the crowding in the dining room became a pressing concern. The original dining room was wide and sunny: the kitchen staff served lunch from the nearby kitchen, and girls sat in assigned seats at long rectangular tables supervised at each end by a faculty member. In 1910 there were three options: soup luncheon for 10 cents, meat luncheon for 25 cents, or full-course luncheon for 40 cents. By 1920 the girls could order lunch for the year at 50 or 60 cents a day. There had been a logistical problem with the dining area from the very start, when it was discovered that there was no separate entry for ice and food deliveries to the kitchen area.

The third Director of the School, Frances Dorwin Dugan,* in her semi-annual reports to the Corporation, mentioned that the dining room was so

---

* Frances Dorwin Dugan was Director of the School from 1939 to 1951. She was hired to teach English in 1918 and was assistant director 1922–29, associate director 1929–39.

~ GENEROUS-MINDED WOMEN ~

overcrowded they had started to use the Glass Room for a lunchtime club meeting room. The Glass Room had been one of the open-air terraces on the Riverway side of the upper corridor. Although it had been enclosed after one year so that it could be more usable in cool weather, its northern orientation required extra heating. There was also a plan to enclose the terrace facing the courtyard, a move that would obstruct windows and require additional foundation masonry; this project was dropped. Frances Dugan suggested to the Trustees the need for more classrooms so that teachers could have their own desks in their individually assigned rooms for teaching and meeting privately with pupils, a proposal that suggests pedagogical changes as well as growth. Few teachers, however, could claim their own space; teachers at Winsor had to be energetically peripatetic, often teaching in two or three different classrooms assigned to their department.

THE NEWLY INCORPORATED SCHOOL on Pilgrim Road opened in 1910 with 225 students; the architect had planned the original building for as many as 265. At the time of Mary Winsor's retirement in 1922, the number had reached 264, where it remained for ten years. Enlarging the School slightly to 270 between 1931 and 1935 may have been accepted because additional tuition revenue would have been helpful during the Depression.

A little-known outpost building became a part of Winsor's extended campus in the early 1940s. The School added a residential building for a small number of students in 1943; parents were seeking to eliminate long commutes from outlying suburbs, and graduates in other parts of the country

The original dining room, shown here in 1922, was used until the Dexter Wing was built in 1963. The students ate lunch at assigned tables with a faculty member at each end.

The swimming pool was a revolutionary feature in the new School. By the 1970s, shortly after this picture was taken, it was inadequate for competition and expensive to maintain. It was covered over in 1982 and is now office and storage space.

wanted to send their daughters to Winsor. Two Frenchwomen, former school heads from New York, found a house to rent across the Riverway in Brookline and finally purchased the house at 16 Hawes Street in 1946. The fourteen or so places available at the Winsor Residence were open to girls who met the high requirements for character, many of whom went home on weekends. Winsor purchased the house in 1951 and maintained this small boarding school experiment until 1954. Two Winsor sports teachers, May P. Fogg [1938 to 1960] and Maggie Boyd [1952 to 1955], served as directors of the Residence.

Every Director has noted the effect of the increased enrollment numbers. Once the student body had grown to 300 between 1939 and 1949, the School never had fewer than 300 students, except for three years in the mid-1970s, when enrollment dipped in part because co-educational schools—including several boys' schools that had begun to admit girls—became attractive to the Winsor applicant pool. In the late 1950s growth continued, and, with 100 more students than the 225 with which the School had opened, the Trustees began to discuss expansion. It was not until 1962, however, that they made plans for a major addition to the old building. Virginia Wing, Director from 1963 to 1988, recalled that from the time she joined the Winsor faculty in 1952, there was discussion about how and where to expand the building.

The Dexter Wing, completed in 1963, was often referred to as "the new wing" even after newer wings came along. It was named for Franklin Dexter, a Trustee and the first chair of Buildings and Grounds. The spacious new dining room overlooking the courtyard and fields opened the school to sky and air and light. Attached on the Riverway side were a new kitchen and delivery platform and a separate but adjacent private dining room, named in memory of Martina Brandegee Lawrence 1925 but popularly known as the PDR. Beneath all this was an entirely new corridor of five classrooms (named the Case, Thorndike, Winsor, Harwood, and Hiam Rooms for donors to the building fund), restroom facilities for both men and women, and a peaceful and well-appointed retreat for weary faculty. The new classrooms' windows opened onto the courtyard, and two of them had large oval tables, an arrangement conducive to discussion-based teaching strategies, especially in

The Residence at 16 Hawes Street, Brookline.

English classes. The addition was designed by the firm Bastille and Halsey and seemed very modern in comparison to the old building. The exterior was white rather than brick, and its windows and rooflines were a departure from the old academic building with its late-Victorian period touches.

One of the most beautiful spaces R. Clipston Sturgis had designed, the library on the second floor, remains essentially intact. A lofty room with overhead beams and Arts and Crafts–inspired windows, it would at first seem unchanged to a visitor from the past. It is a gracious book-lined room, hushed and peaceful. The furniture has changed, lighting has improved, and shelves have been added through the years, but its character has been preserved.

The first and most significant library expansion occurred in 1980 when two additional floors were created by the clever design of the architect Conover Fitch. Fitch (who was the husband of Priscilla Hall Fitch 1937 and the father of four graduates)[26] radically converted the large study hall directly beneath the library. The room's ceiling was high enough that he was able to insert a mezzanine, providing a middle floor of stacks and a catwalk at one end for the storage of periodicals. About half of the lower floor remained

The Dexter Wing (on the left) was completed in 1963.

*New classrooms in the Dexter Wing allowed the expanded use of round tables,
as seen in this 1984 photograph.*

*A rare 1910 photograph of the library shows the atmosphere and beauty
of a room that has always been special.*

at the original height, and the open mezzanine looked unobtrusively over
a new circulation desk, display rack, card catalogue, and additional book-
shelves. The space was strikingly modern in some ways, but it also looked
as though it had always been there. The upper-level library continued to feel
like its distinguished self and was kept quiet for Upper School studying. The
lower library immediately began to be filled with the movement and chatter
of Lower Schoolers who, along with inspired and likable librarians and an
online catalogue, have made it a cheerful and cherished part of the School. A
two-floor semicircular extension added in 1998 holds shelves and study areas
and seamlessly blends the new with the old both inside and outside.

These two library renovations also added much-needed rooms: a separate Lower School library on the lower level, and five large and airy classrooms cleverly situated in "discovered space" between the old building and
the "new wing."

One of the most dramatic changes to the original edifice was the closing
of the science laboratories along the Upper School hallway and their reloca-
tion to a state-of-the-art science wing, completed in 1986. Mary Winsor had
always spoken with pride of her science courses: physics and chemistry had
been taught since 1896, and a biology lab "with individual gas jets" had been
installed at the Beacon Street building in 1899.[27] One of the advantages of
girls' schools has been freeing science and math from being labeled "for boys
only." The beauty and excitement of science attracted many girls throughout
Winsor's history. By the 1980s teachers and students and parents realized that

~ THE SCHOOLHOUSE ~

57

An aerial view from the late 1980s shows the new science wing on the far left and the gymnasium on the far right. Pilgrim Road has been closed, but the parking lot divides the campus.

taking rigorous science courses was not for the few but for the many and that colleges looked favorably on girls who challenged themselves in advanced physics and chemistry.

The love of science was a genuine one for Winsor girls, many of whom from the earliest days have gone on to careers in science—as physicians, researchers, naturalists, explorers, and, of course, teachers. Elizabeth Jackson 1929, for whom one of the biology labs is named, became a biologist who earned the Medal of Freedom for her work studying and preventing infectious diseases among the Allied troops during World War II. When the Massachusetts State Science Fairs began in 1949, Winsor and four other schools exhibited science projects, and Museum of Science personnel erected a planetarium in the lower gym. Winsor seniors have also competed for national prizes in the Intel—formerly the Westinghouse—Science Talent Search. Claudine Madras 1992 was the second-place winner out of 1,705 applicants nationwide in 1992, and the School has had four semifinalists: Liane Young 2000, Justine Nagurney 2002, Lara Maggs 2009, and Elizabeth Byrne 2010.

Science teachers eagerly participated in planning the seven new laboratory spaces with a view to creating rooms that girls would enjoy using. Science teaching (and science itself) had changed so much between 1910 and 1986 that it is astonishing that teachers had been able to use the old laboratories and classrooms so well. Some of the counters and desks of the impressive new facility were scaled for younger girls, and there were areas where the Lower School classes could sit casually on a carpeted floor to see demonstrations and hear special speakers. Broad shelves by bay windows provided a home for plants, and prep areas between the laboratories delighted the teachers. Led by the head of the Science Department, Ileana Jones [1974 to 2004], teachers worked with Charles Tseckares of the architectural firm Childs Bertram Tseckares and Casendino, offering their expertise and experience to create an outstanding facility.

The building of the science wing was a more ambitious undertaking than any previous construction. It involved emptying the equipment from the old science laboratories and refitting those rooms for class and homeroom spaces; there was no more room on the School's grounds for expansion unless playing fields were taken, and the final plan was a challenging one: to build an elevated structure above the Dexter Wing, although it had not been built to support the weight of an additional floor. The science wing would rest on supports installed in the ground around rather than on top of the dining room. This renovation succeeded in uniting the architectural styles of the old and new buildings by enclosing the 1960s windows of the dining room with graceful, elongated, gothic-inspired arches that somehow enhanced, rather than obscured, the view into the courtyard.

The addition was a stunning success and brought the School into its second century with a new spirit. The closing of Pilgrim Road from Short Street to Longwood Avenue in 1983 had united the campus; girls no longer had to watch for automobiles as they crossed the street to the gymnasium. Richard D. Leggat, president of the Board from 1979 until 1988, first recognized the need to make this far-reaching and historical change to the Winsor property. Eventually the parking lot along the courtyard was grassed over, and parking was moved to the Webster lot directly across from the front entrance, which had been acquired by the School in March 1911 and functioned as a play space for the Upper School. The president of the Massachusetts State Senate at the time was William M. Bulger, a colorful and erudite man whose youngest daughters, Mary and Kathleen, graduated from Winsor in 1984 and 1985. Senator Bulger treasured the education in ancient Greek his daughters received. When the School wanted to close the section of Pilgrim Road that bisected the campus, he expedited the process.

The new teaching spaces in the science wing were superior to anything else in the School at the time, and the large rooms they replaced on the second floor of the old building began new life as homerooms for the Upper School, more necessary than ever with the larger student body. The population was still growing, along with the curriculum, the sports program, and the extracurricular activities of the School. Needs became more specific: it

A sketch of the renovated gymnasium in 1993 by the architectural firm of Childs Bertram Tseckares and Casendino.

was now clear that the 1923 gymnasium was old-fashioned and deficient, the assembly hall too crowded, and the stage too cramped for the kinds of theater work the girls were capable of doing.

The renovation of the gymnasium in 1993 turned out to be another exercise in working around and transforming an existing space. Again an architect from Childs Bertram Tseckares and Casendino, Robert Brown, accepted the task, a major part of which was to figure out how to have an up-to-date gymnasium floor as near as possible to regulation size. The Board had considered tearing the old gym down and starting a new one from scratch but because of the prohibitive cost decided in the end to create a larger and more up-to-date gymnasium on the upper level. On the lower level are new locker rooms and workout rooms, and a large, glassed-in space for the sports faculty's office. There are other amenities—a trainer's room, special locker areas for visiting teams and coaches, and an entire new, bowed-out front for the northwest wall of the building, enhancing the original entrance. On the upper level is a comfortable lounge and kitchenette. This sunny room was intended for students, but they did not take to it, and it now functions as a pleasant space for health classes and small luncheons and meetings. At street level is a foyer with a spacious reception area. The renovated gymnasium building was dedicated in January 1994 with a ribbon-cutting and special tour for the whole School.*

The renovated basketball court was still not regulation size, and, although it could be used for practice and for the Lower School, the Upper School varsity and junior varsity teams competed at nearby Simmons College. In 1989

* The upper gym was named in honor of May Priscilla Fogg, the longtime head of the Physical Education Department and an internationally respected leader in her field.

Simmons had constructed a completely new athletic complex containing state-of-the-art training equipment, hardwood courts, an indoor running area, and a swimming pool. Winsor students were also lucky enough to be able to use the new Simmons swimming pool for both practice and competitions, and in return Simmons used the Winsor playing fields. This was just one of several "exchanges of facilities" Winsor has made with other area institutions, including nearby Wheelock College, as well as private clubs in order to offer sports such as squash, ice hockey, and curling to students. Winsor also belongs to MASCO (Medical Academic and Scientific Community Organization) in the Longwood Medical Area and sends a representative to its meetings. Mary Winsor and the Incorporators would be astonished at the growth and complexity of the Longwood area and of the planning required by needs such as parking, traffic flow, emergency evacuations, and security.

Yearbook pictures of the crew in the 1974 Winsor yearbook indicate the early interest in offering a crew program. As it grew it became popular and thrillingly successful. Unfortunately, Winsor did not have a boathouse on the Charles River, and various historical ramifications made it unlikely that any new structures would ever be approved along the historic Charles. The solution was to share the Belmont Hill School's boathouse, an extension of the

*The Winsor and Belmont Hill Schools share this boathouse
on the Charles River in Cambridge.*

Carolyn McClintock Peter Hall, 2005.

brother-school agreement worked out in the 1970s. (The all-boys school was founded in Belmont in 1923.) After lengthy negotiations with the Cambridge Historical Society and the Metropolitan District Commission, Winsor in 2001 won the right to renovate and expand the Belmont Hill boathouse, and both schools were the beneficiaries of a $1.1 million improvement to the facility.

The school population had continued to grow from around 360 in the 1980s to 400 by 1993, and at the beginning of the new millennium the number settled at around 420—a much larger school than anyone would have predicted fifty years earlier. The crowding was noticed especially in the "new" dining room, but a more crucial need was for classroom space. Furthermore, the School's sixth Director, Carolyn McClintock Peter [1988 to 2004], and the Trustees were mindful of Winsor's impressive standing among girls' schools—indeed, among all schools—and of the ongoing need to maintain the attractiveness and usefulness of the facilities. In 2002 they embarked on what would be the School's most ambitious construction project since 1910: Peter Hall. Its main feature is a spacious dining room and kitchen, but it also includes additional science laboratories, faculty offices, a photography laboratory, and a faculty workroom. A maintenance area and delivery platform complete the building.

All rejoiced when the spacious and light-filled new dining room opened for business in April 2004. The expansive addition was piloted by Carolyn Peter, whose vision and energy had steered not only this project but also the renovations undertaken in 1993, 1998, and 2001. There was still more to be done, however: the old dining room would be transformed (amazingly, by the next fall) into five large, light-filled classrooms and the Valeria Knapp Trustee Room for special meetings.*

Because some of the building projects went on during the school year, a sense of community necessarily emerged, for few in the School could have been unaware of the workmen who were pounding nails, carrying out debris, sweeping up, and walking about to oversee the process. The entire school community had a stake in what was being done, and all contributed, even if it was by walking the long way around to a class without complaining because a hallway was blocked or had disappeared. During renovations there have always been special people involved—plasterers and plumbers and painters—who briefly became a part of the Winsor family.

In their own special category, however, are the tireless people who have for more than a century maintained the building day after day when the carpenters and craftsmen have departed: the men who shoveled snow and moved furniture, supplies, and boxes of books from old to new locations; the housekeeping staff who washed the blackboards and picked up litter and polished the brass and guarded the front door and served lunch for many years. Many stayed until they were beyond retirement age. Gradually, a paid after-hours cleaning crew replaced the housekeeping staff, emptying bins, vacuuming, and dusting.

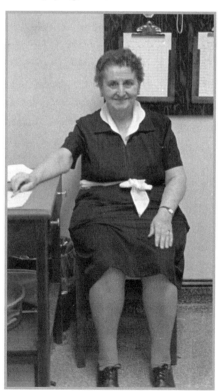

The head of Buildings and Grounds, A. Paul Trifone (honored by a plaque in the maintenance area), kept the buildings spotless during his long tenure, 1957 to 1988. One of his specialties was his insistence on the regular waxing and buffing of floors; the linoleum in the dining room and the original terrazzo floors in the older part of the building received such assiduous care that they have continued to shine far into the twenty-first century. But he was much more than a supervisor of floor polishing: he served as clerk-of-the-works for the Dexter Wing as well as for the science addition and the library renovation. When the original copper roof leaked, the material was sold in 1912 so that a slate roof could be installed. In the 2000s, when the slate needed to be repaired, Kenneth Wonoski, the director of Buildings and Grounds (who had so impressed Trifone during his work on the building of the science wing that Trifone recruited him as his suc-

*Valeria A. Knapp 1916 served as the fourth director of the School, from 1951 to 1963. She arrived in 1922 as a Lower School teacher and became associate director in 1940. She was the headmistress of Concord Academy from 1937 to 1940.

Mary Mahoney at her post just inside the front door.

cessor), learned how to refurbish a slate roof so that this expense could be lowered.

All of them were part of the continuity of the personnel and became friends to all. In 1982 the yearbook was dedicated to Mary Mahoney, the School's first security person, who sat patiently just inside the front door for many years.

> She's the first person we see when we arrive at Winsor and she's the last one we say good-bye to each day. In between, Mary always shows the warmth and caring often taken for granted, but always needed, in the school day, whether she's making sure we get a note from the board, re-minding us to bring home a sick friend's lessons, or merely trying to re-member all our names. We think our mothers would find it comforting to know that, in their absence, someone tells us to put our hats on when it's cold. We find it comforting, too.[28]

At Miss Winsor's Back Bay schools, when the daily session ran from ap-proximately nine o'clock in the morning until one in the afternoon, the girls walked home to lunch. As the afternoon program grew at the new Fenway location, the girls could bring their lunches or purchase them at the School.[29] An in-house kitchen staff prepared meals until food preparation was con-tracted out to a food service company in the mid-1970s. Their staff have quickly become part of the School family and made lunch so varied and in-teresting that it is almost part of the curriculum. Molly Johnson, who came to Winsor in 1976, provided such wonderful offerings that the School pub-lished a small cookbook, *Fringe Benefits,* featuring her special recipes. Her imaginative successor, Regis Downes, helped the School celebrate the Red Sox opening days and eventual triumph in the 2004 World Series by featur-ing "ball park menus," continuing a long Winsor tradition of supporting the neighborhood team. Both students and teachers have been enthusiastic fans of the Red Sox, who won the World Series five times between 1903 and 1918, and then again in 2004 and 2007. The February 1934 *Lamp* even mentions a four-alarm fire at Fenway Park the preceding month.

The Directors' reports to the Corporation continually raised issues about daily upkeep and ongoing repairs, summarizing for the Board of Trustees the physical needs of the plant, both minor and major. In November 1910, just after the new School had opened, the Board's treasurer, Charles Hubbard, wrote to R. Clipston Sturgis about "two or three matters at the school which have been called to my attention": "The first and most important seems to be the heat radiated from the steam coils under the windows in the classrooms, which are within two feet or so of the scholars. . . . I had supposed that this direct radiation would be used daily only in very cold weather, but it is ap-parently on all the time."[30] Hubbard went on to suggest "a metal screen lined with asbestos on the radiator side." He added, however, that there was a need for more heat in the vocal training room and in the third-floor playrooms, and he proposed steam pipes under the eaves. Some things do not change: the excessive warmth of the senior homeroom and the wintry temperatures in the music and art rooms were concerns well into the twenty-first century.

Winsor has been blessed with affable, diligent individuals whom the students know by name and who are considered so much a part of the faculty that when the School began to recognize the twenty-year tenure of employees, an annual celebration instituted by Carolyn Peter, the maintenance staff who day after day care for the structures so laboriously built were also honored at the formal dinner. It is likely that very few people know completely the kind of effort required after buildings are built, expanded, and redesigned. (A student once asked one of the maintenance men what he and his coworkers did in the School. He is said to have replied, "Whatever the teachers don't do, we do.")

The development of The Winsor School on the 7.4 acres it occupies on what is now a very valuable piece of Boston property has resulted in a campus that is efficient, compact, and attractive. With the final refurbishment of the oldest section of the building in 2007 and 2008, a long conversation about whether the School should take advantage of the value of its land, sell it, and build anew in the suburbs came to a close. There were clear advantages to Winsor's urban setting: its proximity to a broad and diverse student pool in Boston and the willingness of those living outside the city to be a part of a vibrant urban school community. In addition, the area around Winsor has become a teaching and learning center: its hospitals, schools, research institutes, museums, and parks are so close that the possibilities for Winsor education extend beyond the actual campus.

From the air, Winsor's green courtyard does indeed look like a gem dangling from the meandering Emerald Necklace. The actual footprint of the School grounds has not changed since 1923, but its inner architecture—a complex configuration of corridors and classrooms that are actually on thirteen different levels—has gone through many refittings. Sometimes it has been a tight fit, but to walk through the building is to see the personality of the community—girls studying together in a cranny, classic wooden garden benches in the hall for teacher conferences, colorful club bulletin boards, and irresistible examples of student work. Winsor's spaces are not as elegant as those at some other schools, but it would be hard to find a more well-kept and efficiently used building. For over a century it has been an incomparable learning environment for a rich curriculum.

It is extremely important that we, in our large and flourishing School, housed in a beautiful building with superior athletic facilities, never lose the personal relationship which is the keystone of true education.

—*Valeria Knapp*

What does it really mean when we say that we care about the individual? It should mean everything, for this is the strength of an independent school: to meet a child where she is, to work with her so that she becomes the kind of person and the kind of student who will go on learning all of her life.

—*Virginia Wing*

E L Brown VIII	MON.	TUES.	WED.	THURS.	FRI.
8.50-9.10					
9.10-9.30		Chem		Chem	French
9.30-9.50					
9.50-10.30	French		Chem		Latin
10.30-11.10	Chem		Eng	Eng	
11.10-11.30	Recess	Recess	Recess	Recess	Recess
11.30-12.10	Latin	gym	French	gym	
12.10-12.50	Eng	Lat		Latin	Eng
12.50-1.30		Read	Latin	Rowley Dike	Chem

French - Miss Dellinger
Chem = Miss Rowley
Eng = Miss Dike
Latin = Miss Griswold
Read = Miss Bowerson

A senior's schedule card from 1921. The same format is still being used.

The Curriculum

⟨☙❦☙⟩

"THE GLAD DISCIPLINE OF BODY, MIND AND SOUL"

SCHOOLS AT THE BEGINNING of the twenty-first century have retained a number of features from far earlier times. Today, as in the 1900s, students follow a schedule of classes that directs them to different rooms for different subjects taught by different teachers; each teacher assigns homework—mostly reading and writing; there are periodic assessments in individual subjects and, in later years, college entrance examinations. Even when Winsor was a very small school, there were report cards, study halls, tests and quizzes, tutoring sessions with a teacher, stress over examinations, and, of course, homework. The broad categories of courses over the years have remained: reading and writing, literature, mathematics, history, science, and foreign language have been the core subjects for American students for more than a century. Even modern pedagogical practices such as small-group work, concentration on the "whole child," and field trips have long been a part of American curriculum. Interdisciplinary courses and independent projects are also not modern innovations, and educators a century ago recommended the consideration of "multiple intelligences" and experimented with nongraded courses.

The Winsor School's teachers were from the early years knowledgeable about their students' differing learning styles and displayed a remarkable awareness of child development. They have consistently adjusted curriculum from a student-centered vantage point, sharing ideas with each other informally and in meetings. Not only have they attended conferences in different parts of the country, they themselves have sometimes been featured presenters describing their own innovations at Winsor.

New course content and some completely new courses did alter the educational picture from time to time, and an examination of The Winsor School curriculum reveals how and why such changes came about. Some of the

November 29, 1897.

Elizabeth

Examinations.

English Composition. Usually good, should be excellent — a+

Reading Grammar. Fairly good

Spelling. Usually good — a.

Poetry. Pretty good — B.

Literature. Excellent — {B+

History. Fair. Written work not done. {a—

Art.

Geography.

French. Gr. Very good — a.

German. Gr. Fair — B—

Latin. Very good — c.

Greek.

Mathematics. Very good — c—

Science. Good — B+

Drawing.

Attendance. Absent three times.
Tardy three times (excused once)

Elizabeth's Class III Report Card.

relevant factors were national trends, college requirements, the advent of standardized testing, and the school accreditation process. For Winsor, with its enlightened and civic-minded constituencies, social and political pressures could not be ignored and, because it is a girls' school, the specific needs of girls and young women were always in the forefront. Schools are peculiarly tied to their historical context, and Winsor, like all schools, responded to society's needs during wartime, the so-called *Sputnik* era, the struggles of blacks and women for civil rights, the emphasis on multiculturalism, and the demands of the parents who sent their daughters to Winsor.

The effects of technological innovation have been the big story in the twenty-first century. The computer has greatly facilitated communication with parents about their daughters' progress, allowing immediate and extensive contact between teachers and parents. Grades and individual comments are now quite a bit more substantial than they were in the "Report Card for Parents" from 1897 in which Mary Winsor wrote, "Elizabeth's work is not first rate." The modern trend toward detailed written reports about a child's work has become popular with parents, but Mary Winsor's pithy observation said a great deal.

Elizabeth's report card also shows the courses she took in 1897: English (divided into two separate courses, one for writing and grammar, one for reading and literature), history, art, geography, French, Latin, mathematics, and science. In 2010 the usual ninth-grade report card (actually a two-page document with a paragraph from each teacher) listed English, history, science, math, a foreign language, a fine arts course, and sports. For students then and now, there were few individual deviations except for the foreign language, the early choices being Latin, French, and German. By 2007 they were Latin, French, Spanish, and Chinese. The most recent revision of the curriculum in 2004 was entrusted to the Long Range Curriculum Planning Committee (LRCPC), and its final recommendation mandated the same ninth- and tenth-grade subject areas for everyone, something that had not changed in decades, the only areas for choice being in foreign language and fine arts. That 2004 revision also brought a change in graduation requirements, most notably that girls take a semester in the history of a non-Western country: "Class VII students will take one semester of non-western history, also taught in conjunction with a non-western literature course focusing on the same geographical area."[1] The LRCPC worked for over two years on their recommendations not only for changes in course offerings and graduation requirements but also for a philosophy of curriculum that would be "a designed continuum of developmentally appropriate learning experiences across departments."[2] It is likely that Mary Winsor would have supported that goal, for curriculum review was not invented by modern educators, and she, who had no college degree, was making additions and adjustments to her course syllabi from the beginning, turning whenever she could to experts in the field of education but also relying on her own and her faculty's instincts and observations of children. The Directors who followed her had college degrees and all had classroom teaching experience.

American educational practices have traditionally been controlled by citizens on the local level, even as national endeavors such as No Child Left Behind and Race to the Top have tried to establish some kind of uniformity across the country. (Most recently, in March 2010, a group of governors and higher education leaders released a new set of core standards to regularize all teaching and learning across the country. Adoption is voluntary, and Texas and Alaska refused to sign on.) But educational reform on the national level is not a modern innovation. In 1892 a coalition of distinguished educational leaders across the United States established the first national committee to assess public education This was six years after the opening of Mary Winsor's Back Bay school and about fifteen years before a group of Boston parents and their supporters committed to building their new girls' school on the Riverway. The public secondary school was gradually evolving into a recognizable entity in the country, and despite the regional variations and the different atmospheres of independent and public schools, there was general agreement that all institutions should share similar ideas about curriculum and standards. As more and more high school graduates went on to college, institutions of higher learning had a stake—and a say—in defining what level of achievement merited admission.

The Committee of Ten, as the 1892 group was called, included professors and teachers from colleges and universities; Charles W. Eliot, president of Harvard University and later a Winsor Incorporator, was its chairman. Members included the presidents of several colleges and state universities, the heads of the Girls' Latin School in Boston and the Lawrenceville School, and William T. Harris, the U.S. commissioner of Education. Subsidiary "committees of ten" were appointed for each subject area of the curriculum, and these divisions themselves revealed how alike the emphases in secondary schools are then and now. The report included ideas that were in some ways radical, but for the most part the committee appears merely to have codified a prevailing educational philosophy of curriculum—one that holds sway today.[3]

By the end of their negotiations, the Committee of Ten had, for example, established many of the structures and course areas we take for granted in our schools: a division into eight "grammar school" years and four of high school; common times for college admission tests; the basic subject areas of English, mathematics, science, history, foreign language, the arts, and physical education. Some of their recommendations were unusual for the time: that interdisciplinary courses should be created between English and history as well as between math and science; that foreign languages should start in elementary school; and that Caesar's *Gallic Wars* should be removed from the intermediate Latin curriculum. From time to time over the years, these ideas have come up during curriculum revision as "fresh, new" ideas, but many of them existed even before the meetings of the Committee of Ten.

Several of the subcommittees focused on "the importance of forming from the start good habits of observing correctly and stating accurately the facts observed." They encouraged such student behavior in the earliest grades, and then, as now, those early years were skill-oriented. They saw schooling as a continuum—in both form and content—from first grade through high school graduation. It was common in the nineteenth century to educate the more able students for university degrees that led to future careers in the church or law, while a second tier of courses was given to those preparing for business or trade. The committee's final report, however, stated that it was essential to educate as many young people as possible with a rigorous and complete course of study in order to prepare everyone for the role of informed citizen. Although the educators advocated liberalizing the curriculum by offering modern languages as well as classical ones, they urged that specialization in the curriculum not begin until the college level, at which point the high school graduates not enrolled in college would learn trades or, in the case of most girls, marry and raise families. The final report was submitted in December 1893, running to fifty-six pages and including a minority dissent from the key recommendations.

The curriculum of Miss Winsor's small Back Bay school was in keeping with the recommendations made in the 1893 report. Although we have no early course catalogues, record cards for each girl exist going back to 1900, and the courses can easily be deduced from the handwritten list of teachers beginning in 1886, which gives names and subject areas in their order of hiring. Mary Winsor herself, her sister Elizabeth (a favorite of the girls), and Euphemia Johnson taught English and history, but specialists were hired for mathematics, German, French, and drawing. Latin and science teachers are listed for the first time in 1896, teachers of diction, current events, and gym by 1900. Between 1901 and 1910 Mary Winsor, influenced by her own educational philosophy and by the desires of her clientele, hired teachers of ethics, the history of art, singing, history, civic problems, Italian, and Greek.

When the newly incorporated School opened in 1910 with its larger student population and more extensive facilities, it gradually added faculty for economics, physics, debate, and individual sports. Some of these additions did correspond to the Committee of Ten's suggestions that were taking hold across the country, but because the parents had wanted their daughters' education to be as strong as their sons', the curriculum at elite Eastern boys' schools was a factor in what was offered at Winsor. Most parents also wanted outdoor exercise, and the new school's playground, gymnasium, and swimming pool required more sports and gym teachers; special instructors for posture and dancing were added in the 1920s. The arts program, which had begun with singing and drawing, expanded to include an orchestra, a choral class, modeling (sculpture), the history of art, drawing and design, and drama (taught by the diction teachers). In 1917 one teacher served as both housekeeper and domestic science teacher.

Beginning in 1910, each catalogue of course offerings contained a pullout sheet that described in detail the curriculum for each of the eight grades—a

Year.	English.	English.	History.	Geography.	Mathematics.	Science.	French.	Latin.	German.	Greek.
I.	"Open Sesame II." Hyde's Grammar, Dictation, Spelling, Themes.	Stories from the East, Norse, Mythology, Homer, etc.	General (biographically treated).	Butler's Elementary.	Arithmetic, (Walsh).	General Elementary Lessons.	Dictation, Regular Verbs, Longman's First Reading Book.			
II.	Grammar, Analysis, Spelling, Definition, Poetry and Composition, Themes.	Historical Selections from Irving, Longfellow, Holmes, etc.	United States.	Political, Physical.	Arithmetic, (Walsh).	Tree Study.	Irregular Verbs, Longman's Second Reading Book, Chardenal.			
III.	Spelling, Poetry, Lewis' First Book in English, Composition and Themes.	Selections from Historical Poems and Plays, (Scott, Shakespeare, etc).	English.		Arithmetic, (Walsh).	Elements of Chemistry.	Chardenal, Longman's First Conversational Reader, etc.	Tuell and Fowler's Beginner's Latin Book.		
IV.	"Open Sesame III." Spelling, Poetry, Lewis' First Book in English Themes.	Stories from Herodotus, Antigone, Julius Cæsar, Coriolanus, etc.	Greek and Roman.		Algebra, (Smith and Wells).	Elements of Physics.	Rollins' Reader, Chardenal.	Tuell and Fowler's Second Year Latin Book, Grammar.		
V.	Spelling, Poetry, Abstracts, Note Taking, Themes.	Song of Roland, Morte d'Arthur, Chaucer, Spenser.	Mediæval and Modern.		Algebra or Observational Geometry.		Composition and Sight Reading.	Second Year Latin Book.	Eysenbach's Grammar, Guerber's Märchen und Erzählungen.	
VI.	"Heart of Oak," Talks on Principles of Composition, Themes.	History of English Literature through Milton	English.	Art.	Geometry.	Physiology.	College Reading: French History, Modern Authors, Composition.	Cicero and Vergil, Composition.	Eysenbach, Prose Reading.	White's Beginner's Greek Book.
VII.	Daily Themes.	History of English Literature through Wordsworth.	United States.	History of Sculpture.	Reviews.	Biology or Astronomy.	College Reading: Classics, Lyrics, etc. Composition.	Cæsar's Civil War, Cicero and Vergil, Composition.	Poetry, College Reading, Bernhardt's Composition.	Gate to the Anabasis, Gleason. First Greek, Reader, Moss. Pearson's Composition. Xenophon.
VIII.	Weekly Themes on College Reading, etc.	Poetry and Essays of the Nineteenth Century; or College Reading.	Current Events.	History of Painting.		Physics with Laboratory Work.	History or Literature.	Horace.	Literature and Composition.	Homer.

Schaeffer's "Bible Readings for Schools," and R. G. Moulton's "Bible Stories" are in daily use.
The Course in Drawing includes studies in the harmonious arrangement of line and color in decoration, as well as drawing from the object.

large grid that in many instances also listed the books used. The ten major areas of study listed were English, literature, history, geography, mathematics, science, French, German, Latin, and Greek. There was also handwork, which varied from year to year and by class but included at least two of the following: drawing, color work, watercolor, writing (probably penmanship), cooking, leatherwork, sewing, stenciling, carving, copying at the art museum, modeling or sculpture, and typewriting. All girls were required to take gymnastics. Such a course load seems overwhelming until one learns (from the 1912–13 listing) that not all the seventy-two courses offered met five days a week. What today would be one English course was divided into two courses, meeting a total of six periods a week in the Lower School. The courses that met five periods a week were Latin, Greek, German, and geometry in the Upper School; the only five-period course in the Lower School was beginning Latin in Class III.

Merely reading a Plan of Study is misleading because many courses now considered major, deserving of at least four periods per week, were given only one to three forty-minute meetings per week. Science courses ranged from one class meeting per week for the fifth-graders to seven for Class VIII chemistry. In the other Upper School science classes, astronomy had one period per week, physiology two or three, physics three, and junior-year chemistry four.

In 1910 every girl took the following courses every year: English, literature, history, arithmetic, French, and fine arts or home economics. Every class except Class IV took science, presumably because the IVs started Latin in that year. In the last three years in the Upper School, German or Greek could be substituted for French or Latin. A course called Elements of Domestic Economy was added that year for Class IV, for one period a week.

A close reading of the Plans of Study reveals some interesting things. Class IV had math for two periods a week, but Class V had five periods for algebra, cutting English and history back to a combined total of four days a week. As was noted somewhat bitterly in the schoolwide curriculum discussions in 1970, the humanities were usually given the lion's share of hours, and science and math suffered. Balance among subject areas and the amount of time allowed for each became dominant themes almost every time the curriculum was subsequently revised. Through 1920, the Plan of Study included two extras: "Each class has instruction in the Bible, sight singing, the use of the voice in reading and speaking, and in gymnastics." Also included was a column headed "College Entrance Requirements," which gave the units required in each Upper School year for students who were planning to apply to Radcliffe or Bryn Mawr.* Beginning in 1914, College Board course requirements were also listed, and in 1916 the specific prerequisites for Smith, Vassar, and Wellesley were added.

The Winsor School from its earliest day emphasized good writing. Katherine English, a member of the faculty, in 1955 compiled a history of the research paper known as the Long Theme: "From 1910 to 1955, a passing of forty-five years, every girl† [who graduates from] . . . The Winsor School has written a Long Theme—Boston themes to some of you. . . . Here we have almost the longest tradition we have had at Winsor—perhaps the strongest."[4] It was Elizabeth Anderson Dike [1910 to 1934] who put her stamp on the project by requiring her students to research topics that were tied specifically to Boston, feeling that the girls knew very little about their hometown. Eventually, the students were allowed to choose their own themes, and the project was no longer known as the Boston theme. Records of assemblies going back to 1910 reveal that the girls heard each other read at least some of their long papers in front of the whole School. When the paper was called the Boston theme, the topics were varied and specific:

* It is not known why the requirements for only these two colleges were given, for girls were clearly applying to and attending other colleges.

† Originally in Class VIII (seniors), then for many years in Class VII (juniors).

What Mr. Charles Eliot did for Boston (on the Metropolitan Park
   System)
The Horace Mann School (for the deaf and hard of hearing)
The new technology buildings (at MIT)
The history of the telephone (invented in Boston)

Katherine English's account of the course suggests that some students enhanced their presentations with visual aids, for she refers to "exhibit after exhibit in the reception room." Beginning in 1972, the entire process (a semester
course) was called Expository Writing or just Expos. Students often groaned
over its demands, but alumnae have again and again remarked that it was
their most important course at Winsor and praised their English teachers
profusely. The course was moved from Class VII to Class V (with modifications for that age group) after the 2004 curriculum revision.

Such an overview reveals the complexity of analyzing any school's curriculum, even a century ago. What is clear is that Winsor almost from the beginning was preparing those girls who wished to go to college to take and pass
the college entrance examinations, a complex process at the time since each
college had its own set of requirements. At the same time, however, Winsor
girls who were not college-bound could earn a diploma in a "non-college"
track. In the early 1900s the listing of which credentials were awarded shows
these categories: College Prep, Regular Course, Regular Course 16 points diploma, General Course certificate, Irregular students, and One-year students
(sometimes referred to as Class IX). The earliest Record Books frequently
listed the largest number of girls in the one-year category—classified as either "advanced work" or "college preparatory"—for Miss Winsor's was one
of the few schools in the area that prepared girls specifically for the entrance
examinations in the late 1800s.

The existence of these six separate tracks reflects how fluid the creden-
tialing practice was at the time. A diploma may have been irrelevant in the
early years, when few girls were planning to seek a college degree. One could
take individual courses at Radcliffe, for example, without taking the entrance
examination. The *Graduate Club Register*s of 1910 and 1915 list many alumnae
taking one or two college courses before marrying.

Winsor's pedagogy and curriculum anticipated nearly every tenet of the
national trends in the early twentieth century. All the early Directors had
time to teach, visit classes, and discuss educational philosophy with their
teachers. The Directors' Reports to the Corporation contain wonderful
details about what was going on in the Winsor classroom in the late 1920s
and early 1930s. During the 1929–30 academic year, Frances Dorwin Dugan
stepped in as interim director while Katharine Lord was traveling in Egypt
and Greece with President Marion Edwards Park of Bryn Mawr. Although
she would not become the next Director for ten years, Frances Dugan already

had a clear sense of Winsor's mission and wise observations about the state of the School. "Class I and
II share a workroom, where you may see . . . groups
of small persons constructing remarkable represen-
tations of Egyptian houses, contour maps, colored
drawings, cut paper designs, or earnestly taking off
on the hectograph topics, poems, or stories which
they have written. . . . The hectographing apparatus*
which the children helped to make is in constant use.
The copies of the best topics in history are honored
by being made available for every notebook and
soon a literary magazine by Class I will issue from
this work-room."[5]

The Directors repeatedly expressed concern for
the needs and care of teachers, as well as for continu-
al overview and adjustment of the school day and activities. Frances Dugan called for more flexible units
"so that Miss Knapp can have long periods with the
children which can be devoted to any subject which
at a given time needs most attention": "Miss Knapp
and Miss Jennings are here every afternoon and are
having many long and satisfactory consultations

*Katharine Lord, second Director of
the School, 1922 to 1939.*

with the parents of the children in I and II." There were trips to museums,
and on the walls in the study hall the teachers displayed the children's murals
of ships and maps and ancient trade routes from the course called Transportation and Exploration.

In the Upper School there were ongoing efforts to improve the Winsor
experience. Frances Dugan described the lecture for the highly successful
current events class: "We have made the first term's lectures center on problems and opportunities here in Boston. We have had representatives from the
Good Government Association, Judge Baker Foundation, the Attorney General of the State, one of the librarians of the Boston Public Library and others.
We hope . . . to go further afield in a study of the United States in Foreign
Relations." In her 1932 report, Katharine Lord, the School's second Director
[1922 to 1939], said she wished every member of the Corporation could hear
"the power and maturity of some of these girls in a discussion of the question
of debt and reparations" in the current events class. To a great extent, however, as early as 1929 the perceived success of the Upper School depended a
great deal on admissions to college: "We sent seventy-six girls [both juniors

---

* A hectograph or gelatin duplicator was the predecessor of the spirit duplicator, whose pur-
ple printing is rarely seen in schools anymore. A 1918 Portable Flatbed Gelatin Duplicator
Hectograph was recently for sale on eBay for $999.00. One brand of the machine was Ditto.

and seniors] up for the college examinations and twenty-seven had honors in one or more subjects. . . . No girl who was recommended for an examination failed. From our graduating class last year, which was not a strong class intellectually, we had twenty-one girls trying College Board examinations."[6]

On specific curricular change in the Lower School, Katharine Lord said: "The new science class that we planned in IV has gone very well. The widening of horizon by discussion there is very valuable for that age, [which] is particularly difficult, and I feel as if we were giving the right kind of chances for some of the why's and how's to be assessed. This term we move into straight mathematics and we are waiting to see whether the scientific approach will not have given algebra new meaning."[7] At educational conferences Katharine Lord as well as her faculty heard about new ideas at other schools and shared Winsor pedagogical practices. Winsor continued to be proud of its attention to individual children's learning needs, of its consultation with psychological professionals on readiness and child development, and of the emphasis on both physical and mental health:[8] "When a child needs help either in personal adjustment or in work, and the two are closely tied together, Miss Dugan or I or the room teachers make time to do very careful planning for her."[9]

In 1932 The Winsor School became one of thirty private and public schools taking part in "The Eight Year Study" conducted by the Commission on the Relation of School and College of the Progressive Education Association. The funding of the study by the Carnegie Foundation made it possible for Winsor educators to meet and work with colleges around the country. The aims of the project were somewhat radical, considering the hold colleges already had on high school curricula. "The purpose of this Study was to find out whether the traditional college entrance requirements and examinations made any difference in success in college, and what secondary schools would do if these requirements and examinations were abandoned."[10] There was general agreement among parents and educators that the curriculum needed to be updated, but most schools feared that altering their curricula in any way would jeopardize students' chances for admission to college. In her April 1933 report, Katharine Lord introduced the plan to the Corporation: "A group of progressive schools has been working to bring about better relations between themselves and the colleges for which they prepare. They think great improvements have been made in elementary education and could be made in secondary education if the colleges did not hold them so tightly. A very large group of colleges have agreed to take people without examination and without restriction of subject matter from a small group of schools who were chosen by a central committee and who presented plans of work approved by the committee."[11]

At this time the colleges and universities set the standards for what secondary school students needed to learn. In 1930 each of the eastern women's colleges had its own requirements and even gave its own tests, finally agree-

*Mary Gay, shown here in the art room in 1922, taught art at Winsor for twenty years
and was one of the architects of the New Plan, which emphasized creative cross-
disciplinary teaching and course content.*

ing to accept Scholastic Aptitude Test scores in 1942. Eventually, standardized testing would become a significant factor in determining college ac-
ceptance, although Winsor's reputation among the colleges was such that
its graduates did not have to submit SAT scores at first. But a strong belief
in making schools more responsive to students' needs—not merely running
them through a regimen—reflected the progressive agenda that every student have at least one teacher who knew her well and could guide her.

Winsor joined the project with enthusiasm, entrusting its execution to
several faculty members whose dedication and creativity contributed to the
plan's success at Winsor. The entire teaching staff of the School was involved
in the proposal that was finally submitted. Katharine Lord appointed Mary
Gay, Hannah Rowley, Florence Waterman, Frances Dugan, and Valeria
Knapp to work out details and teach the new curriculum to one half of the
ninth-graders in the college track.* The students in the experimental pro-

---

* Mary Gay taught art for twenty years, Hannah Rowley, science for twenty-three years,
Florence Waterman, Greek and Latin for sixteen years; Frances Dugan taught English and
was an administrator for thirty-two years, and Valeria Knapp 1916 taught history and English and was an administrator for thirty-eight years.

CHART OF THE NEW PLAN PROGRAM

Grade	MAIN UNIT	ASSOCIATED STUDIES	
IX	COMMUNITY LIVING AND UNITED STATES HISTORY Historical Background Social Civics General Science Units Composition and Literature	MATHEMATICS LATIN II FRENCH MUSIC STUDIO	
X	THE ANCIENT WORLD Greek Roman Medieval History Literature Art History English Composition	MATHEMATICS FRENCH PHYSIOLOGY or LATIN III	Music: Theory and Practice Studio
XI	DEVELOPMENT OF THE MODERN WORLD Part I. Renaissance to 19th Century History Art History Astronomy English Literature French Literature English Composition	LANGUAGE Latin IV, V or German I, II or Greek I, II or Spanish I, II	MATHEMATICS or a Third Language for the Linguist
XII	DEVELOPMENT OF THE MODERN WORLD Part II. The Last 150 Years European and American History English Literature French Literature English Composition Biology (except for girl concentrating in mathematical sciences)	PHYSICS or CHEMISTRY	

Note: Physical education is required throughout the school. Art and music are required through grade IX, optional in grades X, XI, and XII. Special current affairs forums and a choral class are open to grades X, XI, and XII.

The curriculum outline for Winsor's New Plan, from Thirty Schools Tell Their Story.

gram would stay in it throughout their four years in the Upper School. "The great problem now as I see it is to make time enough for the teachers to carry out the work without killing themselves," Katharine Lord observed, but she felt the effort was worthwhile because the colleges were already showing interest in the new curriculum; it appeared that it might well be a definite advantage to be involved in the experiment.*

The first year of the experimental curriculum was so successful that it was put in place for all Winsor ninth-graders (Class V) in subsequent years; however, the rest of the plan was used only once at Winsor, as originally conceived, in the tenth, eleventh, and twelfth grades. There was a distinctly American flavor to the project in that most of the schools concentrated on the importance of community. The country's educational institutions had traditionally been expected to be models of democracy that would prepare students for citizenship as well as for success in higher education and careers. A well-established current events group, begun in 1929 by Katharine Lord and an enthusiastic new history teacher, Alice Jenckes (who remained at Winsor for thirty-seven years and for whom the history chair is named), was so popular that it had to be limited to fifty students. Including the arts was also a priority for Winsor. The Upper School electives in music, art, and drama were an integral component of the Winsor curriculum and had had a secure place in the life of the School from the beginning: musical performances and dramatic presentations on historical themes were a regular part of weekly assemblies and served as a common experience for the girls as well as their teachers. In addition, bona fide artists taught art classes and inspired many graduates to continue their art education at the School of the Museum of Fine Arts.

For half of the college-preparatory girls the ninth-grade New Plan history curriculum combined a study of the community of Boston with American history. "It is fundamentally elementary instruction of economics and government using the city of Boston and, for the sake of perspective and depth, going back in the second half-year to the city-state in Greece," Katharine Lord told the Corporation, emphasizing that the children would work with, rather than under, the teacher.[12] Winsor had a long history of drawing in parents and friends of the School and actively sought local professors and authors to address the experimental classes. Winsor's final report of its New Plan in *Thirty Schools Tell Their Story* was a detailed overview not only of courses given (the titles of which in fact did not differ greatly from the standard college-preparatory program at Winsor) but also of the philosophy behind the choices. Winsor's faculty team for the New Plan worked to incorporate ideas such as "integrated curriculum" by designing cross-disciplinary courses, but they discovered (as did many teachers in future decades) that such interdepartmental planning was especially time-consuming.

Aside from gradually adapting some of Winsor's Upper School courses

---

* Some of the other fine schools were the Francis W. Parker School in Chicago, Milton Academy in Massachusetts, New Trier Township in Illinois, and the Dalton School in New York.

to the successful aspects of the New Plan, Winsor did not make major curriculum changes in the late 1930s. Katharine Lord called the implementation of the experimental program "stimulating" for the teachers in her 1936 Report to the Corporation, saying they had learned "how to plan cooperatively and criticize objectively their own and each other's work." Winsor teachers were sought after to write articles, describe their new courses, and serve on educational commissions in the 1940s. Katharine Lord was proud: "I do not think the school is dropping behind educationally." The workload for the teachers involved in the New Plan had been excessive, however, and there were other pressing concerns in the School, such as parent-teacher communication, the creation of more cohesiveness in each grade-level class, and adjusting the after-school sports offerings in response to parents' requests.[13] Although the "Thirty Schools" experiment invigorated Winsor and led to some changes in the English and history curricula, the ongoing requirements for continued participation seemed to overwhelm the small school's staff. Nonetheless, students who took the New Plan history course remembered it for many years, grateful for its breadth and intellectual challenge.

In the end, Winsor did not make radical changes in the curriculum, although it did continue to build courses around the theme of community, not just in regard to the School but also relating to the city of Boston. Both students and faculty were eager to broaden to a national and global level the perspective of what constitutes a community. Katharine Lord valued the current events forum as a place to train the girls to bring facts to support opinions and to challenge weak arguments by "questioning to get at the facts." Winsor was educating the daughters of the financial and intellectual leaders of many Boston institutions, and although it may have seemed at times like an oasis or an ivory tower, the School made significant and regular attempts to look outward. On a national level, the big news was the election of Franklin Roosevelt (whose niece Eleanor II graduated from Winsor in 1938) and the attempts to pull the country out of the Depression. From overseas the girls were hearing the names Gandhi, Huxley, Jung, and Hitler. Women's names were also in the news, providing new models for the girls: the aviator Amelia Earhart, the first female Cabinet member, Frances Perkins, the authors Virginia Woolf and Agatha Christie, and the singer Marian Anderson, the first black artist of any nationality to perform at the Metropolitan Opera.

The international rather than the local political point of view might also have been appealing because at this time, ironically, the city of Boston—the Puritans' "city on a hill"—had pretty much been taken over by Irish immigrant politicians, and for the first time, the old families of Boston (the "Brahmins")* were not in power in the city. The first Irish mayor had served from 1885 to 1888, and the first native-born Irish Catholic mayor was elected in

---

* This term is still used to refer to the oldest families in the city; it was a class designation rather than an economic one.

1905. On the state level, Republicans, some of whose daughters, nieces, and wives attended Winsor, still had control, their influence reaching to Washington. The School's connections to those at the head of universities in the area and to wealthy financiers and industrialists reflected the social and political divisions that would mark Boston's culture for many years. The widespread (and long-lived) notion of Winsor's elitism was a result of this divide, and although the School struggled continually to define itself as a place of intellectual rigor and academic excellence rather than merely an upper-class girls' school, its reputation as a school for the well-to-do prevailed in spite of Winsor's providing scholarships for deserving girls from its earliest years.

The majority of Boston's young people attended their neighborhood public schools. Several ethnic and racial groups in the city promoted their own schools, although the public schools were free and open to all, including black children; when the system was integrated in 1855, the black citizens closed their own schools, but independent schools for Catholic and Jewish children stayed open.[14] Robert Middlekauff points out that the student population of the public schools was thereby decreased and to a great extent homogenized. In addition, he notes: "Private education thus freed public finances from a heavy burden. In relieving public education of the necessity of expanding its scope, private schools had yet another effect . . . they helped confirm the traditional conception of the role of public-supported education."[15]

In the 1930s the Irish, for doctrinal reasons, did not aspire to attend private schools, which were mostly built and dominated by Protestants. The immigrant communities were increasingly conscious of their group identity and of stark differences in values and beliefs between themselves and the old aristocracy of Boston.[16]

Boston parents who were choosing Winsor did not really want it to change, nor was the curriculum of The Winsor School being challenged by other points of view. Few Catholic and Jewish girls attended Winsor, but some did, for they were not intentionally excluded. Boston was a complex metropolitan area in which separate nationalities tended to live together for social, economic, and geographical reasons. Eventually this situation would be called de facto segregation and would result in tremendous upheaval in Boston proper and in its suburbs. Eventually, also, it would stimulate a significant rethinking of every aspect of Winsor's program.

There were around 270 students in the School when Frances Dugan became its Director in 1939. Although global events portended grave perils ahead for the entire world, the beginning of the Second World War in Europe caused only small changes at Winsor. When the United States entered the war, students, parents, and teachers were inevitably affected. In 1940 Frances Dugan admitted six British refugee girls who were to live with Winsor families. "These girls give us a better appreciation of the meaning of home and family."[17] (In 1955 Valeria Knapp would announce, "The dignity of the Library

The library in 1961.

has been enhanced by the gift of a chiming clock made in 1819 by the clock maker to the Queen and sent to the School from England by Colonel and Lady Bevan in gratitude for the education received by their daughter Jennifer 1946, during the war years.")[18] Frances Dugan felt the teachers should not overstress the war with the younger girls, but for the Upper School classes she believed discussion "cleared the air." She encouraged their understanding of and belief in democracy, and the entire community supported charitable activities for refugees, needy families, and, as always, the Hampton Institute. (Winsor's connection to the Hampton Institute and the Calhoun Colored School is discussed more fully in chapter 6.)

Slowly the reality of the war intruded. Defense programs restricted the purchasing of new equipment, and everyone was encouraged to support the rationing effort. At Winsor, Wednesday-afternoon first-aid classes allowed seniors to get their certificates; younger girls had a course in cooking and other simple housekeeping chores. In 1942 the lower corridor workroom was given over to war work, and Winsor girls cooperated with Groton boys to raise money for a mobile kitchen for the British. Then more serious concerns intervened. "After the false alarm soon after Pearl Harbor, we organized with great care our air raid drills." Frances Dugan took steps to equip the building with emergency equipment and rations, including "a big supply of lollipops."[19] Because boys were going to war in July, College Board exams were given in April, and the first machine grading of the exams occurred—a change Frances Dugan saw as a mistake.[20]

The strong Winsor curriculum was not much altered, and a solid education was considered a sound investment for a postwar future when many well-trained minds would be needed. Winsor continued to stress the discipline of learning, putting heavy emphasis on acquiring a time-tested foundation of skills and knowledge rather than following what a child's "momentary inclination" might be. More and more women were entering the workforce, proving their usefulness and strength. Graduates who took examinations to join the WAVES (Women Accepted for Volunteer Emergency Service, the navy's women's reserve) and WAACs (Women's Army Auxiliary Corps) praised their mathematics training at Winsor, and alumnae who went to college were grateful for the excellent preparation that opened more opportunities to them. As interest in studying German waned, a limited Spanish program was added.

At school assemblies the entire community heard speeches by faculty as well as by outside speakers. These weekly events have always been a significant piece of the Winsor curriculum. At Monday morning meetings (which in various years were held on Wednesdays or Thursdays) guest speakers often came in to make students as well as faculty aware of a world growing more complex and threatening. Many spoke on academic subjects, especially scientific ones, and several came also to the Current Events Club on Fridays, where a smaller, more motivated and involved audience engaged the speaker in discussions that continued in the subsequent club meetings. Such talks and the topics covered are still considered part of the broader curriculum of the School, and it did not seem that anyone begrudged the fact that an hour a week was taken from classes for these assemblies.

The girls' reactions to the speakers are preserved in the *Lamp*s from those days. The *Winsor Lamp* was much more than a literary magazine in its first incarnation: it maintained detailed records of assemblies, sporting events, and graduate news, with thoughtful comments on the weekly morning lectures given by alumnae, local academicians, Winsor faculty, and authors. The girls' contributions to the magazine reflected a growing awareness of the international community and of their own local community's needs for social workers, nurses, and doctors. During the Second World War the girls heard speeches from diplomats and professors, including Margaret Mead, from the president of Radcliffe, who spoke on careers and education for women after the war, and from former students who were serving in the military and doing defense work.* After the war they even heard about the Nuremberg trials from Nazi camp survivors.

---

* Three of these were Lieutenant Anne Conant Weaver 1937 of the WAACs; Julia Deane Crowley 1940, chairman of the War Service Committee at Radcliffe; and Ensign Nancy Homans 1935 of the WAVES.

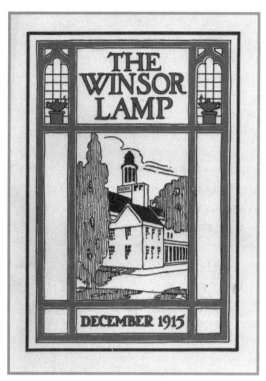

The cover of the first edition of the Winsor Lamp.

The graduation issues of the *Lamp* printed in toto the commencement speeches by the guest speakers (often a clergyman, professor, physician, or other prominent male)* as well as the student valedictories. The senior speeches contain the occasional platitude about beginning a new phase of life, but each one reflects its era and many are both sophisticated and extremely serious. When Winsor was founded, it was rare for women to speak publicly, but from the beginning the School encouraged speaking skills, anticipating a future in which women would face no barrier to their eloquence.

After the war, the Winsor Upper School curriculum changed in three different ways: biology, chemistry, and physics became full laboratory courses meeting seven periods a week; more Spanish was added; and students began to be prepared for the standardized Scholastic Aptitude Test rather than for an individual college's own tests. There were few changes in the Lower School, where eighth-graders still had no history course and only two periods a week for science. Bible study was dropped for everyone except for one year in fifth or sixth grade, but, in a trend that continued for decades, little was actually deleted from the curriculum when new courses were added.

Lower School courses throughout these years were quite ambitious, especially in Classes II and III, where the curriculum covered, in various configurations from year to year, ancient, medieval, and American history with coordinated reading from, for example, the *Odyssey*, Shakespeare, Dickens, and Louisa May Alcott. Mathematics, which would culminate in Class VIII with solid geometry and trigonometry, remained a four-period-per-week course every year no matter what other changes were made. As for the "real world," that is, the war, Frances Dugan continued to adhere to her philosophy of providing a nonthreatening perspective on learning and on valuing individual differences. Course content and skills were important, but so was the School's mission of character development.

Winsor graduates from the eastern women's colleges occasionally spoke at the assemblies and wrote articles for the *Lamp* encouraging the older girls to acquire college degrees at that time, when men were not able to do so

---

* The first female graduation speaker was Vera Micheles Dean in 1946. She was a part of the United Nations Relief and Rehabilitation Administration in 1943 and 1945.

because of the war. In fact, most Winsor graduates were going on to higher education by this time, and they were continuing to enter the professions previously "owned by men" in spite of men's efforts to restrict them. Their successes had always been announced with pride each year in the Directors' reports, and it was clear that preparing young women for college was a major goal of the School. In December 1943 Frances Dugan announced to the Corporation that every senior who applied had been accepted by her first-choice college.

The Plans of Study for the decades following World War II reflect few dramatic curriculum changes. The war had brought scientific advances—supersonic airplanes, the first microwave oven—and Winsor continued to offer biology, chemistry, and physics for girls in Classes VII and VIII. The number of girls choosing to take more than the required two years of Upper School science increased throughout the 1950s. There was no science offered for ninth-graders, and tenth-graders were limited to physiology (The Human Body and Its Functions); eleventh-graders took chemistry, and seniors had a choice of either physics or biology. In 1960 an Introduction to Science course replaced physiology, giving students an overview of the topics to come.

The *Lamp* editorials and accounts of assembly speakers describe postwar world events—the creation of the United Nations, the assassination of Gandhi, and the gradual encroachments of Communism—which would fuel both progress and peril in the 1950s. The students eagerly formed a Student Federalist Group in the School, and members attended conferences at Phillips Exeter in 1946.

Nor was Winsor immune to popular culture. In 1953 the movies *Roman Holiday, From Here to Eternity, The Robe,* and *Julius Caesar* were released, and there was yet another popular attraction: television. About this Valeria Knapp was sanguine: "Actually I think we are over the worst of the mental inertia accompanying the television craze." That was in 1957. Between 1950 and 1954 the number of Americans owning television sets had increased from 1.5 million to 29 million. In the mid-1940s the *Lamp* began to publish movie reviews—the first being *Caesar and Cleopatra*—and educational films were sometimes screened in assemblies. It was

Frances Dorwin Dugan was the Director from 1939 to 1951. (Photo by Bachrach.)

still more common, however, for plays by students to be featured at assemblies; girls of all ages acted in the performances, which were often student-written. Thoughtful but brief reviews of nearly every dramatic presentation on Winsor's stage appeared in the "Calendar" section of the *Lamp*.

The 1950s found Winsor maintaining a demanding curriculum that had scarcely changed. By holding fast to what it had always done well, Winsor was already prepared for the next educational crisis. This was the *Sputnik* era, and it forced educational institutions at every level and size to rethink and if necessary tighten and enhance their programs. Public schools in particular were being challenged to upgrade courses so that the country could compete with the new enemy, the Soviet Union. Federal monies became available, and just below the surface were the first rumblings from the Civil Rights movement, which, although not yet rising to the impassioned cries for equality of opportunity that peaked in the 1960s, were bringing the biggest educational changes of all. In the near future, students would be demanding courses that were more "relevant," in particular courses that acknowledged the histories of minorities and disadvantaged groups. As educators looked anew at the old courses, the questions being asked at Winsor were: Should language offerings be expanded, should Latin and Greek be dropped to make way for Spanish or Russian, and should the traditional graduation requirements be adjusted? What would fall by the wayside in the curricular shuffle? And—most important—who would make these decisions?

The U.S. military had begun using standardized tests during World War I, but their widespread use elsewhere began in the 1940s. Winsor's earliest permanent record cards reveal careful documentation of tests named Binet, Otis, Cleveland Arithmetic, and Peet-Dearborn, which were given every year. The SAT had been in existence since 1901. Its purpose was to measure mastery of specific academic subjects and thereby predict success in college. In the 1920s the redesigned SAT was said to measure innate intelligence and aptitude. Although there had always been tests and quizzes at Winsor, students began to express a particular disdain for and slight dread of the standardized IQ and national achievement tests, perhaps in part because of their impersonal aspect. As early as 1958 there were test preparation businesses, and in 1984 the College Board itself began to offer coaching materials to improve a test taker's score. The national frenzy over standards accompanied the triumph of the scientific method in nearly every area of American life in the 1950s—child rearing, housekeeping, both mental and physical health—and the rise of the "expert," who was usually a man. When educators discovered the copious data from nationally given exams at all levels, they started to use the statistics to formulate a more scientific approach to teaching. Hardly any mention of these tests (other than the College Board examinations) occurs in the Directors' Reports, and the School was unwilling to devote teachers' time to the analysis of scores: the interpersonal knowledge gained from small classes and caring teachers was more valuable, and eventually Winsor stopped giving the yearly Educational Records Bureau tests. The ERBs were given nationally so that students—and schools—could be compared. Sometimes these scores became part of the child's permanent record.

With the advent of computers, the analyses became very sophisticated, giving exact details of any given student's performance on any single test item and recommendations for improvement. Winsor found the tests less and less useful, mostly because teachers monitoring their students' performance through small classes and one-on-one help sessions were quite aware of individual deficiencies and were able to address individual needs. (Even when public schools were, in the twenty-first century, forced to prove their success by repeated testing, Winsor sought to avoid both the practice of "teaching to the test" and the temptation to reduce arts, science, and history courses to accommodate a testing regimen.)

Of course, students have continued to take the Scholastic Aptitude Tests and individual subject tests administered by the College Board. Winsor also stopped giving its own admissions tests and began to use the Independent School Entrance Examination (ISEE) and the Secondary Schools Admissions Test (SSAT) in the late 1980s.

A 1952 report based on a study by educators from three elite private boarding schools and three Ivy League universities led to yet another form of testing, the Advanced Placement (AP) courses and examinations.[21] Because this groundbreaking innovation was proposed by a group of educators with such prestigious credentials, it was hard to ignore and caught the attention of college preparatory schools and the teachers of advanced or honors classes. Their book, financed by the Ford Foundation, identified ways to make the final two years of high school and the first two years of college a more cohesive unit, but the authors admitted that their recommendations were in part based on "current practices in our six institutions" and that it would not necessarily be useful for other types of schools.[22]

Although it was not intended to evaluate a student's potential for success in college, the Advanced Placement program soon became another way for colleges to evaluate and sort secondary school students, especially the strongest ones. Ostensibly designed to elevate the quality and scope of the high-level courses high school seniors were taking, the Advanced Placement examinations were meant to be a way to award college credit and replace a required college course, allowing a student to advance at once to a more challenging course. If she had taken and passed enough AP exams, she could even enter college as a sophomore.

As she was stepping into her new role as Winsor's fourth Director of the School in 1951, Valeria A. Knapp, herself a 1916 graduate of the School and a teacher there since 1922, included in her Report to the Corporation "a brief restatement of the educational philosophy on which the School was built and

Valeria Addams Knapp served as Director from 1951 to 1963. (Photo by Bachrach.)

which has weathered well the changing times."[23] For the Lower School she identified the teaching of basic skills, knowledge of the world through history, science, and literature, and active participation in art, music, and sports. There were more choices in the Upper School, a curriculum so flexible that "the forty-three girls in this year's Class VIII have thirty different programs scheduled." "[We are] constantly thinking and working for the growth of the individual, are quick to appreciate unique contributions, and rejoice with the child when a particular hurdle is overcome."[24] In her previous report, Valeria Knapp had shared with the Corporation the good news from the colleges to which the girls had matriculated, a practice begun by Mary Winsor herself in her reports and continued by other Directors. The success of the Winsor curriculum—not just the courses but also the "habits of heart and mind"[25] built into the character of the School— was proven year after year by the number of admissions to excellent colleges. The fact that the Directors' fall reports consistently emphasized these achievements shows how important a goal preparation for college continued to be.

By Valeria Knapp's time more alumnae than ever were pursuing degrees beyond their bachelor's degrees; she announced their names with pride, as well as the names of former students who were on the Dean's List or had been elected to a prominent student government position and thereby reflected Winsor's training for leadership. As though to deflect the significance of an AP transition-to-college program, she expanded further on Winsor's special characteristics—the "very happy relationships between faculty members" that made interdisciplinary courses work, the heterogeneous abilities mixing to increase "friendly intercourse" among the students, and the faculty's new emphasis on encouraging students at every grade level to do independent work. The School was doing well as its experienced teachers observed the varying needs of their students and developed new courses and pedagogy. Perhaps the School felt its college placement success was a validation of its already demanding classes that were equivalent to the Advanced Placement courses, for its catalogue did not designate any class as "AP" in the majority of departments until the 1970s. The mathematics department added calculus in 1962 and designated the senior course as AP in 1971. A two-year AP sequence in French was listed for the first time in 1974; U.S. history, Latin, and Greek offered an Advanced Placement option in 1978, and AP biology was first given in 1979.

As important as college admission was, Frances Dugan in her final report offered the following disclaimer: "I hope you keep in mind the fact that our educational policies are not bound by the college entrance boards and that education here is a rich and vital experience in itself."[26] A year later Valeria Knapp elaborated further on the School's mission, omitting any reference to college. "In conclusion may I emphasize that back of the rich program of courses the School offers and the multiplicity of extracurricular activities to suit individual needs is the primary concern of developing healthy, well-balanced, resolute individuals with strength and resourcefulness to overcome the difficulties which will constantly beset them."[27]

Nonetheless, since Winsor graduates did indeed go on to earn advanced degrees, the School enjoyed a reputation as a good place to prepare for college. But the landscape was subtly changing: Winsor and schools like it could no longer count on "sure acceptances" by the eastern women's colleges, some of which had adopted the new process known as Early Decision. High test scores alone could not ensure admission to the most selective schools, and high school in general was becoming a more competitive place. In a trend that continued into the twenty-first century, some girls participated in more extracurricular activities than they could comfortably contribute to, and many led a social life that included dances with boys' schools and, for a dwindling few, coming out teas. From time to time, Directors alluded to the stresses of Winsor girls' lives and even tried to rein in the activities—especially school-week entertaining.

To emphasize its concern with global issues, the School for several years supported bringing a foreign student to Winsor for the academic year and sending a Winsor student abroad, usually in the summer after her junior year. Between 1957 and 1973 ten foreign exchange students spent one year each at Winsor. The 1950s also saw the beginning of what would eventually become an extremely popular and successful extracurricular activity, the Model United Nations student conferences. Julia Lawrence 1949 had visited the United Nations in her senior year and reported back to the School with so much spirit that that she motivated six seniors to make the visit the following year. In the wake of her untimely death, the Class of 1949 in her memory funded the sending of a senior to visit the United Nations during spring break for the next ten years.[28]

The high school version of Model UN began in 1952, growing out of the college program, which dated back to simulations of the League of Nations in 1920. Winsor students and their teachers had from the beginning closely followed world events, and in the 1950s Soviet troops in Hungary, Fidel Castro, desegregation, and the polio scare could not be ignored.

In 1959 Valeria Knapp asked the faculty to take a new look at the curriculum: "Is the development of the course material sound and adequate for students who will make their contribution to this country and to the closely interrelated world in which they will be living during the last third of the 20th century? Are we giving them methods of attack on work which will stretch their minds and strengthen their intellectual drive?"[29]

In the spring of 1960 a visiting committee came to the School to evaluate it for accreditation, the first of what would be a once-every-ten-years process. The School had prepared its own account of itself from which the visiting committee would take its cue in determining whether the School was achieving its goals. The very first self-study, completed in the late 1950s, is not in the archives, but the report of the visiting committee, based on that self-study, gives an extremely favorable assessment of the School as well as suggestions for improvement.

The visiting educators gave credit to the outstanding faculty for the success of the curriculum, praising its "loyalty" and "keen interest in the philosophy and objectives of the school." The committee felt, however, that the salaries of the teachers were "not commensurate with the quality of teaching." The curriculum itself was found to be in keeping with the mission statement, and the 100 percent college-acceptance record validated the course of study. The committee supported the School's own long-range plans for changes in the science and history departments and made specific suggestions for an upgrade of the library, the reinstatement of German,* and a longer lunch period for the Upper School, where, it felt, there were "over-crowding and tension." Although Winsor had always stood firm against the ranking of its students and had resisted ability grouping except in math and language, the committee wondered whether homogeneous grouping in English and history might not better prepare the more capable girls for the Advanced Placement program, but they were unable to suggest ways for achieving this.[30]

In 1959 James B. Conant, who had been the president of Harvard University from 1933 to 1953, published his appraisal of the state of secondary-school education, nearly seventy years after President Eliot's Committee of Ten had issued its recommendations. The book aroused further the national concern about education that the launch of the Soviet Union's *Sputnik 1* had provoked. Seeking to raise at once the level of public schools to prepare all students—not just those from elite private schools—for the best colleges and universities, Conant emphasized the need for physics and calculus and in addition thrust himself into some nascent controversies, such as the introduction of foreign languages, the optimal size for a high school, and the ineffectiveness of racial integration. (By 1964 he had reconsidered the Civil Rights issue and, in his book *Shaping Educational Policy,* he recanted his view that "artificial in-

---

* Three years of German had remained in the course of study until the 1956–57 school year. It was added again in 1973. It was dropped permanently in the late 1980s.

tegration" was a flawed approach to remedying the inequalities of black and white schools.)[31] Like earlier sweeping overviews of American schools, the Conant Report documented prevailing practices in American public high schools across the country and set forth recommendations for them. The report received a great deal of attention from public school boards, but its influence on schools like Winsor was negligible; the School was already doing the things Conant was recommending.

Winsor had the advantage of being a small, selective school, a girls' school, and a purely academic institution that did not attempt to train its students for a vocation such as clerical and secretarial work. All independent schools had the luxury of predetermining who would attend their schools. None of the schools Conant had examined was single-sex, but an intriguing aspect of his study was the gathering of separate data for boys and girls in the same high school. The report concluded that girls "of high ability" in public schools were not being educated as thoroughly as boys; this situation would therefore diminish the number of candidates (presumably women) who could teach advanced science, mathematics, and foreign languages in the future. Conant did not mention the effect of teachers on school performance but did point out the importance of training young women so that they can teach science.

Almost without exception, he found that "academically talented boys" took more rigorous subjects than girls of similar talent, especially in science and mathematics. Girls more often studied a foreign language longer, but Conant bemoaned the meager number of language offerings across the country. Winsor's girls were again ahead of the curve in all areas. By building methodically and consistently on what it had always done well, Winsor was keeping pace: the girls in the senior mathematics course began to use *Elements of Calculus and Analytic Geometry*[32] in 1962, and physics as a laboratory science had been in the curriculum since the 1930s. Conant, a scientist by training, helped establish the high school science requirements that were the cause célèbre of the *Sputnik* era, and federal money became available for educating mathematics and science teachers for the new courses.

Winsor's leaders also recognized that there was more to a good school than its printed curricular offerings and began to look at its infrastructure and its nonacademic program as well as at its admissions policies, which, because of standardized testing and outreach, had broadened the demographic picture of its students. In the next decade, the makeup of the student body would become gradually less white, less upper middle class, and less Protestant, and the inevitability of these changes was what the School grappled with in the 1960s.

Virginia Wing, who was the School's Director from 1963 to 1988, in her first Report to the Corporation in 1963 asked a provocative question: "What kind of school is Winsor?" As she took up the reins as Director, she tried to clarify, just as Valeria Knapp had done, the goals, the makeup, and the repu-

Virginia Wing was the fifth Director of the School, from 1964 to 1988. (Photo by Bachrach.)

tation of the School. She was uncomfortable with the contradictory rumors she heard from outsiders about Winsor: that it was a finishing school not interested in college preparation; that it was only for the very bright who could excel on the standardized tests (all others need not apply). She wanted it to be known that Winsor admitted Catholic, Jewish, and black children and was *not* a place where "everyone made a debut." Virginia Wing was forthright in acknowledging the cauldron of racial and class unrest that was boiling in the city of Boston. Her outreach endeavor, the Educational Enrichment Program, described in chapter 6, provided an opportunity for the School to interact with different areas of Boston and perhaps broaden its admission pool.

Like all previous Directors, Virginia Wing at first oversaw the entire admission process, interviewing candidates, reading their applications, and making the final acceptances. Even after an Entrance Committee began to share the responsibility in the 1960s, she continued to take this task very seriously, feeling strongly that the School needed to attract and enroll able students from the broader community, especially students whose parents shared and supported Winsor's high academic standards. She had real misgivings about standardized testing, which she felt was unfair to some girls and revealed nothing that a wise teacher did not identify better through the daily observing and testing of her students. Regarding the National Merit Scholarship Qualifying Test, she stated, "The Semifinalist record of a school is not a reliable indicator of the school's effectiveness or educational quality." The practice in the national media of ranking and rating schools by their students' test scores was beginning to put educators on the defensive, but Virginia Wing knew from experience that the academic and professional success of Winsor graduates had not necessarily been predictable from their standardized test scores. She was also ahead of her time in recognizing the cultural bias of some of these tests as well as the bias of some observers who assumed that broadening the applicant pool would dilute the quality of the student body. The heads of the independent schools insisted that standards would not be lowered as the racial-ethnic picture changed, for able girls could and should be found from all sectors of society, and that most institutions (including Winsor) would and could raise additional money for the scholarship aid.

Widening the demographics of the School led to a careful appraisal of courses, especially in English and history, where the accounts and achievements of minorities and disadvantaged groups were gradually included. It seems obvious, in retrospect, that teachers should and would revise courses to include a wider spectrum of world writers and historical figures, but an examination of the catalogue listings reveals that the inclusion of even women's accomplishments and perspectives did not happen instantaneously. Winsor continued to be traditionally conservative when changing a curriculum that had served its students well over the years, but the faculty carried the load in the development of a more diverse plan of study.

An unexpected factor in changing the curriculum was a generation of younger teachers who came from various parts of the country and had often not been educated in independent schools or on the Eastern Seaboard. Some had had direct involvement with the Civil Rights movement and the Peace Corps. They had heard the cries for equality of opportunity that were beginning to shred the fabric of Boston's neighborhood and schools in the 1960s. These young newcomers were not hesitant about sharing their ideas with older teachers and administrators. There were also voices from another unforeseen constituency, the students themselves—smart, confident girls who were not immune to the atmosphere of discontent among their peers across the country. They were the generation who would idolize a new young president, then grieve after his murder, and finally embrace his legacy, the Peace Corps. They would know of the space race and the Berlin Wall. They would become increasingly aware of freedom marches, federal troops protecting black students, and the deaths of Malcolm X and Martin Luther King Jr. The first black girls were admitted in the mid-1960s: Patricia Elam, Ellen Pinderhughes, and Pamela Parks McLaurin all graduated in 1971. Patricia Elam earned degrees in law and fine arts and became a writer of both fiction and nonfiction. Her novel *Breathing Room* was published by Washington Square Press in 2001. Ellen Pinderhughes is an associate professor in the Eliot-Pearson Department of Child Development of Tufts University. This department is named for Abigail Adams Eliot 1910 and Elizabeth Winsor Pearson, who started their first nursery school in 1922. (For details see chapter 6.) Pamela McLaurin became Winsor's director of admission in 2002.

The assassinations of Martin Luther King Jr. in April 1968 and of Robert F. Kennedy in June 1968 reawakened the nation's grief over the 1963 assassination of John F. Kennedy. Virginia Wing did not ignore student protests over the wars in southeast Asia and the lottery system for the draft that were occurring on many college and university campuses. "The concerns of young people, their sense of wishing to be involved in the larger world, their confusion about what is really important and about how their goals should be achieved all reflect the perplexities of a wider community in which even the most thoughtful adults are often discouraged or unsure of their own reactions."[33]

During the Civil Rights era, the calls increased for "relevancy" in courses, and Virginia Wing praised teachers "who willingly interrupt a lesson when children need to talk through troubling issues." She proposed that in the following school year "we deliberately set aside more time to bringing in adults to talk with students about some of the concerns that both young and old share in the world today."[34] Students throughout the country were on the front lines of the Vietnam War protest. In April 1969 thirty Harvard students registered their protests against the war by occupying University Hall on the Harvard University campus. Meant to be a peaceful demonstration, the takeover escalated when more and more students entered the building and police were called in to arrest the protesters. In 1970 the discovery of the bombing of Cambodia (kept secret during the previous fourteen months) created even more uproar on the nation's college campuses. Virginia Wing assented to students' requests for a day during which they could discuss the situation, and they organized a panel of speakers who could provide insight on all sides of the war issue. The participants ranged from Howard Zinn to a member of the John Birch Society.* Another speaker was John Kerry, who had been given an early discharge from the navy in order to run for a Massachusetts congressional seat and was just beginning his antiwar activities. Winsor parents and alumnae also participated.

In the 1960s Winsor had added a Class IV science course, a Global Geography course in Class II, elective seminar classes in Upper School English, and full laboratory courses in chemistry, physics, and biology; it had already dropped German and nearly all Bible study. These modifications to the curriculum were not made precipitously but only after reflection on the School's stated mission and careful consideration by faculty. There had been some outside influences: the French courses were using the oral-aural method, and in English courses seventh-graders were using the new SRA reading approach, which allowed girls to proceed at their own pace.[35] On the other hand, some things stayed the same: for example, every Upper School student continued to have a biweekly conference with her English teacher, and Class VII was still required to write a research paper. (There is a full discussion of the research paper in chapter 7.)

"Tampering with curriculum is foolish business, but studying thoughtfully the need for improvement can be a stimulating project," Virginia Wing admitted to the Corporation in 1967. When the Dexter School, in Brookline, opened its computer center in that year, Winsor was able to share it, and Virginia Wing cautiously observed: "I should add that to what extent knowledge

---

* Howard Zinn was a political science professor at Boston University and an activist on labor and antiwar fronts. The John Birch Society, founded in 1958, was avowedly right-wing, its purpose being "to bring about less government, more responsibility, and—with God's help—a better world by providing leadership, education, and organized volunteer action in accordance with moral and Constitutional principles."

about the use of the computer will contribute to the mathematics program is a question which we cannot yet answer, but at the very least we expect that the students involved will learn to understand the machine and to realize that it is not a monster but a servant which has to be programmed by human beings."[36] She was less circumspect when labeling some of the new trends in education "fad ideas," and she feared that schools that quickly adopted things like "independent study" might find it hard to maintain high standards. With this caveat, she announced that the faculty was moving carefully to establish a program for senior projects that would address the demands of students for relevancy and independence as well as the importance of learning more about the city of which the School was a part.

In 1970 the Winsor School completed its second self-evaluation for accreditation by the New England Association of Schools and Colleges (NEASC). (A visiting committee was on the Winsor campus in May 1970 when National Guardsmen killed the four students during a protest at Kent State University. The visiting committee noted that the Winsor administrators handled the crisis with "wisdom and tact," and although the traditional evaluation seemed almost inconsequential, the committee carried on its work.) The visiting committee, comprising a school head as chairman and experienced teachers from independent schools similar to Winsor, studied the School's mission statement and self-evaluation report. During their three-day campus visit, committee members were to consider how well the School was achieving its own stated purpose. The 1970 committee commended the School for success in achieving its goals. Although such committees usually made suggestions for modifying some aspect of a school, its recommendations were not binding. The real impetus for change grew out of a school's own reflections on its final self-evaluation. Since the Winsor faculty had always been assiduous about examining and improving curriculum and pedagogy, all members of the community valued the exercise of doing the intensive self-study every ten years.

The 1970 self-evaluation and report of the visiting committee made some observations that reflected the grave and unsettling events in the world and the need for an evolving curriculum. The committee admired the "stimulating healthy exchange of ideas among students" in history classes and recommended adding courses about Asia, Africa, and Latin America and, perhaps, seminars on the media, propaganda, and the Arab-Israeli conflict. In the fall of 1971 the History Department offered several one-semester courses, including World Religions (Judaism, Roman Catholicism, and Protestantism), Asian History, The City in Modern America, and The American Political Tradition. Two other courses stand out: Anthropology, for seniors only, and Elements in Elementary Teaching: Both Theory and Practice with Seminar and Field Experience. In the mid-1970s the department added more electives: Minorities in Literature, Russian Studies, Women in the United States, Chinese History, and African History.

By the 1972–73 school year, the English Department had revamped its Upper School curriculum, offering mixed-grade, seminar-type courses to girls in the three upper classes. The topics, which changed somewhat from year to year, included Creative Writing, Society and Its Outcasts, Shakespeare, Persuasion, and Modern Drama. This format was continued, the revolving seminar subjects reflecting more modern and less traditional themes, until the major reworking of curriculum in early 2000. The content of English classes in the Upper School gradually included more reading by and about women and minorities, and a Russian literature elective was an option in 1974. The Lower School program continued to center on American history and the city of Boston, but Class III met some non-Western cultures as they studied how geography affected culture. This additional attention to minorities as well as to China and Africa did not come because of any national mandates for change; Winsor history and English teachers took on the responsibility for exploring, planning, and implementing new areas, even designing and printing their own reading materials when an ideal textbook could not be found. New teachers brought the new perspective of their younger generation, offering ideas for new content as well as different techniques in pedagogy, and department heads listened and signaled a willingness to change. To take advantage of the interest and expertise of new faculty, for example, the English Department discovered it could offer eighteen different seminar-style electives.

"Jan Term," a four-week inter-semester program in January, was instituted in 1974. (In the 1980s it was reduced to three weeks.) Teachers offered tutorials, seminars, and up to fifty minicourses, ranging from astronomy to yoga. Students could also undertake full-time independent projects outside school or be part of a trip to "swim with the dolphins" in Florida or complete a practical course such as driving or typing. Parents and alumnae received information on the varied courses and could attend some classes. The freedom from grades and tests, the flexible daily schedule, and the innovative courses pleased both students and teachers, but eventually the demands of new Advanced Placement courses (which had continued during Jan Term) and questions about the wisdom of giving up academic time convinced the faculty to vote for its end in 1996. Some of the courses, however, became part of the regular curriculum in subsequent years, and a number of offerings showed that the faculty was anticipating trends in curriculum.

As early as November 1969 a Long Range Planning Committee composed of some faculty and corporation members had identified the challenges facing the School:

> There is no aspect of education which is not now undergoing profound change, and indeed the very philosophical premises upon which most schools rest are being questioned. The impact of student unrest has

brought into focus some very legitimate issues which no school can for long ignore. Among these are the desire of students for participation in the direction and administration of their own educational experience, the demand of black students for programs which meet their special needs in an integrated school, the doubt about whether the standard academic curriculum is truly relevant to today's reality.... Of all the changes now taking place in the educational milieu the most visible is the trend toward some form of coeducation.[37]

After thoughtful deliberation, the committee recommended that Winsor remain a girls' school at its present site. Two years later the issue was again raised when Winsor began a discussion with the Noble and Greenough School in Dedham about the possibility of a coordinate or coeducational arrangement. The debate about coeducation among most schools dealt mainly with two issues: the merits of educating both boys and girls in the same classroom and economics. Noble and Greenough had already decided to adopt the coed model and was debating internally the best way to accomplish that objective. Winsor had to decide whether a merger or some other organizational structure on the Dedham site made sense. Both schools recognized the need for a relatively prompt and decisive resolution to these questions and set a timetable in the fall of 1971 to do the research and hold appropriate meetings, both separately and jointly, culminating in a final decision the following fall.

A basic tenet underlying the discussions was that both Nobles and Winsor were highly regarded and strong enough to remain independent institutions. That is not to say that, given the times, there might not be challenges, but that economic factors need not be the raison d'être for a decision. The boards of the two schools completed their deliberations on schedule and the Winsor Executive Committee voted to recommend to the Winsor Corporation that the School remain at its urban location and continue its mission "to further the development of competent, responsible, and generous-minded women." Thanks in part to the skillful leadership and goodwill fostered by two dedicated Winsor parents, Robert A. Lawrence, head of the Nobles Board, and Robert D. Brace, the president of the Winsor Board, the constituencies of both schools generally commended the manner in which the decision was reached and moved on to plan for the future. These men exemplified the tireless and energetic contributions made not only by fathers but also by sons, husbands, and brothers of Winsor women.

In the fall of 1980 the School completed another self-study, the faculty again suggesting specific updates to curriculum. The curriculum in 1980 differed from that of 1970 not so much in the courses offered or in the quality of the overall educational experience, but in its opening up to respond to the deep and challenging changes in society and the world. Having decided to continue in its urban location and to remain committed to the education of girls, Winsor began to fine-tune the content of courses. Competing and complicating claims filtered through the system: the School had to continue to be attractive to its constituency while still broadening the definition of who that constituency was. It also needed to confront budget deficits by embracing the process of fund-raising for scholarships, teachers' salaries, and an expanded program both curricular and extracurricular.

Winsor distinguished itself in the 1980s by adding unique programs such as the Mountain School experience, an innovative coeducational program in Vermont where junior girls could spend a semester on a working farm. Winsor was the first of several schools that joined Milton Academy in this endeavor in 1984 and thereby was able to assure places each semester for Winsor students. A multilevel sports program made it possible for any girl to play a team sport, and a rich and varied fine arts program offered sixteen different possibilities in the Upper School. In academic courses the students began to have more choices. Whereas in the 1972 catalogue the English Department listed six one-semester seminars for students in the upper three classes, for the 1980–81 school year girls were able to select from twenty-five classes; the most popular topics determined which courses were actually taught. More emphasis was placed on language skills in this new decade, partly because of a student body drawn from more disparate schools. The differences in the preparation of new girls affected also the mathematics and language programs, where those who had spent most of their time in Winsor's own

Lower School were ahead of some newcomers. In response to this situation, younger students could boost their grammar, spelling, and reading skills in a special language skills class, and there could be as many as four levels of homogeneously grouped sections for math, French, and Latin. Other subjects remained heterogeneous, and there were often mixed grades in English and history courses.

Virginia Wing asked thoughtful and sometimes radical questions about the directions the School might take. Young women had many more life options open to them, sometimes perhaps too many. She early on identified the need "to find balance for the goals of young women." She noted in 1982 that "they can't all be engineers or lawyers," and she heartily validated those who wanted to marry and be mothers.[38] In the not-too-distant future, it would come about that many women felt they could, in fact, earn an M.B.A, an M.D., or a J.D. and be wives and mothers, too. Even acknowledging these new possibilities for women, Virginia Wing did not think that the emphasis at Winsor needed to change: many girls were already taking math and science, and Winsor's objective—"to challenge able girls intellectually and personally to grow towards self-reliant and responsible adulthood"—was still relevant.[39]

Winsor's curriculum reflected some national trends. Emphasis on and interest in science were especially notable: the number of faculty in the Science Department had doubled by 1983, because 70 percent of each class took more than the required two years of science. The Math Department was offering Introduction to Computer Skills, History offered electives in the Arab world, Russian history, Chinese studies, and current events at various times. The course Facing History and Ourselves, adopted in 1982, quickly became a favorite, adjusting to current world events and encouraging every student's active involvement.

Virginia Wing expressed concern about two other factors that were affecting the curriculum: college pressure (which she compared to "marketing") and the influence of standardized testing on teaching and subject matter. She deplored the tendency to teach to a test that tied the teacher to materials "which often lag behind the curricula" and, in the case of science, for example, were devoid of "material of vital importance such as environmental issues."[40] Concerns about college entrance and testing were not new for the School, but a wider applicant pool for precious college spots, especially at the eastern men's schools that now admitted women, was exacerbating them.

Faculty members became more involved with curricular change in the 1980s by serving on a number of ad hoc committees. In the same time period, teachers in public schools also began to lobby for more say in planning curriculum, but municipal bureaucracies found it difficult to accommodate faculty input. In the early 1980s Virginia Wing appointed the Long Range Planning Committee to consider the kinds of unsettling change the School might face in the future—in demographics, fund-raising, plant maintenance, faculty availability, administrative needs, and, of course, curriculum. Trustees and parents and even a few faculty members from other schools served on this committee, and several subcommittees were assembled. The subcommittee on curriculum, after months of discussion, recommended that Winsor establish a standing Curriculum Committee of experienced teachers who knew the School well and would guide it through the increasingly complex thicket of curriculum reform.

Virginia Wing's final year as Director was 1988, and some major decisions were put on hold until her successor, Carolyn McClintock Peter, could be involved. In January 1989, Carolyn Peter established the Standing Curriculum Committee "to act as a vehicle for evaluating the curriculum and anticipating changes." Previously there had been several short-term committees that looked at a particular area such as the Class IV program or the schedule, but they lacked the authority to mandate changes. In addition, a serious concern developed among some faculty about the makeup of such committees; it came to be an accepted tenet that all such committees should have a representative from each academic department on every committee, even—or especially—on the Curriculum Committee. At the same time, Carolyn Peter announced that she had created a new position, director of studies, whose responsibility was to lead the Curriculum Committee and to have oversight of the curriculum in Classes I through VIII.

Carolyn Peter felt that the upcoming ten-year self-study in 1989–90, the year after her arrival, would be a blessing for a school that was looking for new ways of doing things and willing to make its own suggestions for change as well as to hear the recommendations of the visiting committee. The English Department, for example, felt strongly that its conference system—"In the Upper School required, biweekly, twenty to forty-five minute conferences with each student provide opportunities for informal assessment"[41]—was one of its strengths and should be continued but also acknowledged that they each needed "to learn more about writers from diverse cultures," an idea praised by the evaluators from NEASC. Carolyn Peter was committed to the active recruiting in Boston schools begun under Virginia Wing and to the enrollment of minority students. Both actions would lead to a more multicultural curriculum and a need for more scholarship funds.

Changes rarely happen quickly in established institutions, and at Winsor the final decisions about curriculum had traditionally been subject to approval of the Director and the department heads, whose perspective had been formed by their long tenure in the institution. Winsor found that opening the discussions about change to the wider community required "a careful balancing of the wisdom of the past with an impetus for its evolution in the future."[42] In faculty meetings and on professional days, some of which were led by outside consultants, teachers and administrators debated the School's mission and character to determine what should or should not be retained.

Many in Winsor's broader community agreed with the faculty that technology, diversity, and the inadequacy of the physical plant could not be ignored. All these issues would affect the program of courses the School could offer.

The 1990 visiting committee was enthusiastic about the quality of the faculty—"The present faculty and staffing pattern is an extraordinarily rich one in comparison to most other schools in this area and in the nation"— and its efforts to teach a multicultural curriculum. The committee encouraged the development of more courses about the Middle East, Japan, and India that "go beyond the ancient cultures."[43] Although most of the history courses in the late 1980s dealt with European and American history, Class IV in the 1987–88 academic year studied the Middle East and Africa, and in their study of religions, Islam was included.[44] Upper School students could elect the widely respected course on genocide, Facing History, or The Arab World.[45] The committee praised the English Department "for focusing on the need for young women to read literature written by female authors ignored in many other curricula."

Some of the suggestions from the committee reflected Winsor's growing tendency to broaden the definition of curriculum to include school community concerns. Their report commented favorably on the diversity of the student body while noting that financial limitations kept some students from certain Jan Term experiences.[46] It also suggested the expansion of programs started in the 1980s on drugs and alcohol and that an effort be made to increase the number of students involved in community service projects.

In schools throughout the country it had become a fact of academic life that parents and society in general expected more from the schools. Winsor had taught ethics almost from its beginning and had dealt energetically with social issues through clubs and assembly programs, and it had recently confronted drug and alcohol use and the stresses of a highly competitive and demanding high school. The committee helped focus these challenges by suggesting changes to the counseling and guidance system, the role of the Room Teachers, and the expansion of teaching roles to include nonacademic areas. Concern for the wellness of "the whole child," a trend that culminated in the School's 2010 plans for a new gymnasium building, resulted in the hiring of a school nurse for the first time in 1990 and a long overdue examination of the sports facilities and the playing fields.

Throughout the 1990s, under the spirited and steady leadership of Carolyn McClintock Peter, Director from 1988 to 2004, Winsor moved forward to embrace numerous renovations to the physical plant and a broadening of the definition of "curriculum." A priority for Carolyn Peter was to increase the ways the School might become significantly more diverse in the racial, cultural, and socioeconomic makeup of its student body. The enrollment had grown; the student count during the 1960s and 1970s fluctuated between 300 and 330, and it had reached 364 when Virginia Wing left in 1988. The School

Carolyn McClintock Peter served as Winsor's sixth Director, from 1988 to 2004.

grew again throughout the 1990s as it extended its effort to attract able students from lower-income families. The Development Office added personnel and committed itself to meet the challenge of raising funds for additional scholarships and expansions to the buildings. The number of faculty and staff also increased. When positions for employment opened up, the Director and the department heads sought applicants of color, and they eventually created a hiring protocol to further support the mission of diversity and inclusion. Carolyn Peter announced to the Corporation in April 1991: "The course offerings of several academic departments now include to some extent the history and cultures of Asia and Africa, as well as a broader range of perspectives on American history and culture. In addition, we have tried as a community to address the experiences and beliefs which interplay to create attitudes of exclusivity, stereotypical thinking and racism. . . . My sense is that the School became more open, more welcoming, more reflective about justice and equity."[47]

In 1991–92 the enrollment was 380—the number would reach 400 in 1993–94 and increase further after that—and still growing, testimony to Winsor's strong reputation for academic rigor and a signal that the School was going in the right direction by restructuring its student counseling and advising practices. Although Winsor had always been a nurturing environment with careful attention to each student's needs, the scope of those needs had increased, and in schools everywhere it was expected that teachers, coaches, and administrators would be ever conscious of the whole child when revising curriculum. In order to know each child well—a cornerstone of Winsor's mission—the School expanded opportunities for parents to have one-on-one contact with individual teachers via back-to-school nights and scheduled conferences. The School continued to invite parents for one Upper School and one Lower School Parent Visiting Day each year, while at the same time including more parent voices in planning. The first full-time director of parent relations was appointed in 1990. To communicate clearly and effectively with the parent constituency required an awareness of their dreams for their daughters and careful weighing of priorities. The successful simplicity of Winsor's early years was replaced by a system that depended on the interaction and occasional disputation among many equally vociferous constituencies of the School—the faculty, the administration, the students, the parents, and the alumnae.

Carolyn Peter also recognized the importance of a new national—and global—awareness about educating girls. The American Association of University Women released their report *How Schools Shortchange Girls* in 1992.[48] The report strongly urged that girls be taken more seriously as mathematicians and scientists; it suggested that the environmental movement was a place where women scientists could contribute. And, as before, when there had been national reports and sweeping recommendations, Winsor could say with pride that Winsor girls were already taking three or four years of laboratory sciences and four years of mathematics, some of which were Advanced Placement courses. In 1993 the School participated in a national movement, Girls United To Save the Environment (GUTSE),[49] by holding a day of classes and workshops about the dangers to the planet and the specific efforts, large and small, that young people can make for the cause. Winsor's cleverly named clubs, the Lower School's CALF (Concerned About Life's Future) and the Upper School's COW (Conserve Our World), were already involved in the cleanup of the Muddy River on the nearby segment of the Emerald Necklace; they participated in bulb planting and cleaning along the Charles River; they spearheaded and kept track of recycling in the School, providing bins for paper recycling in each classroom.

Broadening the racial and ethnic makeup of the School was a goal for both Virginia Wing and Carolyn Peter. Under Virginia Wing, the School began admitting black students in 1964. The first black faculty members joined the staff in 1990, a year after Carolyn Peter appointed a Diversity Committee, whose purpose was to "consider the ways in which the School as an institution and faculty and students as individuals have subtly or overtly expressed support of a hierarchy of race, culture and class."[50] She also arranged the first meeting for alumnae of color, to which she invited students of color in Classes VI, VII, and VIII. Feedback, frank and sometimes hard to hear, moved the School toward developing a more multicultural curriculum and put in motion a schoolwide discussion of diversity: the Parent Support Group for Diversity, student assemblies on racism, professional development for faculty, and an exchange program with the island of Guadaloupe.[51]

Beginning in 1991, the School called in outside personnel who ran periodic workshops called Confronting Racism: An Educational Imperative for the 90s. The faculty attended in small groups of about twenty, and eventually all members of the faculty and staff participated. This two-and-a-half day off-campus exercise challenged the participants and inspired soul-searching conversations among the adults throughout the School. A series of schoolwide discussions for students, START (Sensitivity Training/Anti-Racism Training), began in 1995; the students simulated the effects of some girls being labeled "elite" and being given special advantages.

In 1992 the School undertook a self-evaluation by participating in the Multicultural Awareness Project.[52] In her Report to the Corporation in April

1993, Carolyn Peter described the MAP assessment as a "process in which we have reviewed the programs, policies, climate, and practices of the School in the light of its diversity and the diversity of greater Boston and the world." A first step in the process was the School's creation of questions about its own diversity status. "Does each student feel valued by the school? Is each student reflected in the curriculum? What do students need to learn in secondary school about the diverse multicultural world in which they will live?" As a result of the MAP, said Carolyn Peter, there were "new challenges for the School: a more diverse faculty; a curriculum which serves as both window and mirror to all its students; a community which respects our common humanity and celebrates our diversity."[53]

The faculty met the challenge to build a curriculum that throughout the 1990s became more consciously multicultural than ever while maintaining high academic standards. Faculty devised innovative teaching methods—some of which were inspired by the new possibilities of technology—and Carolyn Peter praised "the untraditional ways the Winsor faculty is teaching a traditionally rigorous curriculum." It was the era of "connected teaching and learning" to ensure that a child could see how she was connected to the curriculum.[54]

By 1990 the Computer Curriculum Committee, made up of faculty from several disciplines, had set up one-semester courses to teach BASIC programming and the use of online library databases. The Technology Planning Committee was formed in 1996 as the School continued to formulate the rules that would govern the student use of the Internet on the School premises. Parents served on this committee and worked to locate funding for the huge task of facilitating the use of computers in classrooms and offices. Carolyn Peter pointed out to the Corporation that technology would have a significant influence on the curriculum, "forcing us as individuals and as schools to think about education and learning in dramatically new ways"; she praised the thoughtful balance of conservatism and innovation that characterized the approach of the Winsor faculty to the challenges and possibilities of technology.[55]

The 2000 Self-Study described a robust technology division in the School, led by the director of Library and Information Services, a technology coordinator, and the computer curriculum coordinator, who met regularly with faculty to discuss new initiatives and strategies. The use of computers was curriculum-based. "Any introduction of computers into the curriculum must work to enhance the existing programs, not replace them."[56]

Updating the technology facilities was a continuous project throughout the first decade of the twenty-first century. Staff was added as needs for various aspects—technical support, Internet access, student accounts, curriculum development—became crucial to every person in the school. As teachers incorporated the use of computers in myriad ways across the curriculum, the School made every effort to assure that no student lacked access to the technology required by any assignment or project.

One of the most challenging aspects of computer use in schools involved the students' use of what by 2008 were called social-networking sites. Through assemblies, programs for parents, and discussions in classes and homerooms, the School sought to make students aware of the potential risks in sharing their personal information online. As was the case with nearly everything connected to computer technology, the changes were multitudinous, swift, and unpredictable. The School was able to respond because of careful preparation in the mid-1990s. By hiring knowledgeable technical personnel and including the entire school community in planning and implementation (which had been the trend in curriculum development throughout the previous decade), Winsor joined the educational computer age with verve.

Technological changes also required money, and, as always, generous gifts and grants helped support this program. By 1994 Winsor was in the midst of the most ambitious fund-raising drive in the School's history—a capital campaign that would meet its $10 million goal in 1997. Admission rates increased yearly; the yield from admissions (the percentage of those who are admitted who actually enroll) was 80 percent, higher than Harvard's. Teachers benefited from higher salaries and the opportunity to apply for a Virginia Wing Grant; the Trustees had established the Virginia Wing Fund for Faculty Enrichment to compensate faculty members engaging in research, study, and travel.

The course listings in the 1997–98 catalogue show a curriculum richer and more varied, especially in English and history, than that ten years before. English had added books by and about women in the Lower School and in the Upper School had moved beyond Jane Austen, Edith Wharton, and Virginia Woolf, adding Maya Angelou, Maxine Hong Kingston, Louise Erdrich, and Adrienne Rich, among others. In Lower School history, students still studied ancient civilizations (and Boston's), but they encountered new people and places such as early Africa, Eskimos, China, the Anasazi, Western Africa, and medieval Japan, as well as the ancient civilizations of the Mediterranean.

The Upper School History Department had become the acknowledged leader in making curricular changes and pressing all departments to maintain focus on Winsor's creation of a multicultural program. Facing History secured a permanent place in the history curriculum. Its "Taking a Stand" project made each student a participant in her community by examining how one individual's effort can make a difference. In the 1980s offerings varied from year to year and might include one or more of the following: Russian History, Medieval History, Current Issues, Chinese Studies, and The Arab World.

With the new millennium, the School also made a major change in the daily schedule, a move made after long deliberation by a faculty committee.

Winsor's website, www.winsor.edu, not only provides information about the School for the wider world but also gives students, teachers, and parents minute-to-minute communication about School events, courses, and even homework. A constantly evolving gallery of photographs becomes an online record of events such as Spirit Week (top photo) and commencement.

The new schedule that began in the 1999–2000 academic year sought to lessen the stress of changing classes by instituting fewer periods and lengthening the lunch hour. The goal of equal classroom time for all subject areas in the Upper School was achieved, and the global awareness of the new millennium inspired a serious look at the overall curriculum at Winsor.

In the spring of 2002 Carolyn Peter appointed ten faculty members to the Long Range Curriculum Planning Committee and charged it with answering three challenging questions: What is the vision for the curriculum of the School in ten years? What skills, knowledge, and qualities of character do we want each Winsor graduate to have? How do our graduation requirements reflect the Winsor missions and vision? The committee worked for two years and gave its final report in June 2004.

The report defined the School's "Philosophy of Curriculum," defining *curriculum* as the total classroom learning experience. The statement identified four principles as key in the twenty-first century: Connected Curriculum, Skills, Preparation for Responsible Citizenship in the Global Community, and Independent Thinking and Learning. The significant changes for the Upper School were the moving of Expository Writing from Class VII to

Class V, the addition of a required semester of non-Western history, and an additional semester of science. The fine arts requirement was restructured. Mandarin Chinese would begin in Class V in 2004–5, the foreign language requirement was clarified (requiring only three years, rather than "mastery"), and a mandatory Independent Senior Project would be required each spring.

The scope of the report was extensive, covering "Standards of Effective Pedagogy" and definitions of how Winsor students learn best and what conditions assure "effective learning." The report broadly defined *assessment* and decreed homework amounts for each class. It also outlined a formidable list of tasks that lay ahead for faculty as they discussed and implemented the changes, which would begin to affect students in the Class of 2009. An important facet of the new plan was the institution of grade-level meetings for faculty in Classes I through V, designed to coordinate all subject areas according to the new philosophy of curriculum.

The LRCPC's curriculum can be seen as containing many of the trends and practices in Winsor's earlier adjustments to the curriculum. The broad outline of subject areas remains the same as it was in 1910: faculty collaboration continues to be the heart of curriculum development; pedagogy is based on the idea that girls have individual learning styles; and an informed and responsible view of the world underscores the "fundamental interdependence of all people."[57]

She could probably fill the school with pupils paying a much higher tuition rate than at present; but neither Miss Winsor nor the promoters of the school wish to have it consist exclusively of the daughters of the rich.

—1908 letter

The whole School has expressed simultaneously emotions of rapture, incredulity, astonishment, and envy at the remarkable prowess of Class VI, who held on December 8, at Eloise Lawrence's house on Commonwealth Avenue, a fair for the benefit of the Playground fund. They made $1000.

—Winsor Lamp, 1924

We want to make better use of our urban location and to move more steadily into a policy of cooperation with our neighbors.

—Virginia Wing

Julia Lyman (later Simonds) with her Class of 1917 (left to right): Ellen Curtis, Rose Townsend, Julia Lyman, Eleanor Cabot, Molly Hill, Mary Winsor, Mabel Thomas. Because she was an example of service both to the School and to her community, combining "the energetic pursuit of excellence with devoted service to humanity," her family established the Julia Lyman Simonds prize given each year to the alumna who exemplifies these qualities.

The Spirit of Service

❦

"THE FUNDAMENTAL INTERDEPENDENCE OF ALL PEOPLE"

*W*ITHOUT THE GENEROSITY OF OTHERS, Winsor would not exist. Gratitude for the gifts of money, time, and talent pervades the written records. In return, the School has maintained the practice of giving to others, beginning with its support of the Calhoun Colored School in Alabama and continuing with granting scholarships to students who need them, raising funds for international relief, participating actively in community projects, and inspiring its alumnae to put themselves on the front lines of humanitarian endeavors throughout the world.

The Winsor School's early benefactors were part of an energetic movement in civic renewal that was occurring in cities across the country at the turn of the century. This urban creativity sprang from the aesthetics of the Arts and Crafts period* and has been called the City Beautiful Movement. The precise origin of the phrase "city beautiful" is unclear, but it evolved at the turn of the century in discussions about urban planning, beautifying city environments, and awakening civic pride; it eventually became a convenient label for a school of thought that was not just about a city's streets and buildings but also about citizen involvement and community building. City planners hoped that creating useful, lasting, and attractive public spaces would make cities enjoyable places where citizens could live and work: the beauty of parks and the dignity of classically influenced buildings would call forth the best from people. An "ideal" urban atmosphere would be one where civic pride and moral virtue could thrive together to create a fair and democratic society for everyone. Men and women of wealth and vision gave large sums of money to achieve this dream and also donated their time, participating on planning committees, sharing their technical expertise, and drawing others

---

* The movement, from which the Mission style arose in America, developed in England in the late nineteenth century. It was as much a social movement as an artistic one.

into the process. Museums, libraries, hospitals, research facilities, housing projects, and bathhouses received money from private individuals.

The Incorporators of The Winsor School were part of the City Beautiful dream, willingly contributing to many great causes that would better the city. For their daughters they envisioned a school committed to strong academics and healthy habits of living, but the passionate idealism of the times decreed also that these curricula for mind and body be suffused with three human values without which a society could not exist: caring for others, generosity to those in need, and a sense of community. These were to form the curriculum of the spirit at Winsor, and the new School immediately began to instill in its young students the philanthropic habit of community service—the practice of giving what one has more than enough of to those who have less. It is said to be a peculiarly American tradition and one on which a democratic country continues to depend economically, socially, and spiritually.[1] "This school, dedicated to sound minds and sound bodies, is also concerned with developing in young people a sense of community responsibility. It is one of the assets of a day school that in their most impressionable years the girls can have a part, however small, in community work—work not just for themselves or their small group."[2]

The first money raised for the School was intended for a scholarship fund, about which Mary Winsor remarked: "Perhaps the most important of all our gifts were the Scholarships: nine full Scholarships, endowed by certain donors to the original building fund, and numerous partial ones, contributed during the war, when times were bad. They have proved of inestimable value to the long line of people who have used them."[3] From its inception, the incorporated School was meant to be not just for daughters of the well-to-do who were financing and supporting it but also for deserving girls whose fathers were professors and engineers and artists and clergymen unable to afford the tuition for such a school. Each original donor of $10,000 had the right to name a scholarship recipient, subject to Mary Winsor's approval, if he or she so wished. In her address at the Fiftieth Anniversary of the School in 1936, Mary Winsor gave heartfelt thanks to the many donors and advisors who had continually offered monetary or physical help or expertise in the early years.

Every Director of the School, in her semiannual Report to the Corporation, expressed the ongoing need to increase the Scholarship Fund. Since Mary Winsor herself interviewed each child and chose the recipients, she might have been expressing a sadness that she felt upon meeting a spirited, intelligent fourth-grader who would enjoy and be enjoyed by the School, had there been money enough to support her.

In her Report to the Corporation in 1932, Katharine Lord reported that $2,350 in scholarships had been awarded and that she expected more demand for aid the following year. "It may be interesting to know that in one case where there was great financial difficulty last fall and the scholarship was given, it was paid back this spring, though I am sure there are still hard times for the family." She added, "In another case where the older daughter is coming out, the younger is put into public school rather than ask for scholarships."[4] "Coming out" was the vernacular for making one's debut in society. Families often spent lavishly for the teas, parties, and cotillions that accompanied a young woman's debut.

The Directors provided the money discreetly and kept a close eye on the recipients' progress at the School. They were expected to do well, and often scholarship help was not given until the girl had proven herself. The Executive Committee in fact decreed at one point that no scholarships should be given to girls in their first year at Winsor. Katharine Lord brought up in the same report a concern about class diversity: "It seems to me very important, that when a child is here on a scholarship, the family's and the child's values are clear, because I have seen children much upset by being brought into a group who were spending money more freely and therefore came to value unduly the things money can buy."[5]

In the early years the School was entirely dependent on tuition and private contributions from parents and alumnae. The Scholarship Fund increased during the Depression, and the School tried to support students who had previously been able to pay their way in full. Several letters in the archives convey the gratitude of the recipients and their parents: "I wanted to tell you myself just what the scholarship meant to me and how deeply grateful I am to you. I had always been fond of the Winsor School, but when the possibility arose that I might not be able to continue there, it seemed more than I could bear to give up my school life and all my friends there. Therefore when you offered me the scholarship, you may be sure you saved me from a great sorrow."[6] In Katharine Lord's view, such support reflected the "investment we are making in these students." During the 1940s partial scholarships were given to some of the English refugee children who were "foster sisters" in Winsor homes.

Eventually, scholarship funds were increased by grants from private organizations, such as the Dorothy Melcher Sneath 1918 Scholarship Foundation and the Independence Foundation. As the School increased its effort to attract and enroll middle- and low-income students, especially those from the city of Boston, there was need for increased scholarship aid. The scholarship budget in 1970 was $35,570 and benefited "about ten" students.[7] In the 1970s, with the effort to enroll more students from the city of Boston itself, Virginia Wing noted the increase in the number of scholarship students, students whose parents were enthusiastic about education, students with varied cultural and social backgrounds, and students from the middle-income group.[8]

The American Field Service foreign exchange program, which the School

Janet Sabine 1921 and her sister Ruth 1924. Mary Winsor received expert advice on the new music rooms from their father, Wallace C. Sabine, who made history when he designed the acoustics for Symphony Hall in Boston and devised the formula for the "sabin," a unit of acoustical sound.

joined in 1957, required fund-raising to pay the foreign students' way.* The exchange students lived with Winsor families, whose hospitality was also a gift to the School. In 1964 the School made a switch to the International Student Placement Service, a smaller organization that served only a few schools in the country. "In a school the size of Winsor it seems to me important to have as broad a representation of backgrounds and points of view as possible, and one of the ways is to have children from another country."[9]

An early and unique opportunity for the Winsor girls to engage in philanthropy came through the School's connection to the Calhoun Colored School in Lowndes County, Alabama. Charlotte Thorn of New Haven and Mabel Dillingham of Boston, in partnership with Booker T. Washington, started this school for black children in 1896. "They took a great interest in the welfare of the negroes, and having grown up in this New England community they had some of the big-hearted feeling that men and women in this community have."[10]

The Civil War had remained, even after forty years, a defining event for Americans, and Abraham Lincoln was celebrated as a martyred hero, especially on his birthday. In 1909 the centennial of his birth was marked at a special School assembly in which excerpts from his speeches were read, "Hymn of Peace," a famous Jubilee Song,† was sung, and Colonel N. Penrose Hallowell spoke: "He looked as if he could tell a very interesting story about himself too, for he fought through most of those four long years of war." Colonel Hallowell was one of several Bostonians who served on Calhoun's Board of Trustees, and, although there is no specific reference to how the Winsor-Calhoun connection began, it was most likely through the Hallowells.

Calhoun was more than a mere school. It was an entire community that resembled the settlement houses Winsor mothers and students worked in at the turn of the century.[11] The two New England founders drew their in-

---

* The AFS program was an outgrowth of the American Ambulance Service, which originated in World War I and received the services of several Winsor graduates.

† An extravagant five-day National Peace Jubilee had been held in June 1869 in Boston, featuring a band, chorus, and orchestra of about 10,000 singers and musicians. Oliver Wendell Holmes wrote the words to "Hymn of Peace"; see www.americanmusicpreservation.com/nema.htm.

spiration from Samuel Chapman Armstrong, who had founded the Hampton Institute in Virginia in 1868 to educate emancipated African American slaves. The school was in the "black belt of Alabama, where only a few years ago it was a crime punishable with death to teach a black boy or girl a letter in a book."[12] Graduates from the Hampton Institute worked at the Calhoun School, training the new citizens to learn trades, buy land, build houses, start businesses, and develop churches and schools.[13]

The 1906 *Scrapbook* (which was sometimes the *Scrap Book* or the *Scrap-Book*) mentions the Junior Calhoun Club's successful drive to collect contributions for the Alabama school—580 articles of clothing and toys, in addition to nine dollars and fifty-one cents. The announcement was made at a school gathering at which "Miss Harriet Ware read some letters from Port Royal, where the first Colored School was started during the Civil War."[14] One of the annual occurrences at Monday morning assemblies* was a visit from the Hampton Institute Quartet from the Hampton Institute.†

The stories, poems, and essays in the *Winsor Lamp*s of this period contain many references to the plight of ex-slaves and the need to support the efforts to help them. Some of the language could be considered, from a modern perspective, patronizing, but the intention to keep the issue in the students' minds was clear. In 1916 the relationship between Calhoun, the Hampton Institute Quartet, and Winsor was still strong. The *Lamp* described a speech by Ann Scoville of the Hampton Institute and the singing of the Hampton Institute Quartet: "To our great joy, the 'Hampton Quartet' emphasized many points in her address by singing old African melodies with words which gave voice to the thoughts and feelings of the whole colored race. Miss Scoville made us realize that there are over ten million colored people within our borders who need the blessing of education."[15]

At another assembly that same year, the *Lamp* reported that "Mr. Boyd Rhetta, a graduate of Calhoun, spoke to the five lower classes." "The latest development of the work at Calhoun is the buying of land and the building of homes by the school's graduates. One of the first to build a better home for his mother was Boyd Rhetta, who came to Hampton after finishing his course at Calhoun, graduating in 1901. . . . It is encouraging to learn that thirteen Calhoun graduates are either buying land or have already paid for a farm."[16]

Although World War I would create a new philanthropic focus for both students and alumnae, the connection to Calhoun was not severed, and several Winsor graduates went to teach at Calhoun and Hampton, including

---

* At some point the all-school gatherings were moved to Wednesdays, then back again to Mondays. Later still, there were two assemblies—a brief, school-oriented one on Tuesdays and one for longer performances on Thursdays.

† Hampton University still exists and is one of the more famous historically black colleges. The Hampton Institute Quartet began to tour in 1913, promoting African American songs.

Margaret Vickery 1905,* who taught at Calhoun from 1916 to 1918, and Sarah H. Davis 1919, who spoke in a Winsor assembly on one occasion. In 1925 the *Lamp* reported that Blanche Theodora Hill 1921 was teaching at Hampton Institute with her husband. In the 1940s, Marjorie Applegate, who had taught for six years at Calhoun, joined the Winsor history faculty. Winsor maintained a relationship with Calhoun and Hampton for many years, inviting the Hampton Institute Quartet to sing for some years after the Calhoun School closed because of financial problems during the Depression.

Philanthropy was also a major undertaking for Winsor alumnae. From the beginning days in the 1890s alumnae treasured their bond to Mary Winsor and were enthusiastic supporters of the new building in the Fenway. The young alumnae established the Graduate Club of Miss Winsor's School in 1907 and published their first *Graduate Club Register* in 1910. In addition to supporting the Calhoun School, they were seeking "to give members an opportunity to meet Miss Winsor and one another," in other words, to maintain the friendships they had made and to continue a connection to their teachers, who were made honorary members of the club. One of their first official acts was to request—or, rather, insist—that the new school be named The Winsor School, not the St. Botolph School. When they prevailed in this, they set up a committee and raised $5,218 for the building fund. They continued to raise money for the school through plays and outright gifts, and they were given their own Graduates' Room in the new building.

After a few years, the group decided to give all the money they raised to The Winsor School. The graduates expanded their activities: they presented an assembly each year to speak to the students on college life, social work, interior decorating, and even duck hunting; they planned field days and played on teams with the faculty against student teams; they held art exhibitions of their own work; they created an occasion for welcoming to their ranks the next graduating class, a practice that has continued. By 1915 some of the graduates had been elected to the Corporation.

Just as the Graduate Club was increasing its involvement at Winsor, World War I began in Europe on July 28, 1914, offering to Winsor students and graduates new opportunities for philanthropy. Long before the United States actually entered that conflict, Winsor students were collecting clothing and money for war relief. Given their intelligence, energy, and desire to contribute, it is not surprising that a number of young Winsor graduates left their serene, comfortable homes in Boston and traveled to European war zones to be of service.

The Graduate Club published *The Overseas War Record of the Winsor School, 1914–1919* in 1919.[17] The booklet was dedicated to Helen Homans 1902, who began her work in France in March 1915 and was stationed at three

---

* Vickery graduated from the Boston School of Social Work in 1911, later earned a B.S. in nursing, and taught at the School of Nursing of the Children's Hospital.

different Red Cross hospitals before her death from influenza in 1918, just before the Armistice was signed. The club entrusted the managing of the project to one of the overseas volunteers, Eleanor "Nora" Saltonstall 1911, who had been an ambulance driver for a mobile Red Cross unit that worked very near the front lines in France. Her stirring collection of letters, *"Out Here at the Front,"* reveals the traits of perseverance, moral fortitude, and humanity that would compel young women of the period to seek the challenge of war work beyond the restricted women's sphere of their mothers. These young graduates felt themselves to be in and of the world. Their education at Winsor and (for some) in college had broadened their perspective and instilled in them a confidence that they could probably do anything a man could do, society permitting. Nora Saltonstall survived the war but died shortly afterward of typhoid fever on a trip to Oregon. A memorial fund to finance a Winsor graduate's year of study in France, the Saltonstall Scholarship, was established in her name in 1920. Amelia Richards 1913 and Hannah Fiske 1915 also died at the end of the war. The survivors returned with an intimate understanding of war that few other American women had.

Nora Saltonstall 1911 in a portrait by Frank W. Benson, an American Impressionist painter who also taught at the School of the Museum of Fine Arts for some years.

That The Winsor School fostered an ethic of philanthropy is reflected in the phrase from an early catalogue that became a part of nearly every mission statement: "the aim of producing competent, responsible, generous-minded women." The spirit of giving to others, however, had been one of the very few ways the mothers and grandmothers of Winsor students had been able to contribute to community life. The efforts of women during World War I, not only abroad but also on the home front, gave new life to the suffrage movement: women could do men's jobs, so why couldn't they also vote? Windows that had opened to show women challenging careers and causes would never really close. For Winsor students, the returning war workers modeled new female roles. Mary Winsor observed: "I view with astonishment the accomplishments of our graduates. Their courage and power are symbolized, to my mind, by that procession of young women in khaki, who marched down our Assembly Hall on the first graduation day after the Armistice."[18]

Between September 1914 and August 1919 fifty-eight Winsor women were part of the war effort. The earliest, in 1914, were Elsa Leland Pierrefeu 1895,

Mary Dexter Napier-Martin 1904, and Esther Hayden Stanton 1901. *The Overseas War Record* printed in detail the dates and places of service for each of the volunteers and included "Abstracts and Extracts from Letters" from forty-three of them. The part of the book that contains the young women's own voices is wonderful reading. Their experiences ranged from heartbreaking to amusing, but the striking thing is the quality of their writing and their ability to show their intimate personal connections to the people they met. Winsor had taught them to observe carefully and to write beautifully, and because they had learned to speak French at Winsor, their communication skills were priceless.

Some words culled from the letters in *The Overseas War Record* may entice Winsorites a century later to find this little book and read it from cover to cover:

> The other day, when I was bandaging the stump of a soldier's right arm, he said to me so sweetly in French, "I am lucky to have one hand. Yes, I believe I can work with that." A soldier who had both legs cut off and a wound in his head besides is doing very well. It is wonderful how brave they are.
>
> *—Isabel Perkins Anderson 1894*

> Each day hundreds arrived from the front, the most pitiful old men and women with small children. They arrived, crowded into third-class carriages, tired and discouraged, their homes gone and their only possessions a small parcel of clothes and a pet dog or cat, in one instance a goat.
>
> *—Elizabeth Ayer Inches 1908*

> One of the consequences of the shortness of coal was that the gas company only furnished gas at certain hours, and of such a bad quality that it was impossible to sterilize anything. If it had not been for the dressings we received from America, especially from the Surgical Dressing Committee, already sterilized, we would have been in a bad way.
>
> *—Isabel Coolidge Cunningham 1911*

> These were black days in the war with daily communiqués bringing news of our lines being driven back upon our lines of communication, when Amiens was under fire and we were nearly wedged off from Paris into a pocket in Northern France.
>
> *—Alice Cunningham 1909*

> I was appointed Chief of the Bureau of Refugees for Paris and the Department of the Seine. . . . There were at that time 83,000 refugees in Paris and 47,000 in the suburbs. The greatest needs . . . were for better housing [and] more medical care.
>
> *—Margaret Curtis 1902*

I have just lived through the most terrific ten days of my life. I didn't know that it was humanly possible to work so hard. I did three thirty-six hour stretches in one week. . . . I have never learned so much in my life, but if I had known the responsibility I don't know that I would ever have come.

—*Helen Homans 1902*

In 1916, I started a hostel [the Lady St. Helier House] for women munitions workers to care for cases of industrial diseases. We take cases suffering from Tri Nitro Toluol poisoning,* mercury poisoning and fatigue, also a few convalescent cases, women suffering from burns, septic finger, or women who are recovering from operations.

—*Grace Monks 1905*

A few volunteers were sent to Great Britain, but most served in France at Red Cross army hospitals; the February 1916 *Lamp* listed the graduates already nursing the wounded in France: Margaret Jackson 1898, Helen Homans 1902, Louise Coolidge 1904, Mary Dexter 1904, Edith Parkman 1909; the piece added, "Three grads have lost their husbands."[19] The young women cared for the wounded and assisted the trained nurses by unpacking supplies for the canteens. These canteens, sponsored by charitable organizations in the United States, were little oases where the volunteers could comfort the soldiers with either a hot drink or a friendly word, but it is clear from

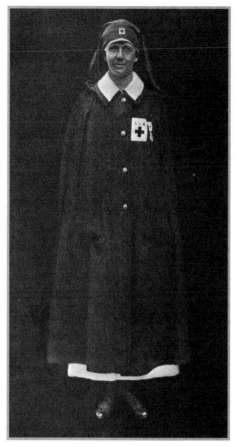

The Overseas War Record of the Winsor School, 1914–1919 *was dedicated to the memory of Helen Homans 1902: "Intrepid and serene she gave her life for suffering humanity in the hospitals of France."*

the women's letters that they often pined for more challenging assignments. Alice Channing 1906 recounted: "When Hannah Fiske arrived with a new Ford touring car, armed with a knowledge of how to drive and keep in order both her car and our delivery car, she became an essential part of the [relief] work."[20]

The American volunteers even paid their own traveling expenses, and their "uniforms"—long dresses, aprons, and head scarves—must have complicated their work in a dirty, crowded, and cold environment where real danger could befall them at any time. They were often closer to the front lines of the battles than anyone (especially their parents) had expected. The

* Trinitrotoluol is TNT. Women workers exposed during the manufacture of TNT could, over time, be severely disabled, and much of what was done at Lady St. Helier House in England was to teach the women how the toxic effects could be prevented.

young women continually received supplies from their families in Boston and shared these provisions of food and clothing with the needy refugees and soldiers. When they wrote back to their benefactors, they pleaded for more contributions and illustrated their experiences with vivid descriptions of the people they were helping.

(Winsor women also enlisted for service in World War II: fourteen were in the WAVES, eight in the WAACs [later the WACs], three in the Marines, and one in the British WRENS. In addition, ten graduates served as members of the Red Cross.)[21]

Following the Armistice on November 11, 1918, some of the women stayed in Europe to assist with refugees. Back in Boston, a new way of life was about to begin for all women as the long campaign to pass the Nineteenth Amendment finally neared its victorious end. The amendment would pass on August 26, 1920, after decades of struggle. References to this victory are surprisingly absent from the Winsor records. There were, however, many names of Winsor-connected people on the list of the Standing Committee of the Massachusetts Association Opposed to Further Extension of Suffrage to Women (clumsily abbreviated MAOFESW) published in 1898, a fact that suggests that Winsor may have been in the antisuffrage camp.[22] The "Remonstrance" (against women's suffrage) was a particularly robust movement in Massachusetts, and its adherents were both male and female. On the listings of members from Boston, Cambridge, and Brookline are Winsor-connected names such as Mrs. J. Randolph Coolidge, Mrs. Charles P. Curtis, Mrs. Charles Eliot, Mrs. Henry Saltonstall, and a Miss Mary P. Winsor.*

In *Anti-Suffrage Essays by Massachusetts Women*, published in 1916, two essays by Winsor women forcefully state the case for protecting women from the degradation and loss of respect they would face if they were allowed to vote. In this book, dedicated to "the 295,939 Massachusetts Men Who, on Election Day, 1915, Endorsed the Anti-Suffrage Sentiments of the Women of Massachusetts," Ruth Whitney Lyman, a member of the Winsor Class of 1898, declared: "The fundamental difference is this—that the suffragist (like the socialist) persists in regarding the individual as the unit of society, while the anti-suffragist insists that it is the family."[23]

Anna Hallowell Davis, the daughter of Sarah W. Hallowell, wrote a long essay for the book called "The True Function of the Normal Woman," in which she stated one of the most common rationales for opposing suffrage:

> A good mother of three or four children already has more than she can do well. If she takes up this whole new department of life and thought, I am convinced she will have to let something else go, and already under the influence of the feminist movement, that "something else" seems to be

---

* There was another Mary P. Winsor around this time, but she was a rather radical proponent of birth control and other liberal causes, including suffrage, and she was based in Philadelphia. Interestingly, Mrs. Frederick Winsor's name was also on the list.

her home. So, this is what the anti-suffragists feel most keenly—that once the franchise is imposed as a duty, they would have to do the things which men already are doing (and doing as well as the women could do them); that they would no longer be free to do what they think is the higher work for them, as women. Therefore, when a suffragist tells me she has a "right" to vote, I say that, in the name of the best interests of the community, I have the right not to vote.[24]

On the other hand, there were Winsor connections on the prosuffrage side. One of the most prominent was Pauline Agassiz Shaw, whose daughter was a Winsor Incorporator and who at one point in the suffrage fight made available a house at 6 Marlborough Street for the Massachusetts Woman Suffrage Association to use as a headquarters. There is but a handful of references to suffrage work in the *Graduate Club Registers,* but most of the graduates named other organizations for which they were volunteering. Charlotte Jones 1899 worked after graduation at the South End Music School (affiliated with the South End House) and was involved in "work for equal suffrage," and Margaret Anthony 1900 was the secretary of the New Bedford Equal Suffrage League.[25] Two Winsor fathers who supported suffrage were Richard P. Hallowell, who served on the board of the Massachusetts Woman Suffrage Association, and Judge Louis Brandeis.

Whereas there is little evidence that the School maintained any position, either for or against a woman's right to vote, it is somewhat ironic to find that during the final years of the fight Winsor women—not only alumnae but students and teachers and parents—had actually not stayed in their spheres but had been extensively involved in serious volunteer work outside their homes. Their activity testifies to Jane Addams's comment in a speech in England: "I am a strong supporter of woman suffrage, and, although I hope to see the women of England enfranchised, I see around me endless opportunities for social work which could be usefully performed while the vote is being won."[26] After the war Winsor graduates, with a new perspective on the value of their volunteer contributions, continued their social action work. There can be no doubt that the impressive contribution of young women both at home and abroad throughout World War I was a catalyst not only for the passage of the suffrage amendment but for the women's increased determination to be doing something significant with their talents. The historian David Hackett Fischer has noted: "Jane Addams, who observed the suffrage campaign at first hand, believed that the decisive factor was the conduct of American women in the First World War. Women's suffrage, she wrote, came as 'a direct result of the war psychology.' It was an extension of ideas of liberty and freedom that kept expanding in America, during and after the war."[27]

In early 1918 the Graduate Club started a special educational project and released the following announcement in a pamphlet:

The Winsor Training School for Home and Social Service

The School will open on May 1, 1918 at No. 1 Autumn Street, Boston. Ultimately the course will cover two years, but in the present emergency the school will begin by offering a four-months' practical, intensive training in the elements of

(1) Domestic Science
(2) Home Nursing
(3) Child Study

The last month of the four will be spent chiefly in field work connected with the settlements, hospitals, organized charities, day nurseries, and Rutland Street Nursery School, which is to be opened about May 1st, under a trained and experienced teacher.[28]

The June 1918 *Lamp* reported on the visit of Gretchen Howes Waldo 1902 to Winsor: "On May 20, Mrs. Waldo . . . told the eighth class some facts about the Winsor Training School . . . for girls who wish to learn the scientific way of running a house and some of the elements of nursing." Mrs. Waldo suggested to the students that the Training School gave them a chance to prepare themselves "to be useful later in the reconstruction work which will follow the war."[29]

The earliest Winsor graduates were not deterred by the fact that they could not vote or serve on juries or own property, goals the suffrage movement was aiming for, but rather sought out causes with more specific goals. In addition to opening the Training School, they were starting a nursery school at 48 Rutland Street in the South End. The *Lamp* tells of a visit to the Graduate Club from an alumna, Alice Brown DeNormandie 1895, and Dr. Richard M. Smith: "They suggested that the Club finance and manage a Nursery School for little children between the ages of two and five, as one of the best means of furthering their work ['child conservation']. Miss Winsor and Mrs. Pearson explained the practical working of the school and its connection with the Winsor Training School."[30]

Much later in the twentieth century a Winsor graduate, Eleanor Thomas Nelson 1949, founded Workplace Connections, Inc., which provided employer-sponsored child-care services in the city of Boston. Their nine centers became a part of Bright Horizons Family Solutions in 2001. An author of many articles, Eleanor Nelson gave a speech to Winsor girls titled "Teaching the Disabled Child," and she was at the School often when her daughters attended Winsor in the late 1970s. She was a Trustee, led fund-raising drives, and became such a devoted creator of costumes for the Shakespeare play (even after her girls had done their plays) that the costume room was named for her. Her generous bequest established the chair in the Department of Fine Arts.

The ongoing improvement in devices for housekeeping was another factor in allowing young women to be less tied to their homes, as was the fact that many had been to college and not a few of their classmates had pursued "men's" careers in medicine and college teaching. Although the alumnae took credit for their new nursery school as the "oldest nursery school in Boston," they had assistance from other schools' alumnae groups and were using a space that was a part of the South End House Association. This location in the South End has through the years accommodated a settlement house, an art school and music school for children, and other community projects. It still exists as a part of the United South End Settlement.

Two other Winsor women founded a pioneering nursery school in Boston that still exists on the Tufts University campus and bears the names of its founders, the Eliot-Pearson School.[31] The nursery school movement in the United States began in the three fields of home economics, social work, and education in the early 1920s. Early nursery training centers stressed good health and hygiene for children, education for better mothering, and learning and habit training through play.[32] Abigail Adams Eliot graduated from Winsor in 1910 and went on to Radcliffe. After graduation she worked for the Children's Mission to the Children of the Destitute of the City of Boston, and, in 1918, served as district secretary for Associated Charities. After studying at Oxford University in 1919–20, she worked for the Massachusetts Minimum Wage Commission. Mary Winsor's sister, Elizabeth Ware Winsor Pearson (Mrs. Henry Greenleaf), who taught at Winsor between 1895 and 1911 and was a great favorite with the girls, invited her to establish a nursery school in the Roxbury area of Boston. Abby became the school's first director, but she also continued her education, earning first her Ed.M. and then her Ed.D. from the Harvard Graduate School of Education. In 1922 the two young women founded the Ruggles Street School and Training Center at 147 Ruggles Street, a site not far from the Winsor Training School and from Winsor itself. The school developed a laudable reputation as a school and as a teacher-training institution.*

A new nationwide interest in the education and care of very young children, called "child conservation," had arisen in part from concern for the children of immigrants, and Elizabeth Pearson was one of many particularly interested in the work Maria Montessori was doing with disadvantaged children in Italy. The famous "grandfather" of the kindergarten, Friedrich Fröbel, had died in 1852, but his exhaustive exploration of how children learn influenced the kindergarten movement in the late nineteenth century and also echoes through nearly all later "innovations" in modern pedagogy.[33] Fröbel and Montessori advocated the education of all the senses of the young child—an earlier version of "the whole child." The approach was not merely technical, based on close observation of the child's physical and mental de-

---

* The Eliot-Pearson Children's School became part of the Tufts University Department of Child Development in 1951; see http://ase.tufts.edu/epcs.

velopment, but also spiritual: "The principle of the Montessori school is the ideal principle of democracy, namely, that human beings reach their highest development (and hence are of most use to society) only when for the growth of their individuality they have the utmost possible liberty that can be granted them without interfering with the rights of others."[34] For Winsor women, this deeper dimension would have resonated with the kind of nurturing each had experienced at Winsor.

The stunning growth in the population of immigrants after 1840 played a significant role in the development of the social world of Boston in the twentieth century. The geographic boundaries created by the harbors and hills and wetlands of the city resulted in natural divisions that city planners reinforced. As has been mentioned, the Back Bay was intended to be an upper-class neighborhood: not only who could build there but also which churches and clubs could establish themselves were strictly controlled. In addition, newly arrived immigrants, seeking some sort of stability, tended to cluster together in their ethnic groups and to create their own community facilities and maintain their religious groupings in low-rent housing near the harbor. Distinct areas of the city housed Irish, Italian, and Jewish immigrants, as well as southern blacks who were attracted to Boston as a safe haven after the Civil War.

The truly altruistic motivation that made Boston a major force in the abolitionist movement in the 1800s now inspired the next generation of reformers to reach out to the immigrant communities and to the large number of former slaves who came to Boston. To educate the young children of the newcomers and thereby to ensure that they would become productive citizens in the city became a cause for both women and men. Many upper-class women whose clubs and organizations had been a major part of American philanthropy since the early 1800s led the kindergarten and nursery school and settlement house movements.[35]

The *Lamp's* record of the girls' writings and accounts of performers and speakers at Monday morning assemblies show that the School endeavored to widen the students' understanding of the world and the wider community with frequent outside speakers and reports from both teachers and students. There were many speeches by the nursery and training school founders, and there were talks with lofty themes that inspired idealistic Winsor students. "Miss Thomas spoke to us on evolution and the unity of all mankind, showing how the people of one nation, perhaps of many races, came gradually to be bound together by common customs, traditions and ideals."[36] Mabel Thomas [1905 to 1922] was a highly respected Boston educator who came to Winsor after teaching at Concord High School in Massachusetts.*

* Mabel Thomas's letters and papers are preserved at the Concord Public Library. Some of the correspondence is to Mary P. Winsor and other Winsor-connected people. She also founded the Thomas School in Rowayton, Connecticut.

All constituencies of the School—students, graduates, parents, and teachers—supported fund-raising and gave of their time to support not only the School but also outside charities. Winsor students raised money for the playground fund in 1911, and in the spring of 1916 started the Polish Relief Fund "after hearing Mme. Sumoska Adamowska tell of the terrible condition of her country." Antoinette Szumowska-Adamowska was a renowned pianist whose daughter Helenka attended Winsor from 1914 to 1917. Helenka Adamowska Pantaleoni 1917 was the founder of the American division of UNICEF in 1947 and was its volunteer president for twenty-five years. A Monday morning speaker, Edward Nichols from the "Harvard Unit," inspired the girls to raise $305 for the American Ambulance Service. Nichols, a physician who headed a hospital unit serving with the British army throughout the war, was also involved in establishing the American Field Service Ambulance Corps in France, which operated in both world wars.

In addition to contributing to the playground fund, in the 1910s the girls supported twenty-five French orphans, made layettes to send to France in 1917, and created mite boxes (for collecting coins) for Belgian relief. The girls were also making surgical dressings for the Red Cross, doing hospital supply work, knitting sweaters, collecting blankets, and always, it seems, exhorting each other to do more. "In the immense work that the declaration of war has imposed upon our nation we are eager to do our share," said an editorial writer in the April 1917 *Lamp*. Another speaker urged her peers not to be slack in the summertime, suggesting such things as raising hens or vegetables, typing to help out their fathers, learning about first aid and dietetics, and even learning telegraphy at the Charlestown Naval Yard.* A year later, an editorial challenged: "What are you going to do this summer? Will you enjoy yourself or help the war effort?" "Eating ice cream depletes the sugar supply," the writer admonished.

The *Lamp* in its April 1917 edition announced that the School would open the campus to the Girl Scouts during the coming summer.[37] The woman behind this project was Helen Osborne Storrow, who, though not a Winsor alumna or mother, was active in women's civic activities. She was the first president of the Women's City Club and president of the War Service Committee before stepping in as a leader of the Girl Scouts in Boston. Helen Storrow used the Winsor site to expand her training of Girl Scout leaders, offering classes in topics such as nutrition, handicrafts, outdoor skills, and safety. Around forty girls attended the summer training at Winsor for two years, but after that she moved the camp to her property on Long Pond in Plymouth.

During the Second World War the School did similar war work, and ear-

* Telegraphy was a wireless communications method of the early twentieth century; its attractiveness to schoolboys (and girls) made them a threat to armed forces' communication. See Robert A. Morton, "Wireless Interference," *Electrician and Mechanic*, April 1909, 422–27, http://earlyradiohistory.us/1909ama.htm.

lier, during the Depression, both adults and young people raised money for community funds, knitted for refugees, and adopted a needy family through Family Welfare Society of Boston.[38] A Wednesday afternoon program in which seniors could earn certificates for Red Cross training was extended to Class VII and then to the faculty in the early 1940s. Teachers kept up the always popular Current Events Club, and the workroom in the lower corridor became the "war service room for knitters and makers of Jr. Red Cross supplies."[39] In her December 1945 report, Frances Dugan praised the faculty for their community work, saying, "It is a good thing for a school to have teachers who take civic responsibility."

The Educational Enrichment Program (EEP) was initiated in the early 1960s by a few educators from independent schools in greater Boston, and Winsor began to be involved in 1966, when Virginia Wing responded to a letter from the program's National Association of Independent Schools consultant, Edward Yeomans, stating Winsor's willingness to join the effort in the following summer of 1967. She put forth a suggested budget and a proposal for using the School's Community Study course as a theme. "Learning about one's own community offers many vistas, and imaginative teachers should be able to do a lot of work on fundamentals as well as offer the variety of a new look at Boston."[40] She had already approached the Board about using the campus in the summer and indicated that the plan was more to her liking than the minimal one-on-one tutoring that a few Winsor students were already doing in the city.

Winsor began the program with students selected from the Dearborn School in Boston, six teachers (one from the Dearborn School), and seven high school aides. Six of the aides were Winsor students, some of whom returned to help with the program in subsequent years. Eventually students from other Boston schools were enrolled in the program, most of them black girls entering fifth, sixth, or seventh grade who had been identified as "lacking motivation." The curriculum, which was modified continually over the years, was based on English communication skills, math, art, music, drama, and physical activities. The Winsor swimming pool was a huge success, although its small size made it less beneficial as the program's student population grew.

The documentation of the EEP in the Winsor Archives reveals a serious, well-planned program run by dedicated professionals and volunteers who consistently reevaluated every aspect of their work. If something was not working, the staff made immediate changes—in the daily schedule, for example—and the extensive analysis that the director, Janet Smith, submitted at the end of each session contained specific, substantive suggestions for improvement for the following year.* The personal reflections of some of the Winsor aides were consistently positive, demonstrating how seriously they

---

* Janet Smith [1962 to 1973] was a teacher of physics and chemistry and served as assistant to the director from 1968 to 1973.

Through a home-stay and service project that helped construct a school in Guatemala in 2011, Upper School students pursued a Winsor tradition of global outreach and community service.

took their responsibilities and how genuinely changed they felt. They described the experience as an "intense" one that involved "emotion, patience and growth." They made astute observations about how the young girls learned, how difficult teaching really was, and how crucial it was for the staff to create a coherent and communal philosophy about what they were doing. One aide wrote: "It is hard for me to capture the spirit that went along with it. There was a feeling of community among the staff, that we were all working hard for a common cause that is the success of the summer program."[41] The aides became the backbone of the EEP, partly because of their youthful enthusiasm for what they were doing and partly because they constituted a "bridge" between the students and the teachers. Both students and faculty felt they learned much about people and teaching and the specific challenges Boston was facing in those days.

Virginia Wing noted in the spring of 1966: "In the area of reaching out to the community, being part of it and contributing to it, much has been done—usually, however, by individuals and not by a group labeled Winsor."[42] Even the younger children were involved—through the Junior Red Cross—and Upper Schoolers were volunteering in hospitals and schools. Nevertheless, the activities were not yet coordinated by the School, and she noted: "The time has come . . . to put a little more organization into our efforts. . . . Next year Miss Niles* proposes to train here at school the older girls who are engaged in tutoring in Roxbury, and the Lower School Room Teachers are seeking more active ways of involving younger children."[43]

By December of that year, Virginia Wing reported to the Corporation than the EEP had moved from its beginnings as a six-week summer session to being a year-round activity at the School. On Tuesday afternoons from 3:00 to 5:00, forty children and four of their teachers were bused from the Martin Luther King and Dearborn Schools to work with Winsor student tutors. In her words to the Board, Virginia Wing tied this enterprise directly to the School's obligation, as the only independent girls' school in the city, to serve the daughters of Boston's families. Reaching out to the parents who valued education and whose daughters would bring a variety of experiences and backgrounds to the School was from the beginning a goal of the EEP not only at Winsor but also at other involved independent schools.

By the end of the 1970s, the Boston public schools had faced challenges that would affect the entire population of the city for decades. As the city tried to come to terms with its racially unbalanced schools, the Educational Enrichment Program continued, surviving until 1985. Until 1974, federal Title I funds were allocated for the program through the City of Boston, but when Boston refused to desegregate its school system, these funds were no longer available to the EEP. Independently, each participating school undertook to raise money to support the program. Winsor parents and alumnae were very generous, but finally the lack of sufficient financial support forced the end of the EEP. Fortunately, several months later funds were again found to begin a program with similar goals called IndePrep. The leaders of six independent schools (Belmont Hill, Buckingham Browne and Nichols, Noble and Greenough, Roxbury Latin, Shady Hill, and Winsor) served as trustees, and beginning in the summer of 1986 and continuing at least weekly throughout each year, minority students worked on academic skills and learned what to expect when they entered these independent schools. The program continued until 1990, when the Steppingstone Foundation assumed the responsibility of finding promising minority students and preparing them for Boston's exam schools and a range of independent schools in Greater Boston.

In the next ten years, Winsor students as well as their teachers broadened their community service activities. They held fund-raisers to buy school furnishings and equipment and even collected money, hoping to save the Educational Enrichment Program. The School continued to emphasize the importance of giving back to one's own community, beginning with the School itself, through the Community Action Program (CAP) in the late 1980s. CAP organized teams of students and teachers to carry out basic sweeping and trash collection in the parts of the building students used. Largely dependent on the dedication of a tireless mathematics teacher, Byron Parrish,[†] and a

---

* Janet Niles taught mathematics at Winsor from 1943 to 1971.

† Byron Parrish arrived in 1978 and continues to teach at Winsor today.

handful of student leaders, CAP was short-lived and did not appear to encourage overall better habits of tidiness.

The commitment of individual teachers was essential to the growth of the School's outreach efforts, and for a few years a teacher was hired to oversee and coordinate the various community service programs. Mary Johnston [1988 to 1995] offered an English course called On the Edge. The readings for the course were based on social problems, poverty, homelessness, and political oppression. Each student did an internship at a service organization serving such groups as abused children or battered women.

A multitalented science teacher, Ileana Jones [1974 to 2004],* who taught in both the Upper and Lower Schools and served for six years as Science Department chair, was the "environmental conscience" of the School. She developed a course on environmental issues in the late 1980s and inspired the formation of the clubs COW and CALF. After the Upper School named its club COW, the Lower School came up with CALF. The faculty eventually formed TOFU (Teachers Opposed to Fouling the Universe). The student clubs took on the responsibility of many of the School's recycling efforts in the following years.

An after-school tutoring project at the Mather School, a public elementary school in Dorchester, began in the late 1980s with a small group being transported to the school by a teacher on Wednesday afternoons. When numbers increased because of the popularity of the program, the School eventually paid for a bus to transport the Winsor girls. Thereafter, under Tyler Knowles,† an English teacher, the tutoring group grew to over thirty participants and became one of the most popular community service activities in the School. After Tyler Knowles retired, another English teacher, Jennifer Slingerland Skeele 1972,†† stepped up to lead the program. The Mather tutoring program won a national Community Service Award from the Council for Spiritual and Ethical Education in 1998.

Individual teachers also volunteered to accompany the girls to after-school and weekend activities at the Greater Boston Food Bank, the Single Parent Family Outreach in Roxbury, and many other local charities. The Lower School was as enthusiastic as the older classes. Under Cynthia LaMothe,** a long partnership with the Mount Pleasant Home, a residence for

---

* Ileana Jones was among the one thousand volunteers trained by Al Gore to present his program, *An Inconvenient Truth*.

† Mary Tyler Knowles taught at Winsor for thirty-four years. See chapter 7.

†† Jennifer Slingerland Skeele joined the faculty in 1977. Her mother, Jean Slingerland, had taught at Winsor for three years in the 1960s, and Jennie's daughters, Katherine 1998 and Anna 2002, are graduates.

** Cynthia LaMothe [1976 to 2005] taught mathematics and served as head of the Mathematics Department; she also worked tirelessly on many school committees throughout her tenure.

the elderly on South Huntington Avenue, brought various groups into contact with senior citizens for activities such as art, music, walking, and repair work at the facility. Because Mount Pleasant was in the Winsor neighborhood, it was easy for girls to maintain friendships with the residents over several years. On their own, the girls often participated in local efforts such as the Walk for Hunger, Project Bread, and Rosie's Place.

Winsor girls had supported Polish and French relief agencies during World War I, and their outreach eventually widened to include China, Afghanistan, and India. It has been not unusual to see the Winsor hallways decked with boxes labeled "Books for Kenya" or large plastic jugs for small contributions to a fund for Bangladesh, Katrina relief, or Haitian earthquake survivors. The generosity and willing spirit of Winsor girls, begun over a hundred years before, has become an intrinsic part of the community's overall spirit of giving to those in need.

Winsor has also been the recipient of the generosity of others. Since the 1800s money donated by private individuals has funded myriad nonprofit causes in Boston and elsewhere, and Winsor and other institutions in the twentieth and twenty-first centuries have depended increasingly on philanthropic support. Faced with ongoing needs to upgrade the physical plant, raise faculty salaries, and increase scholarship funds, Winsor began to depend increasingly on donations, soliciting from former students, parents and former parents, and foundations.

The earliest donors were the parents and friends of the School who contributed to the Scholarship Fund, which became the tiny nucleus of an endowment. Private contributions from the Incorporators and other friends of the School supplemented tuition payments to pay for everyday budget needs. The Trustees initiated the Playground Endowment Fund in 1923 to pay for the second purchase of adjacent land for a new gymnasium building and playing fields.* Treasurer C. F. Weed announced in December 1923 that $84,709.83 had been given "by graduates, undergraduates and friends of the school, including parents of present pupils" toward the goal of $90,000, which would cover the purchase of the land from the David Sears estate. "The Corporation reached the conclusion that the acquisition of this playground was imperative not only for maintaining the pre-eminence of the school but for insuring the continued usefulness of the present site."[44] The Trustees were by then fully aware of the value of the property and of the soundness of their investment. They were also cognizant of the importance of faculty compensation and realized that the School had to establish and begin to build an endowment fund.

A handwritten addendum to Katharine Lord's Report to the Corporation in April 1932 states: "An endowment campaign to improve teachers' salaries brought in nearly $60,000." In that report she praised the leadership of the

* A similar drive in 1911 had allowed the first purchase of additional Sears land.

retiring Board president, John G. Palfrey, who had served from 1923 to 1932. "Under his care the school worked through a critical period. . . . Mr. Palfrey and the men on whose judgment he knew how to call realized that we must have more grounds and opportunity for play and they, by careful handling of funds and by inaugurating a campaign, bought the new playing fields."[45] Katharine Lord also remarked that specific groups raised money for specific projects: "Besides the showers [given by the Graduate Club], which were mentioned in the fall, and the teacher's room for which the Class of 1931 gave the money, we have had two lectures, one on the Pueblo Indians, donated by Mrs. Weeks, the other the lecture of Mr. Johnson O'Connor* given by a generous mother. This year's Class VIII has given a radio Victrola which we will use for music classes, and they are giving a small French library of French books on France."[46]

Katharine Lord attributed the strong financial health of the School to the expertise and time donated by the Trustees, singling out "Mr. [Charles] Weed and Mr. [Phillip] Stockton for handling the funds through this complicated time." There was no serious money problem in the School throughout the Depression. Fund-raising was an ongoing project because the tuition revenue did not fully cover the cost of a student's education. The need to fill that gap led to the establishment of the Annual Fund. The first Annual Fund appeal in 1952–53 consisted of a letter to alumnae and friends of the School; contributions totaled $4,970, and two-thirds of the 121 donors were alumnae.

In 1961, under the leadership of Ronald T. Lyman Jr., husband of Susan Storey Lyman 1937,[†] the Winsor 75th (Anniversary) Fund (a capital campaign) was launched with two aims: to increase the endowment for faculty salaries and to build the Dexter Wing. The project raised more than one million dollars, and (see the accompanying chart) five more capital campaigns such as this would raise money for the School's most pressing ongoing needs: the endowment, building improvement, teacher salaries, and scholarships. This and subsequent capital campaigns were separate from the Annual Fund, however. Nicholas Danforth, president of the Winsor Corporation from 1962 to 1970, observed in 1966: "The spirit generated by the 75th Anniversary Fund has had as its by-product a tremendous surge in annual giving. I think it apparent that having moved up from a $20,000 a year level just a few years back to $63,000 in 1965 we are clearly on our way."[47]

In all Winsor's fund-raising the leadership of alumnae has been vital. Their affection for their School has been an impetus for the parents and friends who have also worked hard over the years to solicit funds. In 1965

* Johnson O'Connor established a foundation "to provide an aptitude testing program to help individuals discover their natural potential by identifying personal strengths"; www.jocrf.org/about_us/index.html.

† Susan Storey Lyman 1937 was admitted to Radcliffe but married instead after graduating from Winsor. She was readmitted and received her A.B. in 1949, eventually becoming the chairman of the Radcliffe Board of Trustees.

a member of the staff was appointed as the executive secretary of the Winsor (Annual) Fund. Sallie Adams Lawrence 1935 served in this capacity until 1969, when Mary Louise "Jib" King Beale 1941 succeeded her. During this period three graduates, each of whom was the chairman of the Fund, gave invaluable leadership: Lucy Lowell Grimm 1947, Helen Susan Merrill 1947, and Laura Wiggins Putnam 1932.

Margaret Swain Beecher 1924, the executive secretary of the Alumnae Association, was a great help to the fund-raisers because of her longtime relationship with alumnae. She served until just before her death in 1973. Jib Beale then took on her responsibilities, followed by Mina Ellis Otis 1952 and then by Allie Flather Blodgett 1952 as the director of Alumnae Affairs in 1986.

By 1975 the School realized that a full-time professional fund-raiser was necessary. For two years Sharon Weld 1966 filled this position; then Diana O. Garmey [1977 to 2002], who as a parent of two Winsor daughters had been a regular volunteer, became the director of Development. Her job was not an easy one, for it remains a dismaying fact that fewer women than men contribute to their alma maters, in part because they do not control the money. Diana Garmey increased significantly the number of donors and the total amount given to the Annual Fund, and she successfully guided the five capital campaigns.

Over the years Winsor expanded the role of fund-raising. Building on a solid foundation and with an ever larger development staff, the School made great strides in seeking funds from alumnae, parents, past parents, friends, and foundations. Parent leadership in particular was vital to the success of the Essential Winsor campaign in 2000–2003. For the first campaign in the School's history, philanthropic support of parents accounted for the majority of the dollars raised.

The pride that the entire Winsor community took in the success of these efforts and the financial health of the School was summed up in Carolyn Peter's words in her final Report to the Corporation in April 2004: "Since 1988, our budget has tripled . . . from $4 million to about $13 million. . . . Our Annual Fund has more than quadrupled in size. . . . Even more important to the School's future, the Winsor endowment . . . has grown to more than eight times its size in 1988: our $4 million fund has become a $34 million endowment. . . . I am happy to say too that Winsor continues to have no debt."[48]

The spirit of philanthropy seemed to be a natural impulse for the School community from its earliest years. The Incorporators, the faculty, the students, and the parents have continued to realize what it means to be part of a community in which mutual sharing results in mutual benefit and where all have a sense of personal responsibility for the health of the community. They defined "community" broadly, and in acknowledgment of time and money given by others to the School, they gave back on the local, national, and global levels.

WINSOR CAPITAL CAMPAIGNS

The Winsor 75th Fund

1961–63

Chair: Ronald T. Lyman Jr.

Goal: $1,200,000

Purposes: (1) Endowment for faculty salaries;
(2) Expansion of the plant—the new wing—and renovation

Raised $1,065,000

The Franklin Dexter Wing (the "New Wing") was built and adjustments made to the newly freed-up spaces.

The Winsor Campaign

1979–83

Chair: Eleanor Thomas Nelson 1949

Goal: Phase I: $2,500,000

Purposes: (1) Endowment ($1,000,000 for faculty salaries and scholarships); (2) Expansion and renovation of the library

Raised $3,516,081

The library was renovated, pool area converted to office and storage space.

The Winsor School Centennial Campaign

1985–89

Chair: Wendy Colten Finnerty 1964

Goal: $10,000,000—$4,500,000 to be raised immediately in honor of Centennial; balance to be raised in the next decade

Raised: $4,500,000

Science Wing built; almost $2,000,000 added to endowment specifically for faculty compensation and enrichment and financial aid for students.

The Winsor School Capital Campaign: Renewing the Vision

1991–97

Chair: Lee Bigelow Herter 1950

Goal: $10,000,000

Purposes: (1) Endowment, $4,000,000 ($3,000,000 for faculty compensation; $1,000,000 for tuition assistance); (2) Facilities, $3,500,000 ($3,000,000 for gymnasium renovation, $500,000 for fields and tennis courts); Annual Fund, $2,500,000

Raised: $10,642,510

Gymnasium renovated; fields realigned and lighted.

The 1998 Focus Campaign

1998

Chair: Daniel Sullivan

Goal: $3,600,000

Purposes: Library renovation and new classrooms

Raised: $3,586,994

Library renovated; six new classrooms built.

The Essential Winsor

2000–2003

Honorary chairs: Lee Bigelow Herter 1950, Susan Storey Lyman 1937, and Eleanor Thomas Nelson 1949

Campaign Steering Committee: William Collatos, Michael Cronin, Corinne Ferguson, Elizabeth Partridge Heald 1957, Seth Klarman, Marlyn McGrath 1966, Joseph O'Donnell, Carolyn McClintock Peter, Daniel Sullivan

Goal: $30,000,000

Purposes: (1) Faculty compensation (Preserving the Tradition of Great Teaching); (2) Scholarships (Keeping Winsor Accessible to Top Students); (3) Facilities (Enhancing Winsor's Learning Environment); (4) Maintaining Vitality of Annual Fund

Raised: $32,145,310

- -

Chapter 7

Building an harmonious and efficient faculty is a never-ending concern.
—*Frances Dorwin Dugan*

I still put my faith in the ideas of superior classroom teachers. Since I think that we have a few here at Winsor, I hope that we can give them enough time and flexibility of schedule to allow them to be truly creative.
—*Virginia Wing*

Faculty on Terrace 1922

The Faculty

※⟨⟨47⟩⟩※

"To meet a child where she is"

T HERE ARE MANY ASPECTS to running a school, but there is consensus about what lies at the heart of education: those who teach. Even when effective teaching is recognized as essential, the characteristics of a "good" teacher are difficult to define. Winsor not only acknowledged the importance of teaching but also was able to describe the qualities of superior teachers. Most crucially, there was a constant effort to make the School an appealing, challenging, rewarding place to teach.

Every Director of Winsor has been a teacher first, usually at Winsor, and all have been familiar with the ongoing demands on a teacher's time and energy. The second Director, Katharine Lord, expressed grave concerns about how hard each teacher involved in the New Plan (described in chapter 5) was working to stay on top of her creative, self-designed course: "She must have the vigor to keep abreast of the current of modern thinking, by mingling with people not in her own profession, by wide reading, by keeping her eyes and ears open, and perhaps by engaging in some activity other than teaching."[1] In the best progressive school tradition, moreover, teachers had to know and understand each student as an individual learner. Katharine Lord's description of Frances Dugan in 1937 is a reminder of how a teacher's academic knowledge must be balanced with interpersonal skills: "I have never seen anywhere else the kind of close thinking and sensitive understanding given to the problems of the child that Miss Dugan gives. I have seen many difficult girls find themselves under her handling. The teachers through the School are increasingly concerned with the child as a whole, and the children expect to get fair and understanding treatment."[2]

Frances Dugan became the third Director of the School in 1939, after twenty years of experience as a teacher and having served as both assistant and associate director at Winsor. For her the School's strength was its ability to keep "teachers who are intelligent, interesting, skillful, and sympathetic."[3] Her long experience at the School allowed her to make a steady and smooth transition when she succeeded Katharine Lord, but she had the wisdom to recognize that in the fifty-three years since the School's founding the world had changed, and that a changing world would put additional pressures on teachers as they prepared girls for different roles in what she called "grim times": "[The] next decades will need especially courageous, disciplined people who are not afraid of hard work and responsibility, and who have at the same time love of life and a capacity for enjoyment not dependent on material things but coming from appreciations and sympathies which circumstances cannot take away.... Girls [need] the discipline of practical hardships.... We therefore try to give them the discipline of knowledge and hard intellectual work [so] that they face consequences and take responsibilities."[4]

In 1939 it would have been difficult to keep a school such as Winsor isolated from the world. The Depression had brought anxiety to both children and adults, and its effects lingered still. In Europe, Hitler, having annexed Austria, invaded Poland. Teachers themselves were on the front lines with children as the "grim times" increased, and a school needed to be a safe place for young people as well as a forum in which to confront global problems with intelligence and sensitivity. Frances Dugan's understanding of the power of a teacher's influence contained a caveat: "We must be careful that we do not condition children so that we make positive enthusiasm difficult for them." In other words, children deserved to have a childhood even when adults were perhaps disillusioned and uncertain.

Stability and continuity were essential in 1940. Another world war had started, and the United States would be drawn in after the attack on Pearl Harbor in December 1941. Many Winsor families and employees would feel deeply the effect of the war. The nation and the world would move into a stark modernity during Frances Dugan's tenure, as would the educational environment. Winsor's team—administrators, department heads, and room teachers—wisely chose to stay with the traditional curriculum, backing off from the New Plan except in the connected history and English courses for Class V, where it had been popular and successful, owing mostly to the fine teaching.

Frances Dugan found it difficult to hire good teachers. In the early years of the School, Mary Winsor does not appear to have had trouble attracting capable new teachers; for one thing, teaching was one of the few acceptable wage-earning activities for women, and for another, professions such as medicine, law, and business were still unwelcoming to women. As time went on, however, Winsor had to compete with large public school systems whose substantially larger budgets offered appealing salary inducements. In addition, teachers who had gained valuable experience at Winsor were in great demand elsewhere, and it became important for the School to maintain a pleasant yet challenging environment not only to attract new teachers but also to keep its good ones. Winsor was finding it especially hard, Frances Dugan observed, "to compete with public schools in pensions. . . . So far it has helped that many teachers have family income or like our atmosphere." She added, "The favorable conditions which attract teachers are a sympathetic and congenial environment as well as material advantages."[5] The morale of the teaching staff was an ongoing concern expressed by the Directors, and one notes that every remark about the faculty in the Reports to the Corporation was invariably positive. Mindful of the importance of her faculty's self-esteem, Frances Dugan warned the Board, "The straw that sometimes weights a decision to leave, I have noted, can be unjust criticism by one unappreciative parent."[6]

Comments from the Directors reveal a global attitude toward teaching that assessed not only what was happening in the classroom and what was being taught, but also the "how" and "to whom"—an awareness of pupil differences, developmental needs in each age group, the importance of motivation, and "the happy combination of experience and personality."[7] Valeria Knapp asserted that the good teacher gives "sound training in mental discipline with an increasing awareness of responsibility for a community that is widening its horizon at a breathtaking rate."[8]

Graduation from an excellent college or experience in a respected school was the key credential for a teaching candidate, but Winsor expected more than mere scholarship. The following collage of descriptions of Winsor teachers shows some of the other qualities the Directors were looking for:

A sound and penetrating judgment and essential kindness of attitude
A wonderful sense of gaiety and humor, as well as profound integrity
A sense of responsibility for children's welfare
Civic-mindedness
A willingness to spend time talking and listening to children who want
    to talk to adults
Close thinking and understanding of the problems of the child
An ability to help children develop a sense of values
A very vivid person, inspiring poorer students
A person of culture and vigor
A spiritually minded person
Quick as a flash and very ready.*

Winsor sought out and treasured many qualities, but the sine qua non was a superior academic record. Most of the teachers hired in the first decades of the School had earned degrees from the highly regarded women's colleges such as Radcliffe, Wellesley, Bryn Mawr, Mt. Holyoke, Smith, Vassar, and

---

* All quotations are from the Reports to the Corporation by Directors Lord, Dugan, Knapp, and Wing. The last refers directly to Mary Frothingham 1926, who returned to Winsor as a secretary but was finally convinced to go to Bryn Mawr to continue her education.

This detail of the graduation picture of the Class of 1937 includes four past, present, and future Directors of The Winsor School: Mary Winsor, in a white hat, is in the center; to her left is Katharine Lord, to her right, Frances Dugan, and directly behind her Valeria Knapp.

even Oxford. Many had master's degrees, and most had already taught for at least one year at good schools such as Brookline High School and Concord Academy. Marjorie Applegate [1946 to 1949] had taught for six years at Calhoun Colored School in Alabama, and Mary Hinckley Hutchings Crane 1932 [1967 to 1974] had been the Head of Abbot Academy from 1956 to 1966 before teaching history at Winsor. Nonetheless, teaching experience and personality counted a great deal. When Valeria Knapp left to go briefly to Concord Academy, before returning as Winsor's fourth Director, her replacement was Harriet Tyng [1937 to 1946], about whom Katharine Lord wrote the following succinct assessment: "A New Englander of Connecticut family, trained at Barnard, taught in Miss Fine's School in Princeton for seven years, and in a boys' school on the Philadelphia Main Line. She is clear-cut, intelligent, not so impressive in appearance but sure and well bred with people. She has humor, lightness of touch, seems to have a delightful way with children."[9]

Hiring teachers with previous experience was a priority, but the School sometimes hired and saw the value of young teachers. When Valeria Knapp joined the faculty in 1922, Katharine Lord welcomed her by saying she was "proving the value of young teachers. We are singularly adapted to using them with our organized departments and many experienced teachers, and a young teacher has a very definite contribution to give in her freshness, her point of view, and the close relationships between teacher and pupil which she naturally establishes."[10] Winsor took seriously its own responsibility to mentor young teachers, for whom there was a growing need as public schools expanded and it was gradually accepted that all girls could (and should) be as well educated as their brothers. "For independent schools the preferred form of professional training after college is to have a year working under the direction of skilled teachers and learning from observation and practice and to have an opportunity to become informed about educational philosophy in general."[11]

There was also a vital apprentice program for beginners. Between 1934 and 1944 the School hired as many as twenty-five apprentice teachers, several of them Winsor graduates, who worked for one or two years under an experienced teacher.[12] Other schools were eager to hire these Winsor-trained teachers, especially during the severe teacher shortage after World War II. For these young teachers, Florence Waterman (who taught Greek and Latin from 1920 to 1936) gave a course in educational psychology.[13] Frances Dugan expressed the pride Winsor felt when its faculty moved on to positions in educational leadership. "From the Winsor faculty we have supplied in the last ten years three heads of schools, two assistant administrators, and three college professors." (The trend continued into the twenty-first century.) She added, "With my better and more intelligent nature I rejoice that this is true, although I confess my lower nature quivers like a mother hen when I see roving predatory eyes cast over our special preserves."[14]

Winsor graduates have affectionate and almost rapturous memories of those special individuals who taught them. Eleanor Roosevelt II 1938 singled out Isabella McL. Stephens [1936 to 1940] for praise:* "She was marvelous, just in opening up possibilities to you, always pulling you, making history come alive, making you want to do your homework, read your books, get to know people around the world."[15]

Frances Parkinson Keyes, the prolific novelist whose memoir *Roses in December* describes many facets of the early years of the School, recalls the joy of being held to rigorous standards: "But that 'Excellent' in Latin staggered me so that I nearly tumbled over, for I believe Miss Griswold [1899 to 1921] only gave something like three 'Excellents' in Latin all last year, and is considered the hardest marker in the school. Then four 'Excellents' from Miss Kinsman [1900 to 1905] who declared that she would only give Excellent when the work would seem extraordinary."[16] Kate Griswold also gave up time to tutor Frances in Greek.

---

* By highlighting specific teachers in this chapter, one can extrapolate the qualities exemplified not only by those named but by the majority of Winsor teachers. Naturally, it is not possible to describe every outstanding teacher. Some are notable for their long and successful tenures, others for their scholarly background or inspired teaching or willingness to play more than one role.

For decades students have recalled English teachers whose demanding and thorough teaching of grammar, literature, and writing was a treasure to cherish forever.

I was condemned by Miss [Margaret] Todd [1925 to 1960] to 10-word sentences in all themes for a year. I hate to think how awful things must have got to require that desperate restriction![17]

The inimitable Miss [Elizabeth] Hewins [1929 to 1960] was my absolute favorite . . . . Miss Hewins embodied the word "vivid." . . . Formidable initially, seldom smiling . . . [she] warmed up as the year progressed. The highlight of the course for her and for us was the major project of an elaborate, colored map of the *Pilgrim's Progress*. . . . We began to know that her iciness was but a façade for her real love of children, and teaching.[18]

Two years with Miss Ensor were a joy. In her understated way, with a dry wit, she helped us with literature as she simultaneously coped with Britain's wartime suffering.[19]

Olivia Ensor [1939 to 1946], an English teacher and a graduate of Oxford's Somerville College, wrote many historical novels and biographies for young people under her married name, Coolidge. One, *Men of Athens,* was a Newbery Honor Book in 1963.

Ellen Endicott Forbes 1927 was one of seven English teachers who had graduated from Winsor. She taught there in two separate stints, 1935 to 1940 and 1955 to 1967, and was a beloved mentor to younger teachers. After her unexpected death in 1967, a faculty award in her memory was established. Virginia Wing described her as "a real scholar . . . a linguist, an ornithologist, a musician, and above all a gifted teacher of literature and composition."[20] A former student said, "Her love, as I see it now in retrospect, was helping students to develop their own intellectual potential."[21]

The English Department became renowned for the preparation in writing it gave to Winsor students decade after decade. (The evolution of the writing program is described in chapter 5.) It was not just Winsor students who benefited from the expertise of those outstanding writing teachers: in 1978 *Writing a Research Paper* was published and became a classic guide for young writers everywhere. The authors were four Winsor English teachers—Jonatha Ceely [1970 to 1998], Helen Dunn [1971 to 1993], Judy Robbins [1967 to 2006], and Tyler Knowles [1972 to 2006]—and their revisions have led to its continued popularity. In 2004 Vivien Steir Rubin 1977 praised their teaching of literature: "Mrs. Dunn introduced me to the depth of Kafka, Camus and Hesse. . . . Mrs. Ceely took the intimidation factor out of the Great Books, making the Bible, Dante, Milton and Shakespeare accessible and fun. . . . Mrs. Robbins made me feel incredibly important when she asked me what I thought of her fiancé's poetry and Ms. Knowles encouraged me in my own poetry."[22] Emily Perlman Abedon 1986 said of Helen Dunn: "What stands out is how she treated us all: as if our opinions were truly thought-provoking for her. Surely, sometimes, we must have been entirely off base."[23]

In addition to being fine instructors, these teachers, like many others, took on demanding administrative roles: Tyler Knowles was the head of the English Department for many years, Helen Dunn served as head of the Lower School, as did Jonatha Ceely, who was also the college counselor, the head of the Upper School, and associate director. After she retired, she wrote two highly acclaimed novels.*

Three dedicated teachers who gave a total of ninety-nine years to the teaching of Latin and Greek became household names for anyone who attended Winsor from 1908 to 1974. Louise Packard, Agnes Watkins, and Elizabeth Bridge (later Weissbach) kept those "dead" languages alive at a time where some educators around the country were trying to stamp them as "irrelevant."

Louise Packard [1908 to 1949] was a multitalented teacher who found at Winsor a place where she could play various roles at various times and use the full range of her gifts: she taught both Latin and mathematics, sometimes accompanied the Glee Club, and continued to teach half-time after retiring. She was still teaching in 1949 when her sudden death moved the senior class and the Graduate Club to establish the Louise Packard Memorial Scholarship Fund; the archives contain many letters of appreciation from students she taught in her forty-one-year career at Winsor.

Agnes Watkins [1940 to 1963] "considered by Vassar as one of their best people," and "well-liked" at Walnut Hill and Girls Academy in Albany,[24] was able to lure even a recalcitrant student into liking Latin: "Although I disliked Latin, which seemed to me like a crossword puzzle rather than a language, and did it so badly I had to come back on Tuesday afternoons for a while, I appreciated Miss Watkins' patience and gentleness. . . . When I discovered that if I wanted to major in English in college I would have to take an extra year of Latin, I'm sure it was my trust in Miss Watkins that made me willing to. And of course Virgil was nothing like Caesar—I loved it!"[25]

Elizabeth Bridge Weissbach [1939 to 1974] reenergized the study of ancient Greek, which had been offered to sophomores off and on from 1891. "In 1946, learning that she knew Greek, I and some others asked her to teach it to us," recalled one of her students.[26] It is likely that their teacher took on this class of three as an extra, unpaid duty, a continuing practice for the classics teachers who quite often taught more than the usual number of courses in order to keep Homer and Virgil in the curriculum. Virginia Wing in her memorial to Elizabeth Weissbach said that she even turned down the chance for a sabbatical because she preferred to teach.

---

* *Mina* (2004) and its sequel, *Bread and Dreams* (2005), were published by Delacorte.

By the time they were ready for advanced reading in Classes VII and VIII, girls who loved classics often found themselves in tiny classes of two to five, with a teacher who was willing to fit them in as an extra in an already full schedule. Medh Mahony Sichko 1974 and her classmate Vicky Plimpton Babcock 1974 shared such an experience with Lois May Waters, who taught Latin from 1951 to 1989 and taught every level of Latin from the beginners' course in Class III (or IV) up to the Advanced Placement courses in Virgil and Lyric Poetry. "Miss Waters gave us the sense that Latin was a form of verbal archaeology, searching for the truth through the language closest to the historical event."[27]

Alice Jenckes [1929 to 1966] and Nancy Roelker [1941 to 1960] were stars of the History Department, the former staying at Winsor for her entire thirty-seven-year career, the other leaving after earning her Ph.D. to take a professorship first at Tufts University, then at Boston University. The mere mention of their names has evoked sighs of wordless wonder for decades: their World History course, begun as part of the New Plan, was "almost too good; everything at Radcliffe seemed a bit of an anticlimax."[28] These two women taught the same course but, as is true of all great teachers, the style and method of each were unique.

Alice Jenckes, who was remembered as "direct and dramatic"—often jumping up and down to make a point—served as the independent girls' school representative on the committee to design the American History Advanced Placement examination.* Her former students and many friends gave the first endowed faculty chair in her name in 1979.

Nancy Roelker, who carefully introduced the girls to college-style lecturing, was "more cerebral": "From her we got intellectual excitement at the way history fitted together and how philosophies—political, social, and religious—drew on diverse ideas."[29] In 1958 Harvard University Press published Nancy Roelker's book *The Paris of Henry of Navarre*. The Nancy Roelker Fund, established by the Class of 1946 at their sixtieth reunion in 2006, gives teachers the opportunity to pursue advanced study in the humanities outside school.

Alice Jenckes and Nancy Roelker also served as Room Teachers, a challenging role that was essential to the School's philosophy of guiding the growth of both children and adults. Each of the eight classes had a Room Teacher in charge of the homeroom, and each year the class would be turned over to the next Room Teacher. These carefully chosen faculty members came to know the normal pattern of activities and agonies for their own grade level and had the delight and surprise of following each girl's progress. The Room Teachers constituted a small "Student Life Committee" (as it might be called

---

* Several Winsor teachers over the years have been readers for AP exams, traveling to Princeton University in the summer to hand-grade the examinations.

The faculty in 1953–54 (left to right): first row, Mrs. Duggan, Miss Connelly, Miss Bridge, Miss Todd, Miss Knapp, Miss Ball, Miss Waters, Miss Houghton, Miss Littlefield; second row, Miss Ripley, Miss Mellot, Mrs. Hjelm, Miss Hamilton, Miss Church, Mrs. Hastings, Miss Niles, Mrs. Barghoorn, Miss Roelker, Miss Jones, Mrs. Montgomery; third row, Mrs. Saxton, Mrs. Beecher, Miss Wing, Miss Howell, Miss Jenckes, Miss Watkins, Mrs. Newfelt, Miss Eddy, Mrs. Willey, Miss Alger, Miss Dresser.

today) that met regularly and shared insights and observations; they also worked with the girls' subject teachers, encouraging connections and suggesting solutions for academic or social problems. These liaisons often led to the subject teacher's knowing a student more closely than the Room Teacher, a desirable outcome since the Room Teachers could hardly expect to be the only adult to whom a child might turn.

History teachers, like all teachers in the School, were usually assigned to teach in both the Lower and Upper School, but Constance Houghton remained the Class I teacher from the time of her arrival in 1946 until her retirement in 1978; she served also as head of the Lower School. Connie Houghton established a reputation as a stellar storyteller and an expert with the youngest girls in the School. She frequently trained apprentices, most of whom transferred her legacy to other schools, but at least two remained to teach fifth or sixth grade at Winsor.

Winsor was fortunate in being able to hire a faculty with the skills and ability to teach in both the Lower School and the Upper School. Some teachers specialized in advanced classes in the Upper School, and others found themselves assigned to teach various combinations of classes ranging from the fifth grade through senior year. There were advantages either way. Those who taught in both divisions acquired a perspective on the changing pedagogical and developmental needs of girls between the ages of ten and eighteen. It was a special joy at Winsor to watch a young girl blossom, and the transformations were often so significant that faculty exhorted one another not to label a student who was still growing. Winsor did, however, pay attention to educational research in the late twentieth century that emphasized the special needs of preteens. Studies at that time suggested that schools should develop a core group of teachers who would work specifically with the students in the "middle grades." Winsor therefore made changes that led to more teachers teaching in only one division. Although the size of the school and the particular demands in certain departments made this difficult, the number of "crossover teachers" declined. Those on the faculty who continued to teach both Upper and Lower School classes were enthusiastic about the experience even though they often had to attend twice as many meetings and activities for the classes they taught.

Sloan Sable [1978 to 2010] was a crossover teacher whose keen interest in China was a catalyst for the expansion of China-related courses. The Class III history course had traditionally been a skill-based study of geography and the interplay of climate and culture. In 1991 the focus shifted from the early societies of the Pygmies, Eskimos, and Aborigines to a broader study of the ancient cultures of the Mediterranean, North America, and China. In the 2004 curriculum revision, Upper School Chinese History (which had been in the syllabus since the mid-seventies) was paired with an English course on Chinese literature to be one of the required non-Western semester courses. (The other paired courses were on India, the Middle East, and Africa. This change increased the history graduation requirement from two to two and a half years.) Sloan Sable also helped establish Mandarin Chinese as a third modern language in both the Upper and Lower Schools. As History Department chair, she worked to keep history courses current and provocative as the School moved into the twenty-first century.

Winsor's extraordinary mathematics teachers were able to demolish the myth that math was a "boy's thing." In fact, women held all the mathematics positions at Winsor from 1886 through 1941.[30] They were responsible for inspiring many a female student to love going to math class. Elizabeth Pousland started teaching math at Miss Winsor's in 1907, before the move to the Riverway, and stayed until 1941. She felt such affection and appreciation for the School that she established a modest scholarship, even offering her pension to fund it.

The Winter–Spring 2004 *Bulletin*, which contained students' reminiscences of many Winsor teachers, prompted subsequent letters. One praised Louisa Alger [1935 to 1965]: "I just wish I'd written about Miss Alger, who made math very exciting for those of us who loved math and understandable for those who didn't. She kept in touch with me when I went to Wellesley, wondering if I was prepared . . . and came . . . to visit a Saturday calculus class!"[31] When Katharine Lord hired Louisa Alger, she commented that the Winsor job was "below her talents." When Louisa Alger retired after thirty years at Winsor, Virginia Wing feared that, because of limited funds, it would be hard to replace her.

Harriet Littlefield [1943 to 1973] was remembered by one of her students for coming to class "in her colorful dress-and-jacket outfits with her red hair shining and friendly smile on her face. She could explain anything clearly, and really shared her love of the orderliness and logic of geometry."[32] Virginia Wing recalled: "In that period every other year the Faculty presented a lengthy skit for the two oldest classes and produced a marvelous spread of food. I cringe to remember how we stumbled around the Winsor stage, forgot our lines, and appeared in dreadful wigs and blackened teeth. Harriet came to our abysmal rehearsal to cue us and to encourage us. She, however, never had to be a thespian because she always managed to volunteer before anyone else to be the head of the refreshments committee."[33]

Caroline Haussermann [1948 to 1963] had such flair (red nail polish and a deep tan) that her seventh graders made diary entries about how often (and in what way) she smiled at them.[34] She taught physical education as well as math and reveled in the fact that most teachers in the close-knit faculty group went to the girls' games. She cherished her faculty friends and "their dedication to the Truth, their absolute Honesty, their lack of Compromise with what was Right. As far as I knew there were no politics, no trading off of values, no shading of the truth, no hypocrisy. . . . Never again in my lifetime have I come across a society, a group of people who represented so much of what is fine and of value in the world."[35]

One of her students described Janet Sheltus Duggan [1946 to 1983] as "friendly and smiling, approachable, and unforgettable"—a teacher who brought some fun to her Lower-Schoolers. The teaching of the importance of the "-th" in words like "hundredth" elicited a brief moment of "spraying the *'ths'* back between giggles as we answered the workbook questions one at a time."[36] Janet Duggan had come for her Winsor interview in her WAVES uniform and at Frances Dugan's request wore it on her first day of teaching. Steady and cheerful, Janet Duggan was wonderfully attuned to her Lower School students, and even after retiring she remained a trusted tutor for younger girls.

David Myers [1979 to 2007] was one of many Winsor faculty members who came to Winsor with a doctoral degree.* The School's tech guru when computer technology was just beginning to be a major factor in managing records and bookkeeping, David Myers was highly respected by both students and teachers for his excellent teaching and his whole-hearted involvement in all School activities. He has also written and edited textbooks for Houghton Mifflin, including *Precalculus Computer Activities* (1983), one of the publisher's first books featuring the use of computer problems.

Sometimes outstanding teachers were lured from full-time classroom teaching to become administrators, and nearly always they continued to teach one or two classes in their field. By being involved with the weekly meetings of the academic department in which they taught as well as in administrative committees, these individuals dealt with students, teachers, and parents on various levels and acquired a valuable perspective. Diane Bezan [1975 to 2004] was an example of a gifted teacher who was able to take on many tasks within the School. Hired as a part-time math teacher in 1975, she was quickly identified as a multitalented individual with a wonderful ability to listen. She gradually added responsibilities as Class V Room Teacher and the chair of several committees, and in 1989 Carolyn Peter appointed her head of the Upper School. She had been the associate director for fifteen years and was still teaching one class when in 2004 she was diagnosed with a brain tumor and all too quickly succumbed. The grief was overwhelming for Winsor; there was hardly a person who had not known Diane Bezan in one of her many roles. The lovely room above the reception area (originally the Graduates' Room) was named for her when it became a classroom.

Another outstanding administrator-teacher was Barbara Bailey [1980 to 2006], whom Carolyn Peter in 1989 appointed as the first director of studies and made a crucial part of her administrative team. From her first year at Winsor, Barbara Bailey was a highly popular teacher of advanced mathematics and a willing faculty leader who chaired committees with patience and wisdom. Along with Diane Bezan, she helped Carolyn Peter create in 1999 the very first *Handbook for Students and Parents,* a task that required putting into words (often for the first time) the innumerable academic policies and unwritten rules that had become customary practice during the previous century. Barbara Bailey also oversaw the annual summer creation of the academic class schedule and the yearly fall rituals of solving schedule and room conflicts; she was universally admired for her intelligence and tact. She stepped in to serve as head of the Upper School during the leadership transition between Carolyn Peter and Director Rachel Friis Stettler, who came to Winsor in the summer of 2004.

* In the 1992–93 academic year there were nine such scholars on the faculty: David Myers, Sloan Sable, Acha Lord, Mary Manson, Joan Melvin, Larry Metzger, Ann O'Meara, Sally Williams, and Helen Young.

The story of science teaching at Winsor begins with the earliest science teacher listed, Mabel Earle [1897 to 1914], and includes legendary teachers who built a department that eventually offered Advanced Placement courses in biology, physics, and chemistry in addition to electives such as astronomy, environmental science, and psychology. Like mathematics, science was seen as a male interest, and Miss Winsor's School was one of the few places where girls could take courses that would prepare them for more rigorous college courses.

Anna Holman [1921 to 1952], the daughter of an MIT professor of physics, did more than teach physics during her thirty-one years at Winsor. Her interest in photography prompted her to teach the children to run "lantern slides" and moving picture machines. She also advised the lights committee during plays and supervised the standardized testing program. She was the first woman president of the New England Association of Physics Teachers and an alumna trustee of Radcliffe. She famously asked the students to bring in electrical appliances to be dismantled and examined and

Rachel Friis Stettler became the seventh Director of the School in 2004.

even prompted one father to donate his Ford with its V-8 engine. Anna Holman said she kept one step ahead of the girls in this project by using the manual. They completely dismantled the vehicle's engine and then put it back together again.

Virginia Mayo Fiske [1937 to 1942] received her Ph.D. in biology from Radcliffe while teaching at Winsor and left to teach at Wellesley and do research in endocrinology.[37] Her comment quoted in *Women Scientists in America: Before Affirmative Action, 1940–1972*[38] suggested that women professors who were mothers were not fully appreciated: "The administration does show a distinct lack of enthusiasm toward expectant mothers on the staff even though these women as a group are more conscientious than ever in their maintenance of high standards in their teaching." As late as 1972, pregnant teachers were not allowed to teach in the Boston Public Schools.

Helen Hamilton [1945 to 1971] came to Winsor in 1945, and when she died in 1986, Virginia Wing praised her: "A member of the Winsor faculty for twenty-six years, she was the chairman of the Science Department, from 1952 to 1971. To her pleasure and that of her students, one of the biology rooms in the new science center is named in her honor. A frank, amusing, down-to-earth person, she believed in each of her students; there was no way you could despair and give up if Miss Hamilton were on your side. Her enthusi-

Anna Holman's class with the famous Ford V-8 engine.

asm for biology was contagious, and her zest for nature never left her. Teachers like Helen Hamilton are what makes this school so special."[39]

When Helen Young [1972 to 2008] came to Winsor, only four or five girls took physics, but by the time she retired there were two or three sections of physics each year. She was a key to the growth of science at Winsor, as well as a brilliant user of technology and a merry participant in all aspects of School life. Another extraordinary science head was Ann O'Meara [1984 to 2004], who was the first teacher of AP Chemistry and tireless supporter of young women who wanted to go into science.

In the Modern Language Department, the names alone—Marie Sauveur [1892 to 1896], Eva von Blomberg [1890 to 1918], Giuseppe Merlino [1921 to 1932]—indicate that Winsor sought native speakers to teach French, German, Italian, and, eventually Spanish. Sometimes these teachers stayed at Winsor only briefly; they were needed in a school where foreign language was accepted as a crucial part of the curriculum but where exact enrollments for each language varied. French, which was required of every Winsor student in both the Upper and Lower Schools until the 1980s, was the first language to offer an Advanced Placement curriculum, and students had the enticement of the wonderful Saltonstall Scholarship—a year at the Sorbonne after graduation. Ruth Dallinger [1907 to 1944] came to Winsor after completing her Radcliffe degree in French; her thirty-eight-year career at the School is one of the longest. Blanche Montgomery [1934 to 1961] started teaching French during Ruth Dallinger's tenure, and she overlapped with the third of these outstanding teachers, Adele ("Pat") Bockstedt [1954 to 1982], whose wonderful rapid-fire oral-aural teaching kept every student engaged and precluded the necessity of having a language laboratory for spoken drills.

Upper School students have had the opportunity to choose a language other than French and Latin. By 1910 there was a three-year sequence in German, Spanish, and Greek; there had been Italian off and on in the early 1900s, and Chinese was added in 2005. The first German teacher, Eva von Blomberg, began in 1890 and stayed until 1918, and her colleague Elizabeth Amann taught from 1915 until 1941. Winsor considered carefully whether it should employ a teacher who was a German national during the Second World War, but an overwhelming majority of the Executive Committee refused to replace Elizabeth Amann with a non-German teacher. Allena Luce [1944 to 1957], a Spanish teacher, came to Winsor after teaching music and choral singing at the American Grammar and High School in Buenos Aires, Argentina. She had founded the prestigious Lincoln School in Buenos Aires and was its head for many years.[40] Her popular book of Spanish songs, *Vamos a Cantar,* published in 1946 in Boston, is unfortunately no longer in print. A valuable teaching aid, the book was much used by other Spanish teachers.

Winsor was able to draw on the rich Boston arts community for the Fine Arts Department's teachers of drawing, modeling (sculpture), diction, drama, dancing, singing, and choral classes. In an era without television and movies, little plays and musical performances were a favorite diversion not just at school but also in many homes, especially in the summertime. Teachers in all departments reaped the benefits of the strong arts program and had the girls performing foreign language skits and dramatizations of a scene in literature, even acting out scientific principles. Drawing and singing were pursuits deemed particularly appropriate for girls and women, and although

The Faculty Room in 1922.

males' names predominate in the history books, there were many female artists and musicians in the early 1900s who deserve to be recognized.[41]

Some of these fine arts teachers were young women who left after a short time to marry or to throw themselves more fully into their chosen artistic endeavors, and some became legends in the School and familiar names in the outside world.* Teachers, students, and parents valued the arts courses and acknowledged their crucial role in the curriculum. The arts disciplines were intermeshed so that the girls wrote and performed plays that had original stage sets and costumes and even lyrics and music. Valeria Knapp participated in the drama Sarah Bradley 1916 wrote for their Senior Play that year. The *Lamp* printed many of the plays and poems the girls wrote, and the calendar of School events shows that there were dozens of performances each year.

Mary Gay [1915 to 1935] stayed to teach art and history of art for twenty years. During her tenure she helped create the curriculum for the New Plan, but she was also a painter of miniatures, landscapes, and portraits. Elizabeth Saltonstall 1918 was hired as an assistant to Mary Gay but left after three years for a thirty-seven-year career at Milton Academy. She was a talented and admired member of the Nantucket arts community.[42] In drama (or diction, as it was originally called) Florence Cunningham taught at Winsor for twenty-four years, 1923 to 1947. She was also one of the two directors of the Boston School of Public Speaking (and Dramatic Art), located on Boylston Street, and a founder of the Gloucester School of the Little Theater.[43] Florence Cunningham acquired legendary status at Winsor when David O. Selznick lured her to Hollywood to train actors in elocution.[†]

Rose Dresser [1947 to 1973] attended Vassar, worked for several years as an actress, and headed the Drama Department at the Bancroft School in Worcester. A creative person of unusual humor and understanding of young people, she taught the techniques of acting and production most skillfully. More important, her students learned to work with others toward a common goal and have fun achieving it. She filled many roles in the School. She was the first head of the new Fine Arts Department when it was reorganized at Winsor and served as head of the Upper School during the challenging decade 1963 to 1973.

One chapter is not sufficient to tell all the stories about the women—and men—who have taught at The Winsor School. If there were to be an entire book on Winsor teachers, one chapter would have to be devoted to those special men who had the demeanor and talent to work with young women. In the beginning the gentlemen were invited to fill in short tenures in modern

---

* These include May Hallowell Loud, Alicia Keyes, Amelia Peabody 1908, Mary Gay, Elizabeth Saltonstall 1918, David Park, Frank Rogers, Joanna Kao, George Demetrios, and Mabel Sarton. Examples of works by many of these can be found online.

† Despite anecdotal evidence, it cannot be verified that she worked with actresses in one of the productions of *Little Women*.

language and the arts, but many of them were favorites of the girls and made huge contributions to Winsor. The girls always seemed to enjoy their male teachers, but as Virginia Wing observed, "One problem in attracting men to Winsor was many schools pay men more than women and we do not."[44] David Park [1936 to 1941] came to the School by way of his aunt, Edith Park Truesdell [1934 to 1936], a fine artist trained at the Boston Museum School.[45] The Art Department was sorry to lose her, but her nephew, who became prominent as a social realist in the San Francisco Bay Area Figurative School in the 1950s, was an imaginative teacher whose brief years at Winsor ended when he felt he needed to be a full-time artist and moved to California. His daughter Natalie thought those years at Winsor "were an attempt to do the expected and take a proper job as a young husband and father."[46] Park left in the archives meticulous notes and drawings related to the 1940 revival of the medieval pageant. (The pageant is described in detail in chapter 8.)

David Park was only the ninth male teacher hired in the first fifty years of the School, of a total of about 250 hires. The very first man, Malcolm Lang, was hired in 1910 to teach the choral class for one year; he was a member of a prominent musical Boston family and was married to a Winsor graduate, Ethel Ranney 1906. The second, Boston University Professor F. Spencer Baldwin, came in 1911 to teach an economics course; he had three daughters in the School at the time. Neither man stayed more than a year, and it is probable that neither had a full schedule of classes.

Frank Rogers taught art at Winsor for twenty-three years [1949 to 1972]. Frances Dugan was pleased to announce his hiring in the spring of 1949, calling him "a very promising artist himself" with "a real teaching gift." When he died in 1989, he was praised for making the art studio "a place of delight," using readings, music, and his own performances to inspire the students' visual skills.[47] Rogers's works have been shown in a number of venues around the country, including the Boston Museum of Fine Arts. Rogers studied at the Museum School after serving in the front lines in Europe during World War II and was one of several teachers who divided their time between teaching and practicing their art.

One of Winsor's most prolific modern artist-teachers was Joanna Kao [1975 to 2006], who painted several delightful views of the School, both interior and exterior. Toward the end of her long Winsor career she began to use her creative drive to highlight issues of social justice. At Winsor she had been the inspiration for the Asian Club and had started to display her newer works, which reflected her background as the daughter of Chinese immigrants. After her retirement she became a significant figure in educating the wider community about the importance of public art and private identity.[48]

No male teachers have ever been part of the Winsor athletic department, although from time to time in recent years they have served as seasonal coaches. Gifted women with expertise in the physical training of girls and coaching and playing experience in more than one sport have consistently kept the Winsor athletic program strong. As in music and art, earlier accomplishments of women in athletics have been overlooked and even buried, except for those who excelled in tennis and golf or at the Olympics.

May P. Fogg [1938 to 1960] was highly regarded both at Winsor and in the larger sports world, and she brought a new fervor to Winsor athletics. In an article for the May 1949 *Bulletin*, she maintained that when the girls learned sound techniques, they enjoyed the sports more. "The program includes more girls each year and the standard of individual sports has been maintained. . . . The two things which are fundamental, namely a real joy in activity and a high standard of sportsmanship, are the things which we hope we are developing."[49] May Fogg was one of three founders of Camp Merestead in Hope, Maine, which opened in July 1938. Originally an all-purpose sports camp for girls, Merestead evolved into a field hockey and lacrosse summer program for women and girls.[50] Outstanding as a teacher, coach, and athletic director, May Fogg also served for a time as the house director of the Winsor Residence.

Another figure important to women's sports in Massachusetts as well as at Winsor was Barbara Goss, who taught, coached, and chaired the Physical Education Department at Winsor from 1942 to 1962. She introduced field hockey to the Commonwealth of Massachusetts in 1925 and worked tirelessly to gain interscholastic status for girls' sports in the state.

Margaret "Maggie" Boyd [1952 to 1955] was at Winsor for a very brief time, but she was another star of the women's sports world beyond Winsor. Educated in England, she not only established the first National Schools Championship for lacrosse but also promoted and took part in England's first international lacrosse competitions. She received the OBE (Order of the British Empire) in 1971. Her passion for lacrosse greatly advanced the awareness and proliferation of that sport around the globe and brought her fame as the first woman to be elected to the Lacrosse Hall of Fame in Baltimore.[51]

Natalie Park [1955 to 1980] served as head of Winsor's Fine Arts Department during her last seven years at the School, but, interestingly, she came to the School as a substitute in the Physical Education Department. She moved gradually into teaching in her own fields of art and photography. When she died at the age of eighty-nine, the scope of her talents and contributions was celebrated in her obituary in the *Boston Globe*, which noted her membership on the United States Lacrosse team from 1933 to 1939, and her World War II service as a lieutenant commander of naval intelligence for the WAVES.[52]

Until 1991 Winsor did not have a school nurse, relying on the first aid skills of members of the Physical Education Department and its proximity to area hospitals. Carolyn Peter appointed a former Corporation member, Jacquelyne Arrington, whose daughter Courtney graduated in 1985, as the School's first full-time nurse.

An impressive number of teachers spent virtually their entire careers at Winsor. Many—more than fifty—devoted over twenty years to the School. They stayed because they loved the School, the girls, and especially the opportunity to stretch themselves professionally. They were not likely to stay because of the monetary rewards. In her Fiftieth Anniversary Address, Mary Winsor said that in 1886 "the teacher was given her living quarters and a salary of $600." (No further reference to living quarters has ever been found.) There was, of course, no benefits package. In 1908 the money raised by the Incorporators from supporters and friends of the School was designated for scholarships and the building fund for the new Longwood facility. Thereafter, as we shall see, there was an increasing concern for the livelihood of teachers.

Urged on by each Director of the School, the Corporation continually supported higher salaries for teachers. The School as early as 1917 offered sabbaticals*—a third of the academic year off with pay—but it also agreed with Mary Winsor, who felt that all teachers should be required to retire at the age of sixty. (This policy did not prevail, and Mary Winsor herself did not retire until she was sixty-two.) Andrew Carnegie had established the Teachers Insurance and Annuity Association of America in 1918 at Cornell University, but initially it provided retirement benefits only for college and university professors. The earliest funds for teachers' pensions at Winsor were actually raised by the Graduate Club at the request of the Board. Throughout the early 1930s, the Director and the Board began to confront the complex questions of who should be entitled to a pension after retiring, who ought to pay for it, and how much it ought to be. It was a difficult financial period for the country, although Boston's conservatism had prevented the bankers and financiers from being as hard hit by the Depression as many others were.[53]

Katharine Lord in 1932 reminded the Board that she had introduced the pension idea to them ten years earlier. Now, she said, "even poor schools are making arrangements." Two years later the Board set up an executive committee, and in November 1934 it proposed a plan that would provide for the retirement of teachers at sixty-five (although Katharine Lord wanted the retirement age to remain at sixty) and required an annual contribution by the School of $3,070. Samuel Cabot, the Corporation president, suggested that each teacher deposit $100 in a savings account and the School would match it. Many still believed that the responsibility for teachers who had already been in the School for a number of years should lie with the alumnae.

The Graduate Club had given time and energy to its alma mater by supervising the playground and study halls and donating to the Scholarship Fund. Alumnae were also supporting a nursery school they had founded as well as the Calhoun School in Alabama, but they stepped forward again in that same spirit of philanthropy for which Boston was famous and gave $400 to start a

---

* The first teacher mentioned as taking a sabbatical was Sarah Lake [1902 to 1922] of the Mathematics Department, who was on sabbatical during the 1917–18 year.

pension fund. In December 1937 Katharine Lord announced that the "teachers are delighted with Mr. Deane's pension scheme."[54] A November 1942 letter to alumnae from the executive board of the Graduate Club explained: "When the School started a pension plan for its teachers through the Aetna Insurance Company, there were six teachers too near the retirement age to be included. For the benefit of these teachers, a special Pension Fund was started, to which contributions were made by the School, Graduates, and Teachers. The annual demand on the fund is $2160." The letter urged all alumnae to join and pay dues into the Graduate Club. In 1950 the federal government extended the Social Security program to cover incorporated nonprofit schools, and in 1969 Winsor joined the TIAA-CREF fund.

A fund-raising campaign for the endowment in 1932 brought in $60,000; this was earmarked for faculty salaries and scholarships.[55] The Directors tried to motivate the Board by periodically pointing out what other schools were paying their teachers. In 1922 the Rockefeller Foundation Report placed Winsor in the middle of comparable schools—twelfth of twenty-four—paying $1,400 for a trained teacher, with a yearly raise of $100, up to a maximum of $2,500. By 1937 the salary had risen to a $1,500 for a full-time experienced teacher; the top salary of $3,000 was reserved for the department heads. In 1950 Frances Dugan stated the faculty situation to the Corporation: "It is in some ways not an easy school in which to teach. We demand a high standard of scholarship, a good cultural background, a devotion to the profession, and a genuine liking for children. We offer somewhat mediocre salaries."[56]

In 1954 salaries for a teacher with two years of experience in Boston, Brookline, and Winsor were, respectively, $3,500, $3,900, and $2,700. Two years later the Commonwealth mandated that the minimum salary for a full-time public school teacher was to be $3,000.[57] In 1958 Valeria Knapp cautioned the Corporation: "When a vacancy occurs, I assume you wish me to procure as experienced and gifted a teacher as possible rather than tailoring a replacement to a fixed salary." She had two further observations: the top salary then in Newton was $7,200, and, more ominously, colleges were beginning to hire individuals without doctorates—dipping into the pool of women (and men) with master's degrees from the well-regarded eastern colleges, the very teachers sought by independent secondary schools.[58]

The first time an accreditation team came from the New England Association of Schools and Colleges to evaluate the School was in 1960, and one of its observations was that salaries were not commensurate with the quality of teaching, noting that $6,000 was the top of the salary range, and $3,400 was the bottom. This committee also noted that teachers had no formal contract and no sick leave, although they could take courses at Boston University for free. They recommended a faculty salary scale in addition to a guaranteed salary for those unable to finish the year because of sickness and an "augmentation" of the Director's power to give paid leaves for other, usually personal reasons.

The Winsor faculty in 1988–89.

The Winsor 75th Fund was launched in 1961, and as the School reached the age of three-quarters of a century, it embarked on a new era. The stated purpose of the campaign was to raise funds for "an endowment for faculty salaries" and "an expansion of the plant" that would include an entirely new wing of the building and renovation of parts of the original building. The Franklin Dexter Wing opened in the fall of 1963. (A complete overview of the various additions and renovations to the School can be found in chapter 4.) The new dining room, with its contemporary ambience, was a significant improvement to the plant: its high windows opened to a wide view of the courtyard, playing fields, and the neighbors in the adjacent hospital district. Having a pleasant lunch in the sunny dining room and being able to use the previous dining room and kitchen spaces for academics contributed to the quality of life for teachers as well as students. Even the smallest increase in square footage for the growing school population eased the crowding that had, almost from the beginning, challenged everyone in the School.

But salaries were also increased; in 1964 Virginia Wing announced the next year's range—$4,600 at the lower end, $7,800 at the top—while noting that at Brearley the scale ran from $5,000 to $9,500. She also brought up for comparison what she had recently learned about the Smith College Day School in Northampton:[59] that each teacher had a major medical and a group life policy, annual tuition payment of $1,000 for each faculty child in an accredited college, a contribution of 15 percent of annual salary to the pension program, and a reduction of the day-school tuition.[60] Within two years, significant improvements in the salary scale put Winsor at the top for girls' schools, but this was still without medical or pension benefits. Thereafter, raising teachers' salaries to make them competitive with those of the top 10 percent of similar schools became a priority.

In addition to their salaries, all School employees began to receive health coverage. Teachers had access to funds for taking courses to enhance their expertise and knowledge of a subject area: teachers could apply annually for $400 toward coursework for professional development. In 1989 a fund in honor of Virginia Wing became an even more substantial source of money for teachers to travel, study, explore new areas, and enrich both themselves and their students. A committee reviewed proposals each spring and handed out grants ranging from $1,000 to $3,000. In 1996 a unique areawide program, Teachers as Scholars, was established through the Harvard Graduate School of Education; it provides opportunities for teachers to attend a set of all-day classes taught by professors in a wide variety of fields at nearby colleges or universities.* The School not only paid for these courses but arranged substitutes to cover the classes that teachers missed.

Accompanying these changes was a gradual increase in the responsibilities of teachers in all schools, who faced demands to do more than merely teach classes as the twentieth century came to an end. Winsor teachers were expected to monitor five to ten advisees each year, oversee clubs and other extracurricular activities, attend their students' athletic contests and dramatic presentations when possible, respond to the concerns of parents, substitute on occasion for sick colleagues, and serve on ad hoc or standing committees. As they had for many years, they continued to evaluate their curriculum by staying informed through attending conferences and reading. Not every teacher did all these things, and few did them all at the same time, but there was increasing pressure on all teachers to devote more time and energy to the School, and some dedicated teachers were spreading themselves very thin.

Public school teachers faced the same demands, but their salaries rose steadily; Winsor and other independent schools rarely matched them. Independent schools like Winsor were, however, able to offer the teaching conditions and other amenities that were a traditional part of a different "benefit package": small classes (sometimes very small), highly motivated students, congenial colleagues, a minimum of tedious supervisory duties, greater academic freedom, a nurturing atmosphere for both children and adults, and opportunities to try new things.† From the beginning all teachers and staff have been provided with a free lunch, a not insubstantial benefit. For Winsor teachers, the most often mentioned bonus has been the joy of being a part of a group of women (and occasionally men) who were intelligent, caring, and

---

* Teachers as Scholars in a typical year allows up to one thousand teachers from over fifty school communities to attend more than one hundred seminars in the humanities and sciences; see www.teachersasscholars.org.

† Some of Winsor's teachers were married women, who could not have been hired by the Boston Public Schools before 1954.

honest. As those whose tenure in the School was frequently longer than most students, the faculty contributed significantly to what The Winsor School became.

The traditional values and expectations of the School were passed along through generations of teachers as well as through students in various ways that were a result of many conditions: the careful selection of the "right" faculty; the presence of alumnae who came back to teach; alumnae wanting their daughters to have a Winsor education; the School's reputation for having hardworking students and a stimulating faculty; and the long tenure of many fine teachers. Twenty-five teachers spent more than thirty years (essentially their entire careers) at Winsor: over 750 years. The "old hands" mentored every new teacher long before *mentoring* became a verb and a buzzword. Department heads were chosen from among those with good credentials and long tenure, and as a group they maintained watch over the curricular offerings and the quality of teaching in each department. Teachers who demonstrated insight into character development were another select group—the Room Teachers—each overseeing one class level, shepherding them, serving as a link to the administrators and to other teachers, becoming accustomed to the quirks and quiddities of a particular age group.

Over the years, many Winsor alumnae returned to teach, further enriching and strengthening the pedagogic, ethical, and social traditions of the School. The extraordinary number of daughters, sisters, and cousins of graduates became an inclusive rather than an exclusive factor, in that the special aspect of female connection, be it with friends or neighbors or relatives, pervaded the School environment. Girls often came to feel genuine friendship with a teacher, and those bonds persisted for years, nourished by opportunities to reconnect.

In the issue of the *Winsor Bulletin* that honored Winsor's teachers, one student's tribute might best summarize this chapter:

> The dedication, intelligence, and sophistication of the teachers I had at Winsor far exceeded what I encountered later. I am sure that this was partly because our classes were small and our teachers were dedicated so that there could be the kind of individual attention that made a difference in my life. I also believe that having successful women teachers as role models was significant. I had so few female teachers at college and law school, and so many male teachers who did not exhibit the kind of sensitivity and dedication that I had found at Winsor, that it was painful.[61]

If a student had a seat near the window, he was in an envied position. . . . There was the possibility of seeing and even waving to the girls from Miss Winsor's School, with their colorful hair ribbons, cinched-in waists and voluminous folds of skirt.

—Richard P. Flood

The Science Club sponsored as its first assembly of the year—General Electric's "House of Magic" show. We most regretfully made up the period lost in the Magical House.

—Winsor Lamp

III and IV were . . . not only undefeated in inter-school competition but were constantly commended by the coaches of other teams for their sportsmanship and good manners.

—Virginia Wing

At the end of the graduation ceremony in 1993, Carolyn McClintock Peter and Lisa Taillacq watch the traditional transfer of the lamp from Class President Anne Allison 1993 to Class President Octavia Devon 1994.

The Students

❦

"Competent, responsible, generous-minded"

THE STORY OF THE WINSOR SCHOOL would not be complete without the stories of the young women who were the beneficiaries of the foresight of the founders, the generosity of the donors, the labor of those who built and cared for the building, and of course the energy and dedication of the teachers. What was it like to be an American preteen or teenager as the School moved from its unpretentious beginnings to being one of the top girls' schools in the country? How did they adapt to the changes in their world?

As we have seen, the mothers and grandmothers of Winsor students formed women's clubs that ranged from sewing circles to settlement house committees. The early alumnae of Miss Winsor's School continued the tradition. Eleanor Jones 1897 became first the director, then the treasurer, of the Boston Y.W.C.A. Ruth Bowman Whitney 1898 studied for two years at Bryn Mawr, married, and became a member of the Executive Committee of the Massachusetts Anti-Suffrage Association. Margaret Anthony 1900 was secretary of the New Bedford Equal Suffrage League. Others pursued a more traditionally feminine route that nonetheless put them in competition with men. The young painter Clara Frothingham 1898 opened her own portrait studio on Marlborough Street. Amelia Peabody 1908 and Dorothy Sturgis Harding 1909 trained at the Museum School after graduating. Amelia Peabody was an accomplished sculptor who also managed a horse farm and funded charitable projects. Dorothy Harding, the daughter of R. Clipston Sturgis, the architect of the new Winsor School, was a renowned designer of personal bookplates; she also designed a settlement house and a building for a book club in North Brighton.[1]

Mary Winsor and her girls did not merely react to a changing world, they found themselves asking for change and seeking knowledge that would allow

Dorothy Sturgis Harding 1909 designed this bookplate in 1936 for Winsor's Fiftieth Anniversary.

them to do more than their mothers had done and as much as men could do. The nourishing environment of the School allowed them to learn and lead, to experiment and sometimes fail, and to appreciate together the privilege of being educated. In some ways, school life now does not differ greatly from school life then, and although the School was continually adjusting to the needs of young women and to the realities of the outside world, it maintained its essential personality.

In the late 1800s it was still more common for young women from the upper classes in Boston to marry than to pursue a career. Mary Winsor, however, had intended her curriculum from the beginning to prepare girls for entrance to college and for "training in some special occupation, by following which she can support herself if necessary." She added: "If women are in these days to be self-respecting they must also have it within their power to be self-supporting."[2] Many young women at the time taught school and did settlement work before marriage, and some ventured boldly into professions such as law and medicine, forcing a change in thinking about who would have the privilege of being a doctor or a lawyer. By the end of the twentieth century, Winsor alumnae would be serving as clergy, conducting and composing music, and performing heart surgery.

By the middle of nineteenth century, as the women's suffrage movement grew, more young women aspired to college. Although this attitude was not uncommon among the educated families of the Northeast, in the country as a whole it was still not the usual thing even for a man to go to college, and only a tiny minority of women did so, even when many degree-granting colleges admitted them. "By the turn of the century, 40 percent of all college students would be women, though that figure represented less than 4 percent of all American women between the ages of eighteen and twenty-one."[3] By 1920 women would constitute 50 percent of college-enrolled students, but this was still less than 8 percent of eighteen- to twenty-one-year-old women in the country.[4] By 1929 the size of Winsor's graduating class had increased from fourteen to thirty-five, and the School was giving college examinations to more girls "than any other private girls' school in the country."[5]

In her brief history of the School written for the Graduate Club in 1910, Mary Winsor announced with pride: "Ever since 1897 the school has sent up candidates each June for the college entrance examinations for Bryn Mawr and Radcliffe, and sometimes for Smith and Vassar also. There are now on an average twelve girls taking the regular examinations every year, and more than that number who are aiming at only the sixteen points necessary to admit them as special students at Radcliffe."[6]

The first Winsor alumna to earn a degree from Radcliffe was Pauline Wright Brigham 1894, who was described in chapter 2. Between 1900 and 1903, eight Winsor girls graduated from either Radcliffe or Bryn Mawr.* At that time, most were aspiring to marry professional men, take a few courses at Radcliffe or the Museum School, and continue their involvement with charities. It was the age when the women's sphere was such a powerful ideal that many upper- and upper-middle-class families still vigorously opposed a woman's right to vote. Girls were carefully protected, educated in neighborhood dame schools that were close enough to their homes that they could walk home for lunch. They were clothed from head to foot in constricting high-necked, long-sleeved dresses (and hats) that might have made any kind of high-spirited romping in public difficult. In her 50th Anniversary Address, Mary Winsor recalled only one complaint about the girls' behavior. A Boston police officer, "an enormous fellow, tall and stout," complained that "one of my girls—and he knew her name from previous encounters—had marked with chalk a cross on his back, too high up for him to rub it out." "I provided reparation by removing the blemish and by offering an apology from the perpetrator of the crime. This offer was accepted, the sinner sent for, and a quaint scene ensued between Dignity and Impudence, one all frowns, and the other all dimples."[7]

These young women's future was protected by the coming-of-age ritual known as coming out, the goal of which was to introduce a daughter to the upper-class social set into which she was expected to marry. A girl was preserved like a fragile flower (early debutantes were, in fact, called "buds"); her name could not appear in the newspaper until she had come out. For some girls the process filled an entire year that had set protocols for teas, dancing, visiting, and entertaining.

Some aspects of Miss Winsor's School were peculiar to this late-Victorian social world into which the girls had been born. In the first twenty-four years of her school, Mary Winsor gradually built a curriculum that went beyond drawing lessons and French to include Latin, history, geography, science, and physical exercise. Mary Winsor herself or another teacher led daily calisthenics in the rather cramped rooms at 95–96 Beacon Street. The 1902 Course of Study notes: "As light gymnastics are an important part of the daily exercises, it is of great importance that the pupils should dress in such a way as to be able to use their arms freely." Although some had a commute that included a mad

* Henrietta Faxon Pease 1894 earned her Radcliffe degree in 1901. Leslie Appleton Knowles 1897 graduated from Bryn Mawr in 1900, Eleanor Hooper 1897 in 1901, and Elizabeth Shepley Sergeant 1898 in 1903. Ruth Maynard Soule 1898, Rebecca Whitney Wright, Margaret White Waters, and Marian Sears Robbins, all 1899, received Radcliffe degrees in 1903.

An undated picture shows the elaborate clothing little girls wore in the late 1800s. At least three of the girls have been identified as members of Miss Winsor's first class in 1886. In the front row on the left is Helen Brooks 1895; in the back row Eleanor Emmons 1894 is at the far left, and Susan Emmons 1894 is third from the left.

dash for a trolley, the girls' only exercise came when they crossed Beacon Street to the Public Garden for recess each morning. The Garden was not a playground, however. "It was the preferred place for girls to walk, arm in arm, at recess, and the only restriction placed on such outings was that Winsorites must not leave the school for them hatless, as bareheaded girls would be 'conspicuous.'"[8]

The School's new beginning in 1910 on the spacious grounds in the Longwood area permitted girls to enjoy and compete in many of the sports that boys regularly enjoyed at their schools. At her Fiftieth Reunion in 1951, Mabel Chick 1901 commented, "I wish we in our day could have had the well set-up school buildings and facilities that the more recent students have enjoyed. The Public Garden in Boston was our only recreation."[9]

The other opportunity for real exercise was during the summer, when girls could play tennis, golf, or shuttlecock (badminton), or swim and sail. Many young women were already becoming proficient in those sports. Helen Homans 1902 won the U.S. ladies singles championship in tennis in 1906, and, later, Sarah Palfrey 1930 not only won it twice but also won in women's doubles nine times.* Those long summers had at first determined the yearly schedule of Miss Winsor's School, which did not open until October and ended on "Last Day" in late May. The school day itself was short in the early years, 9:00 to 1:30. At recess the girls could have cocoa, milk, crackers, and sandwiches, and they could buy a hot lunch at school if they wished, although many of them walked home for lunch, often inviting friends along.

It is hard to refrain from quoting repeatedly from Frances Parkinson Keyes's memories of her Winsor days. Her novelist's eye captured the youthful perspective of her years at Miss Winsor's from 1899 to 1903. Here, for example, is her description of a bathing costume before the turn of the century: "The bathing suit was, of course, made of alpaca and liberally trimmed with braid. It consisted of a waist [a blouse], which came almost up to the neck, and had elbow sleeves. This waist was attached to bloomers and these were covered by a skirt, which came well below the knees. With this costume, long black stockings were worn. Why we did not all drown before we ever learned to swim at all still seems to me a minor mystery."[10]

Frances Keyes, who began to write as a very young child, took seriously the responsibility to learn. When she fell behind because of a bout of scarlet fever, she sought out a teacher to help her get caught up after her illness, upset because other girls were making fun of her. She took pride in doing well on her exams, although, like students everywhere, she grumbled about homework: "Our teachers did not assign history and English lessons by the page, but by the number of inches that multitudinous pages would cover when closely pressed together. . . . Our teacher of mathematics considered ten intricate problems . . . reasonable . . . for daily solution."[11]

There were two new aspects to the lives of American girls once they began to attend schools in large numbers in the early 1900s. At Winsor these became the twin poles around which nearly everything else rotated: close friendships and serious studying. Ask a Winsor graduate what she remembers most about her years at Winsor and the most likely answer is "Friends and the wonderful education."

Something significant changed for American girls when they began to go to school. The family—with all its extensions—was no longer the sole source of social activity. We would be surprised to see how many close relatives intertwined in the first Winsor classes; there were cousins everywhere, and the same families kept marrying one another's offspring, repeating the family names over and over to such an extent that researching them is a challenge. But as the School grew and accepted applicants from more social classes and geographic areas, girls (who thrive on friendships) easily made new friends

---

* Other tennis notables include the tennis coach Hazel Hotchkiss Wightman and her daughters Dorothy Wightman Hood 1940, Hazel Wightman Harlow 1934, and Virginia Wightman Henckel 1932.

outside their family and brought different family groups together as well. The original close-knit circle did not loosen quickly, but girls gradually developed a wider social circle, at least while they were at school.

In some ways, just being aware of their need for friends was a somewhat new feeling for girls, who theretofore had been discouraged from too much self-involvement, which would taint the selflessness required of them when they became wives and mothers. Being at school had given them a greater sense of who they were as individuals, as well as the confidence of new skills and knowledge of the world. On this broader base, they built new friendships through the classroom, the playing field, the stage, and, eventually, dozens of clubs. Those who stayed for six, seven, or eight years at the School, as well as those who came for a briefer time and perhaps moved on to another school before graduation, forged durable friendships lasting lifetimes.

The desire to maintain close connections with schoolmates after leaving Winsor lay behind the founding of the Graduate Club in 1907. Young alumnae, married and unmarried, who had shared so closely their school experiences, wanted to keep those bonds alive so that they might contribute further to the School that had established new directions for their lives. "If we can make [the Club] continue to be a pleasure to us, and above all, make it grow to be a body upon which Miss Winsor may call at any time, we shall be expressing in some measure, at least, our affection for her and our appreciation of the privilege we feel of being her graduates."[12]

Their meetings were not mere social gatherings; they organized an orchestra, supervised outdoor play at the School, staged plays, and held fundraising events for the Calhoun School. They established a constitution and bylaws and invited all Winsor teachers to become members as well, reflecting the sense of closeness among all members of the School community, a bond that has been a factor in Winsor's longevity. In 1911 they commissioned Cecilia Beaux to paint the portrait of Miss Winsor that hangs in the upper library.* Thanks to the Graduate Club (which became the Alumnae Association in 1963), there is a vast amount of material in the archives about what Winsor women were doing fifty, sixty, even seventy years after leaving the School. The earliest alumnae "bios" in the 1910 and 1915 *Graduate Club Registers* shed light on the surprisingly varied lives of women in the first decades of the new century. Thereafter, it was the *Lamp* that published news about graduates—their colleges, their jobs, their marriages, and their children's colleges, jobs, and marriages.

The students started the *Lamp* as their own publication in 1915. "As most of you probably know, there has never, before this year, been a magazine run by the girls of the Winsor School. There has been a Scrap-Book, . . . but the teachers, not the girls, managed the Scrap-Book. . . . [the *Winsor Lamp*]

---

* Cecilia Beaux (1855–1942) was one of the finest portrait painters at the turn of the century.

will be a new experiment and therefore very imperfect."[13] They were proud to publish it without teacher input, and student "ownership" of clubs and publications has continued to be a hallmark of the Winsor club program. The *Lamp* was for many years the closest thing to a school newspaper the girls had. It was published four times a year and covered events throughout all eight grades of the School and presented as well letters and articles by alumnae.

Writing had been an important outlet for women's thoughts and feelings throughout the previous century: prevented from speaking publicly on the podium, women used the written word to find an audience. Numerous magazines by and for women and girls had grown in popularity throughout the 1800s, and the wide variety of subjects Winsor girls wrote about in the *Lamp* reflects this aspect of female culture of the written word.[14] Some of the titles of their writings—sometimes essays, sometimes fiction—were "Slavery" (even forty years after the Civil War), "One of My Favorite Heroines" (Minerva), "The Importance of a Purpose in the Life of a Girl," "An Incident in a Streetcar," and "Glimpse into a French Boarding School." There were more scholarly subjects, such as the Pantheon, a comparison of Frost and Hawthorne, and "Milton's Character as Shown by His Minor Poems."

Winsor girls were good writers and readers who were being taught to admire good writing. The April 1918 issue of the *Lamp* announced: "Hetty Hemenway 1911 has shot into literary distinction through the recent publication of two short stories." "When Miss Hemenway published 'Four Days' in the *Atlantic Monthly* last year, it created more discussion than any other war story of the year. Her new story ['Their War'], which is in a quiet key, represents an advance in her art, and the two stories together represent one of the most important contributions an American has made to the imaginative literature of the war."[15]

Katharine Sergeant White 1909 began her long career at the *New Yorker* shortly after it published its first issue in 1925. Quickly rising to become an editor and star writer at the magazine, she told her old classmates, "I write as much as time allows." She eventually married another writer at the magazine, E. B. White, the author of *Charlotte's Web* and *Stuart Little*. Katharine White's biography, *Onward and Upward* by Linda Davis, includes recollections of her Winsor years.[16]

Another published author was Dorothy Gilman 1908; her description of "Last Day" at "Miss Pink's School" is clearly about Winsor, but her heroine, Leslie, is considered a bit of a rebel because she wants to go to Radcliffe.[17] Gilman received all her schooling at Miss Winsor's Back Bay school, as did Alice Deford 1907, who was the author of the books *Singing River* and *Michael's Life*, and Mary Lee 1909, whose prizewinning book, *"It's a Great War!"* based on her wartime reminiscences, "almost won" the Pulitzer Prize in 1930.[18]

The Virginia Wing Library has a section of shelves dedicated to works by

Winsor authors, and although it includes 238 books, it is not a complete collection. The most prolific Winsor writer was Frances Parkinson Keyes, who wrote over fifty novels. The genres represented in the alumnae collection include health and wellness, biography, cooking, poetry, travel, and, of course, fiction.

Like the *Lamps*, the early yearbooks provide a picture of the girls' activities. The senior class began to publish a Class Book as early as 1921.* The first yearbooks often gave a description of the graduating class's highlights and their memories from each of their years at Winsor. On each graduate's page were a hand-pasted-in picture and a list of her extracurricular activities. In 1922 the editors also wrote pithy observations about each classmate, always including her nickname: for example, Batch, Dorfy, Pop, Mig, Moolah, and Weedy.

> She has a high sense of right and wrong and if she feels a thing is wrong nothing on earth will persuade her to do it.

> She has a winning way with the teachers, and also seems to charm the younger children, for you never see her around school without a troop of juvenile admirers.

Misadventures and pranks were described:

> Bunny not long ago was rash enough to indulge in a "permanent" and now can often be seen standing before a mirror, gazing hopefully at the rising young hairs.

> Throughout her career she has amused the class with her numerous escapades, such as removing the door-handles and getting under the desk in the study.

There were parties and picnics, sleigh rides and luncheons, theater outings and even movies, although the adults took a dim view of the cinema. Surprisingly, some girls had motorcars. "As soon as it was legally possible to get a license, I was given a car of my own, and could drive it myself the last year at Winsor School. It was a quaint kind of vehicle, a Hudson coupe, looking somewhat like a horse-drawn carriage, only with windows on all sides."[19] Of another girl it was said: "Her maroon-colored Cadillac with its snappy 'Rolls Royce trimmings' is the pride of the class." "We are on our way to Murrays, packed like sardines, in Midge's Ford." "Nell" also had a Ford. By 1928 it was worth pointing out that so-and-so "started with a Ford, now has a La-Salle." Apparently girls knew cars.

There was occasional discomfort about socioeconomic differences among the girls. At first even Frances Parkinson Keyes, whose family had a summer house and who had spent several years in Europe with her mother,

* The 1921 edition is the earliest Class Book in the Winsor Archives.

In 1917 the younger girls were still wearing a kind of "uniform"—blue pinafores that they found hot, clumsy, and ugly.

felt excluded: "Those girls with their sleek braids and their neat shirtwaists, who had laughed at my curls and my clothes . . . girls who had permitted my lonely walks, while they gathered companionably at each other's houses."[20] Nancy Hale 1926 had a pure Yankee ancestry reaching as far back as Nathan Hale, yet she sensed that she was different, perhaps because her parents were artists whose lifestyle was somewhat "bohemian."* "Later, in my teens, when I was going to the Winsor School in Boston, such a hierarchy of values still obtained. High on the list of perfections stood Fair Isle and Shetland sweaters. Why were they considered so perfect? They just were. Accordion-pleated dark-blue or dark-green skirts came close. . . . The girls who wore dresses never looked right; and the more dressy the dress, the wronger."[21]

The history of women's clothing is a subplot in the history of girls' schools, for some young women began rebelling in the mid-nineteenth century: here was an instance of a societal change pushed through by the women themselves. At Winsor there was a dress requirement that became part of School lore: "The outstanding memory is that of the dreary, hot, dusty-blue, long-sleeved aprons with class numeral in dull red on the sleeve."[22] In 1911–12 a fervent petition from the members of Class III, pleading for an end to the blue aprons the Lower-Schoolers were required to wear, did not result in the desired rule change. When the aprons were finally abandoned, the following heartfelt ditty appeared in the *Lamp:*

---

* Nancy's mother, Lillian Westcott Hale, was a prominent artist who painted the School's portrait of Frances Dugan.

Ode to the Blue Pinafores

Aye, pull the pale blue aprons off,
    Long have they sored the eye,
And many a girl has scorned to see
    The apronettes go by;
Beneath them beat indignant hearts
    Of girls whose hearts were sore,
But aprons of the lower school
    Shall dim our joys no more.
        —Lucy C. Fiske 1921[23]

The catalogue in 1914–15 stated that pupils in the four lower classes were required to wear aprons during the morning session. "These may be purchased from Wm. Filene's Sons Company. For gymnastic work a special skirt made by Filene Co. is required for Classes VI, VII, VIII; members of Class V wear bloomers without skirts in the gymnasium, and the four lower classes bloomers under their dresses."[24] Mary Hill Coolidge 1917 recalled that for sports the girls "wore blue serge bloomers and middy blouses, and we each had our own special way of tying our ties."[25] In an article written on the occasion of her Sixtieth Class Reunion, she recalled details of girls' fashions from the time she was in the Lower School. "The customs and clothes at Winsor were wonderful. At one time, I think it was when we were in Class III or IV, the Lower School went into light blue uniforms with red numbers on the sleeves to designate each class. They were unpopular and did not last. After the uniform period we mostly wore skirts and white shirtwaists of our own choice with gay wide ribbon belts pinned at the side. We were allowed to lengthen our skirts an inch or two a year so that they might arrive at our ankles in Class VIII."[26] There were strict rules about hairstyle, and one audacious girl "did her hair up like a grownup in Class VII" and had to face Mary Winsor for the infraction.

After World War I clothing began to be an issue not only for schoolgirls but also for adult women. The problem was not one of fashion but of practicality: it was difficult to play tennis or field hockey in a long dress with numerous

1911–'12

The following members of Class III respectfully ask for the abolishment of the blue gingham aprons.

Our reasons are as follows:

    1. They are very hot and uncomfortable.
    2. They are very clumsy and awkward.
    3. They are very ugly.

Winsor's basketball team, 1915–16 (left to right): back row, Sarah Bradley 1916, Katharine Townsend 1917, Margaret Cooke 1916, Helen Morton 1916; front row, Marion Pennock 1916, Caroline Baxter, Valeria Knapp (captain) 1916, Priscilla Badger 1916, Helenka Adamowska 1917.

petticoats. Until 1910 girls wore slightly shorter than floor-length skirts for tennis, but women were expected to keep the entire body covered during golf and tennis. Gradually, they were able to wear an undergarment known as a pantaloon under a full skirt. Sometimes the upper layers were hiked up slightly during vigorous play. Girls' schools and colleges, especially Wellesley and Vassar, moved quickly toward shorter and shorter sports outfits that culminated in the one-piece gym suit many women living in the twenty-first century can still remember wearing in their early school days. The concern about covering the body was not so relevant for girls playing on a female school's protected campus fields or in a gymnasium. Winsor girls presented a cheerful sight on the fields during the 1950s and 1960s when each entering class was given a gym suit in a color—red, blue, yellow, or green—they would keep until they graduated.

Just as their work opportunities improved after the First World War, women's clothing became looser and freer, partly because those working in industries had adopted the practicality of overalls during the war.* The popularity of sports such as golf and skiing among women in the 1920s and 1930s also affected dress modifications. At Winsor in the 1920s girls began to wear wider, shorter skirts for sports as the School continued to expand its physical education program through both intramural and interscholastic team play. "We wore white middies, blue sashes with bells on them, and blue bows on the end of our pigtails."[27]

At Mary Winsor's Beacon Hill locations, there had been gymnastic exercises and something called "fancy dancing." The further development of the School's athletic activities happened gradually. When the School moved to the Fenway location, both the girls and their families became accustomed to the option of the students' staying for the afternoon games period, which in the early years had not been required. By the 1923–24 school year, all girls in Classes I through VI were required to stay three days a week for afternoon sports, Classes VII and VIII two days. Said Katharine Lord: "I believe strongly that the girls should realize that regular physical exercise is a necessary part of their education. I see the girls who stay regularly in better physical trim and with better general morale. They have more interest in school, more ability to work with others and to subordinate the interest of the moment to some more real purpose."[28] Marching, rope climbing, and Swedish floor exercises (the early form of gymnastics) were the major physical education activities for women in the early 1900s. In addition to field hockey and basketball, the girls competed in tennis, swimming, and golf. Many competitions and tournaments, especially for younger girls, were intramural. The individual sports were the ones that the girls would have engaged in with their families—tennis, swimming, badminton, and golf, which became very popular with women around the turn of the century. The younger girls played croquet, Indian clubs, and clock golf (a putting game) with one another. Many of them took up skiing and, perhaps because they were just young girls, allowances were made for them to wear pants, but for ice-skating, tennis, and horseback riding, no such freedom was given. By the year 2010 Winsor sports included squash, ice hockey, crew, and even curling. Lacking the athletic facilities for these and some other sports, the School has relied on agreements with area sports clubs and other schools.

The *Winsor Lamp* maintained a very full record of athletic achievements; games were covered in detail; scores and the names of high scorers, team members, and substitutes were listed. The frequent complimentary nod to the skills of the opponents reflected the kind of sportsmanship Winsor encouraged. There were only a few teams that played against other schools, but all girls participated in some kind of sports and vied among themselves in the annual "Fife and Drum" competitions.

---

* Those gallant young Winsor women who went to Europe as Red Cross workers had struggled to do their jobs in long, full skirts and even veils.

Fall 1923.
Nancy Loring · Margaret Swain · Harriet White · Miss Chaplin · Marion Greene · Barbara Greenough.
Sarah Shurtleff · Jamia Bright · Fanny Curtis · Martha Brewer (Capt) Emily Coolidge · Elisabeth Bradford · Jane Megrew
Frances Dohtier · Polly Palfrey   Ellen Frothingham · Claire Parker.
Winsor 5 - May 3
Winsor 4 - Groton 1
Winsor 11 - Newton 2
Winsor 9 - Milton 2.

The field hockey team in 1923.

In June 1935 the *Lamp* reported that all students in Classes III through VIII would be divided into two divisions called the Reds and the Whites. The names were soon changed, and a girl became a member of either the Fifes or the Drums, keeping her team identity throughout her Winsor years. A younger sister affiliated with her older sister's team, and a daughter with her mother's. When a Fife or a Drum was on a victorious team, she earned a point for her division. The winner was announced on Last Day. In the winter of 1935 the *Lamp* reported: "Since the innovation of the *Fifes* and *Drums* as the two interschool teams, the entire spirit of the school life has changed. Every one, regardless of classes, is united in common enthusiasm for her team, and the increased enthusiasm for sports is very marked in the number of onlookers, especially among the Lower School."[29] The Fife and Drum tradition continued for many years, mainly in the Lower School, but excitement and interest declined as the sports program evolved. An article in a 2007 *Panel* explained: "The disinterest coincided with the increase in interscholastic competitions, . . . the emergence of clubs such as SASS [Students Advocating School Spirit] and the formation of the Eastern Independent League in the early 1990s."[30]

Another indication of the lack of a large organized league of schools for intermural games was the practice of having the Winsor varsity team play either the alumnae or the faculty in field hockey and basketball. An amusing account in the April 1935 *Lamp* begins, "On Tuesday March 19th, the entire school assembled solely to witness that colossal, outstanding event of the basketball season, namely the faculty game." The following description suggests that one should not underestimate the teachers' senses of humor:

> Mlle. Renouard, the inspiring cheer leader was enchanting in white slacks and a pink pajama top decorated with the basketball W. The water-*boy*, Miss Water*man*, was wonderful in red bloomers and a white middy, while Miss Todd, the doctor, officiated in a white medical uniform with facemask and cap. The remaining members of the squad, which was captained by Miss Holman, appeared in pajamas and bathrobes and proceeded to stretch, yawn, do sitting up exercises, and recline on the floor in a very uninterested manner. . . . The cheering section of the faculty deserved special credit: "Chicka dee, chicka dee! Rah! Rah! Rah! Faculty! Faculty! Ha cha! cha!"

The School added track, archery, and roller-skating in the 1930s and began to compete with a wider variety of schools in basketball, playing against even public schools such as Weston, Newton, Brookline, and Winchester. There is a reference in the February 1930 *Lamp* to the IIIs and IVs playing football; since touchdowns are mentioned, this could not have been soccer. The girls did, however, also play soccer as early as the 1930s.

Besides coaching the teams, the sports teachers were expected to teach posture, for which, until the late 1980s, a prize was given at graduation,* and to give instruction in "healthy living." For Upper School athletes in 1930, there was the new All-Boston Private School Team; five of Winsor's "lettered" players made the team, which also selected top athletes from the Dana Hall School, Lasell Seminary, and the Beaver Country Day School. In the spring of that year, Winsor beat Beaver 21–2 in baseball, but Milton Academy prevailed over Winsor in that sport, 12–5. Yearbooks from the 1940s mention team captains for the first time, as well as an athletic association. Lacrosse was added in 1950. Girls attending private schools, particularly schools for girls only, were fortunate to have the opportunity to play such a wide variety of team sports long before Congress passed the legislation known as Title IX. "In the days before Title IX, only one in 27 girls played varsity high school sports. By 2001, that figure was up to one in 2.5, for a total of 2.8 million girls playing high school sports. Similarly, 32,000 women athletes played on intercollegiate teams prior to Title IX, compared with 150,000 today."[31]

---

* The Horatio A. Lamb Prize for good carriage was indicative of the "sound body" culture of the times. It also reflected the concern about scoliosis, which some orthopedists refused to correct by braces.

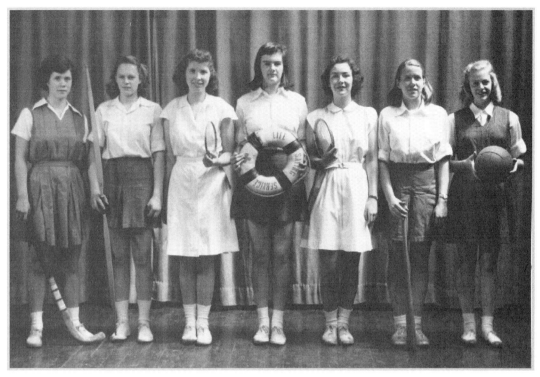

The team captains in 1947–48 (left to right): Midge Rogers, Ellen Dunnell, Cynthia Gruener, Elise (Lisa) Faulkner, Hope Griswold, Cornelia Wheeler, Edith LaCroix. All except Faulkner (a junior) were seniors.

Winsor students honed their athletic skills in the Lower School by playing against each other, and in the Upper School they competed with teams from the schools mentioned above, competition that provided benefits that went far beyond those of health and fitness. Studies have shown that team play provides both girls and boys with learning experiences that contribute to success in later life. Betsey Stevenson, an economist at the Wharton School of the University of Pennsylvania, has noted: "It's not just that the people who are going to do well in life play sports, but that sports help people do better in life. . . . While I only show this for girls, it's reasonable to believe it's true for boys as well."[32] Before Title IX there were scarce resources in public schools for girls to reap the rewards of team sports, but at Winsor and other single-sex schools, girls had been competing on the playing fields and courts since the turn of the century. Once again, Winsor had anticipated a crucial aspect of educational philosophy.

Since physical education and team involvement were required of Winsor students, sports activities were not technically extracurricular. But athletic teams have traditionally been seen as one of the three nonacademic divisions of school life, along with student government and drama. At Winsor there had always been a fourth area—clubs—and the definition of a Winsor club

Playing tennis on the clay courts in the 1950s. The picture shows the blank face of the building where an additional wing was originally envisioned but never built.

is a broad one: it can refer to the weekly meetings of an group interested in a specific topic such as Spanish in which members can explore Spanish culture more deeply, or it can be applied to an ongoing yearlong project such as the yearbook, which requires substantial time and energy. Being elected to the presidency of a club is an honor, as is being chosen by one's peers to head the committee for a fund-rising project such as the Bizarre Bazaar or a class dance.*

Yearbooks in the 1920s list clubs that still exist in some form at Winsor: the Hospitality Committee to welcome new girls, the Second-hand Book Committee, the Charity (community services) Committee, and the Class Book (yearbook) Committee. Ad hoc individual chairpersons for special events earned recognition in the yearbooks. Throughout the next few decades, various clubs seem to have come and gone according to the interests of the girls and the willingness of faculty sponsors: Dance Club, *Lamp* Board, Fife and Drum teams, Orchestra, Science Club (including a Lower School Science Club run by Upper School girls), Student Federalists, and the Lower School Glassblowers Guild in Class IV. The girls loved music, and singing groups organized and reorganized through the years: in the 1950s there were the Choral Club, the Choir, the Glee Club, and the Senior Choir Octet, which anticipated the "Senior Small" (an a cappella group that emerged in the 1990s).

* The Bizarre Bazaar was a fund-raising event in 1925.

Other clubs of that period were the Debating Club, the Spanish Club, the Graduation Choir, the Senior Banquet Committee, the Art Club, and (mysteriously) the Commuting Club.

In both the Lower and Upper Schools the number of student clubs has mushroomed in the last century. Lower School clubs change yearly according to the requests of the students; perennial favorites have been Glee Club, Art Club, and Book Club, each reimagined for the trends of the times: in the 1990s the Harry Potter Club began and continued for several years, the television hit Glee attracted singers, and there is an environmental "art goes green" theme for the Art Club. Leslie Cohn Bernstein 1981, head of the Lower School, noted that the clubs "offer a fantastic community-building opportunity" in which children are free to plan and make decisions and teachers can work with students they might not ordinarily teach. Sometimes there have been as many as fifty clubs in the Upper School alone. The 2010 Visiting Committee noted with admiration the healthy number of active clubs and was impressed with the learning opportunities represented by Winsor clubs. It is not unusual for an Upper School girl to be a member of two or three lunchtime clubs, and some are able to play a sport (though not always at the

Field hockey in the 1950s; the shed left behind by the Longwood Cricket Club
is in the background.

The Small Chorus singing the National Anthem, directed by Lisa Taillacq, is projected on the giant screen at Fenway Park, 2011.

varsity level), serve in student government, and perform in a play. Nevertheless, the faculty takes an active role in teaching these young women that their health and effectiveness falter when they stretch themselves too thin. Younger girls are counseled to avoid doing both a sport and drama at the same time, for example.

The Winsor School was and is something of a rarity: a place where females were and are the leaders, the decision makers, and the innovators. The Directors have taken pride in having added women leaders to the world, announcing with sheer delight the names of girls elected to office in their colleges and of teachers who went on to be heads of other schools. We have seen the major influence the faculty members have had in creating and shaping curriculum, and the frequent return of alumnae who have spoken of their achievements at assemblies. Students have been at the head of activities beginning in Class I, and throughout their Winsor journey they have been continually inspired by their eager, feisty, risk-taking classmates and by strong, supportive, encouraging teachers. Advocates of girls' schools would suggest that few of these girls and women could have gained such leadership experience in a coeducational environment.

Student government became another opportunity for girls to participate in an activity that no doubt would have been dominated by boys in a coed school. From 1912 to 1917 Winsor became part of a trend that would become a familiar aspect of school life for nearly anyone attending any school in the country then as well as now. The idea of student self-government grew out of the progressive education movement, whose agenda was to remove the "dictatorial nature" of most schools of the time and replace it with community-based, shared principles of discipline and school behavior.

Around 1912 Mary Winsor first brought up the idea of using a "city government" metaphor to relate student citizenship to the citizenship of adult life. The population of the new School was double its previous size, and the larger building meant more spaces to supervise, some—mainly the hallways and the library—requiring a fresh approach. Girls had also changed in the period from 1886 to 1912, "from young ladies to girls,"[33] as one writer puts it, having more fun with sports and drama, looking for a role in the world as they anticipated a future life that would be quite different from that in the Victorian sphere of their mothers.

Mary Winsor's earliest student government plan in 1912 was a modification of a newly popular educational idea at the time: that the school could be set up with a "government" like a city; that students would monitor and discipline (and punish) themselves; and that the natural desire to want to maintain order and not be shown to be a "bad" person would keep everyone in line. In the next five years there were occasional problems with the system. An editorial in the 1913–14 *Scrapbook* points out that some of the girls and even teachers had, "from thoughtlessness, disregarded rules in a way which has caused a good deal of unnecessary disturbance." But the girls had learned "that the responsibility for good government must rest on the community at large and not upon a small body of rulers."[34]

In 1917 Mary Winsor proposed a more ambitious plan for self-government—the School City. She did not originate the concept; educational gatherings and school leaders throughout the country had discussed and experimented with it, and many schools, including several public schools in Philadelphia, had adopted it.[35]

A committee of students and teachers began to study the plan and consider its value for Winsor. They wrote an elaborate charter and presented it to the student body for ratification in May 1918. That spring the Upper School students and faculty elected the first "mayor" for the next academic year. The mayor's council would include representatives from each of the ten "wards," (that is, one for each class, plus Ward IX for postgraduate students and Ward X for the faculty). Everyone in the community was to be a citizen who would be ready and willing to take on an elected or appointed position in one of the three branches—executive, legislative, and judicial—and to obey and uphold the laws. The Director, called "the State," appointed the chief justice.

A police badge from the School City government days, ca. 1938.

In the first year there were over 95 city government positions: the chief of police and her officers had power of arrest, although they could only warn teachers; the Health Department oversaw the tidiness of desks and lockers; the fire chief (a faculty member) supervised fire drills and got to wear a special helmet. Certain other officers wore badges. Each student and teacher was to pay a ten-cent tax yearly to help pay for those badges and for stationery supplies.

Arrestable offenses included making noise in the hallways, loitering, especially outside the library, linking arms, running, and eating anywhere outside the lunchroom. Halls were policed and girls could be cited for "not going to the right on stairs, not keeping single file on the study stairs, and not going to the right of the spot." (At the turning points of the hallways large black spots had been painted to remind girls to stay on the right side of the hall at corners; faint remnants of the dark circles can still be seen in one or two places.) Jumping out of windows unless ordered to do so was also forbidden.

The School City was intended as a way to unite the School through the idea of joint ownership of school life. It was a system that could be modified in many different ways if necessary, and it gave the girls practice in working collaboratively and tackling sometimes sticky disagreements. The yearly elections gave a shape to the year in that girls could anticipate which office or duty they might like to try for in the future. The classes vied with each other to have the fewest misdemeanors each week, and those results were published in the *Lamp*.

There was broad support for the School City. A faculty member pointed out that students were getting good training for a future in which women would be taking on more serious responsibilities: the amendment granting women the right to vote was close to ratification. President Woodrow Wilson began to support the amendment, and it was making its way through Congress, about to be sent to the states for their individual ratification. There is some irony in the fact that in 1918, when the School City started at Winsor, American women were still not able to vote, hold office, serve on juries, or speak in public meetings. In the December 1918 *Lamp*, Eleanor Dodge 1920 reminded her classmates that they were receiving training in civics, in the forms and methods of government, in how to conduct meetings, in how to speak in meetings—all skills that would be "of infinite value" when they left school. She did not, however, mention the imminence of women's voting.

As has been noted, there is scant reference in Winsor archival material to the passage of the Women's Right to Vote Amendment in 1920. Names of Winsor parents can be found on the membership lists of both prosuffrage and antisuffrage organizations in Boston, suggesting either that suffrage was perhaps too "loaded" a topic for the community or that the upper-class population at The Winsor School was satisfied with the status quo. The divide was echoed in the second half of the twentieth century when stay-at-home mothers often squared off against mothers with jobs. The fervor of the national movement had waned since the days of the early suffragists, and upper-class women had always been wary of the changes "getting the vote" would bring to their protected lives.

The Nineteenth Amendment became law in 1920, but its constitutionality was challenged in the courts until 1922, when Justice Louis D. Brandeis, the father of two Winsor graduates, Susan 1911 and Elizabeth 1914, read the Supreme Court's unanimous decision declaring women's suffrage to be constitutional. After earning a B.A. at Bryn Mawr and an LL.B from the University of Chicago, Susan Brandeis was admitted to the New York Bar in 1921. She never forgot that she was unable to find a job at a law firm because she was a woman.[36] Elizabeth Brandeis received her B.A. from Radcliffe and, following her father's example, involved herself in labor legislation, playing a major role supporting laws protecting women and minors.[37] Women were becoming more highly educated by schools like Winsor and going on to college as well as to graduate schools; they were also following their mothers into critical social action movements where not having the vote was irrelevant.

The School City plan of student government lasted for thirty-eight years; the last mayor was elected in 1955. The following April (after March blizzards that had "unbelievably" closed the School for two days)* Valeria Knapp called it "amazing that a charter granted to students in the days when there were few if any extracurricular activities could continue to function adequately as more and more demands were made on students' time."[38] A group of teachers, juniors, and seniors who met that spring to consider renovations to the School City government concluded that the School should start afresh "to evolve the best possible government," avoiding the complications that had made the old system cumbersome and in some ways unworkable.

The committee members decided to build on the homeroom committees that had become larger over the years. They first presented their new, simpler plan to Class VII, since these girls would be the leaders the following year in any new plan that was adopted. The juniors were enthusiastic, and a reso-

---

* The second blizzard delayed the College Board exams for a week, and, amazingly, a third storm made that date difficult also, but the exams were given nonetheless.

lution was passed asking the Director to suspend the existing School City charter so that an experimental plan could be tried.

The plan mandated a Student Council for each division; these separate Lower School and Upper School councils would meet together "on stated occasions," but for the most part each would function separately and have separate elections in which the top two vote getters would serve as president and vice president. The senior class president, the homeroom leaders, and representatives from each class would be the voting members of the Student Council, but student heads of the Athletic Association, the glee clubs, the science, drama, and debating clubs, and the editor of the *Lamp* would be present as nonvoting members. Valeria Knapp was quite pleased: "The planning committee has really succeeded in simplifying the government, for instead of having the three branches of the present government, the legislative, executive, and judicial, there will be only one sturdy trunk, the Council, supported by the home room committees, who represent the life-giving roots of the tree."[39] The ongoing issues that Valeria Knapp identified as the "two knotty problems," neatness and noise, could now be approached without having to "arrest" and "try" miscreants in the "court system."

The student council model lasted until the early 1970s, when a town meeting–type of government was briefly adopted. One buzzword of that era was "communication," which the open-meeting format allowed and encouraged, but which came at the expense of the efficiency the old student council method provided. Perhaps every age has its own period of astonishing change that outstrips the changes of other eras, but the period of the late 1960s and 1970s brought significant changes in so many areas that it is worth reminding ourselves of the unsettling events of those years: the divisive war in Vietnam, freedom marches on behalf of minorities, assassinations, travel to the moon, the desegregation of schools, the trend away from single-sex schools, campus riots, and young people's distrust of "old people." Everyone demanded a voice, and consensus was difficult to reach. Winsor made changes as judiciously as possible.

Winsor made many changes during those years: a system was put in place to allow juniors and seniors to leave the campus to do volunteer work, a new faculty-student advisory system began, and the dress code was revised. "After due deliberation and, I fear, to the consternation of a few of you, we have a dress code which allows for trousers although I am still unwilling to include blue jeans in the options for school attire."[40] In response to a student petition, Virginia Wing's successor, Carolyn Peter, thrilled the student body when she announced in an assembly in 1989 that from then on the girls could wear blue jeans, as could the faculty. The stage curtains were drawn open, revealing nearly all the faculty members posing onstage in their blue jeans.*

---

* Hard as it is to believe, 1972 was also the first year women were allowed to run in the Boston Marathon.

Students, invited to serve on ad hoc committees with teachers, were given a greater voice in determining which issues were the most crucial.[41] Along with the town meeting government, Upper School classes elected an Administrative Committee to meet with various adult committees.

In the fall of 1973, a student-faculty committee began to work on yet another revision to the student government procedures at the School. The result was a plan that on the surface looked much like the student council model described above. The innovations were not groundbreaking per se, but they were creative. The leadership group was to be called the "Collect," meaning "a gathering or bringing together."* The members of the community governed by Collect would include not just the students, but also the faculty and administration, to signal that Collect would be a *community* council rather than a *student* council. In addition to student representatives elected by each class, representatives from the "activity groups such as athletic, performing, and publications" were to join the group, and—most novel of all—the faculty would elect three teachers as voting members of Collect. The entire faculty would vote in the yearly elections for a chairperson.

A special newsletter from June 1974 announced that the new constitution for Collect had been approved and the first chairperson elected: "Perhaps the most interesting development so far is that the first 'CP' (Chairperson) is Mrs. Judith Wortham [Robbins], a member of the faculty, elected by a majority of students and teachers in a preferential ballot. . . . The result of the election may perhaps be taken as a hopeful sign of a new community spirit and the elimination of barriers that may have existed among the various groups comprising the Winsor School Community."[42] The same newsletter described two other innovations that reflected the outcome of discussions between adults and students, the still rather new program of joint activities between Winsor and the Belmont Hill School, referred to as "Coordination," and the Jan Term inter-semester program.

Winsor students graduated with some untraditional leadership skills acquired through nonacademic aspects of the curriculum. The importance and value of extracurricular activities has led to some schools' using the term *co-curricular* to signal that activities outside the classroom are not frills but complement the academic offerings. Through them students have a chance to develop interpersonal and leadership skills and to learn through actual experience that communal projects require a communal effort. They learn that a fruitful outcome often depends on an ability to subordinate one's personal needs to those of the group and that each person's part, however small or large, is necessary. Perhaps nothing illustrates these realities of group work better than putting on a play.

A drama production is an ideal cooperative experience in which a group

---

* Pronounced with the accent on the first syllable, this use of the somewhat archaic noun appears to be unique to Winsor and has survived for more than thirty-five years.

works toward the tangible goal of a public presentation. At Winsor from the very earliest years, a variety of dramatic presentations both large and small encouraged even a very shy girl to take a part. The inclusivity of a drama project allowed students to risk trying something new with the encouragement of their teachers and friends, and all could realize that classmates had differing but unique abilities. Drama also can be appropriately adapted for any age group: at Winsor it could be as small as a skit for a banquet or as large as the medieval pageant that had every student (as well as most teachers) in some sort of costumed role. Yearly drama traditions gave a shape to the school year—the Class I musical in the spring, the Class IV Shakespeare Play in midyear, the Dramatic Club's annual winter play, and the senior play or musical in the spring. There were also little scenes written within a class—a dramatization of an event in history or a French dialogue or a spontaneous skit, sometimes even by the teachers.

These miniature enactments were sometimes done for just the Upper or the Lower School, but often the entire School shared the experience. The *Lamp* writers noted and critiqued nearly every drama presented in Monday or Wednesday morning assemblies, reminded of when they had given their own musical or Shakespeare production. It did not happen every year, but another dramatic high point for the students was a faculty skit.* In the earlier years the faculty performed (usually every other year) for the juniors and seniors only, but the Jan Term skit in the 1970s was always a series of school-related scenes with original lyrics written by the faculty. After carefully arranged secret practice sessions and much quick memorizing on the part of the singers, the playlet was presented at the Jan Term Banquet.

That the girls had to play all parts, male and female, was an unexpected bonus of being in a single-sex school: for a brief while, a girl could act and talk and dress like a man by taking a role that she would probably not have been allowed to play in the real world theater. This continued until the 1970s, when as part of the new Coordination Program Winsor joined with the all-boys Belmont Hill School for dramatic productions and a joint newspaper, the *Panel*.† Some of the classics of dramatic literature were mainstays of the drama program: *Arms and the Man, The Enchanted April, She Stoops to Conquer, You Can't Take It with You, Pride and Prejudice,* and *The Playboy of the Western World*. In the spring the production was more often a musical, and as that tradition became established, Winsor often produced a joint Winsor–Roxbury Latin collaboration.

The medieval mystery play *Herod; or, The Adoration of the Magi* was pre-

---

* "Flow Gently, Muddy River," "How Do You Solve a Problem of a Dress Code?" and "Why Can't the Students Be More Like Us?" were performed in faculty skits in the late 1980s.

† The first coordinated edition of the *Panel* appeared in September 1973. Until 1979, when Elizabeth Harding 1982 became a coeditor, the editor in chief was always a Belmont Hill senior.

The medieval pageant was presented in 1928 and 1929 in the assembly hall and then moved to the larger venue of the upper gym, as seen here in 1940.

sented for the first time in 1928. This "somewhat unusual and thrilling undertaking"[43] came about when Sylvia Lee, a Winsor Latin teacher, discovered the twelfth-century Latin text and music for the play in Harvard's Widener Library.* Research revealed its source to be the monastery church of Saint-Benoît-sur-Loire, near Fleury, France. The Latin of the dialogue was not complex, and the hymns incorporated throughout the drama, though written on the original four-line staff, were in some cases traditional unison chants still in use in the Catholic liturgy. It would be an opportunity to engage the entire School in an interdisciplinary project involving Latin, drama, art, music, and history. The December 1928 and 1929 productions were held in the assembly hall, and the 1940 performance took place in the elaborately decorated gymnasium. All the walls and windows were transformed by student-made drapings, columns, and background sets to suggest the interior of a Romanesque cathedral.

One can only marvel at what a huge undertaking this must have been for the faculty as well as for the maintenance and support staff. The bulk of the

* Sylvia Lee taught Latin and Greek at Winsor for thirty-one years, 1909 to 1940.

preparation fell on the teachers of fine arts—drama, art, music, orchestra, and dancing—but because of the broader educational goals of the pageant, teachers of history, Latin, and French created materials for educating everyone about the background of the French mystery play. The "impresario" who directed the entire production was Florence Cunningham.[44] Sylvia Lee worked with the musicologist Richard G. Appel at the Boston Public Library to transcribe the ancient music to a five-line staff. The elegant hand-colored sketches of medieval clothing reflect the intense research by David Park, an art teacher who for the 1940 performance painstakingly traced illustrations and annotated information from hard-to-find encyclopedias and scholarly works about the Middle Ages.

Teachers and students working together created scenery and props, and both students and teachers made their own costumes. The Winsor Archives contain evidence of the extensive research done to reproduce as many authentic details as possible: the colors of the costumes (some actual swatches remain), the exact style of medieval French cathedral architecture, impressive props such as the huge choir book (visible in photographs), monastery chimes or bells, the benches and cushions, the swords and shields, and even, apparently, incense.

Boys on the Winsor stage? No, eighth-graders dressed as shipwrecked sailors in the 2004 production of The Tempest.

The director of the 1947 production was Rose Dresser [1947 to 1973], who found herself directing a revival of the pageant during her very first year at Winsor. The story goes that Frances Dugan asked Rose Dresser to "find out which member of the faculty is wearing that appalling perfume." The incense was not used in this production.[45] Another oft-repeated story was that Valeria Knapp, costumed as a nun for the pageant, attracted much attention when she went out to help direct traffic outside the School.

The pageant was presented four times, but by 1948 it had run its course. It had provided an outstanding example of a collaborative, cross-disciplinary, and communal undertaking, but the experience for participants was uneven. A more successful (from the standpoint of involvement) enterprise was the Class IV Shakespeare Play, in which every girl had a part in one of the two performances and was on a production committee as well. There had been Shakespeare at Winsor before it became an eighth-grade project, and the Upper School Drama Club presented scenes as well as complete plays from time to time.

The tradition of the Class IV play began in May 1931 with *Twelfth Night*. The following year Class IV presented *The Tempest,* which, like all the plays, had to be abridged to fit into the assembly period. Florence Cunningham's quite wonderful notebook on *The Tempest* contains an annotated list of each student's part in the play and her technical assignment. It also shows exactly how and where she cut the play without eliminating plot essentials. The 1932 Graduation Issue of the *Lamp* contains a brief review of the play: "On May 4th Class IV gave us a delightful entertainment in the form of 'The Tempest,' which although it was cut down to fifty minutes, was beautifully done and hung together very well." After the plot summary, the writer continued: "One scene especially delighted the audience, that of Caliban, the drunken sailor (Jane Clark) and the jester (Olivia Russell). In fact we felt that just the right scenes had been chosen to produce the very best results. In fifty minutes we beheld the result of many hours of efficient organization."[46]

The tradition of the Shakespeare Play has been maintained even as the growth of the student body has made the casting much more difficult. Its survival reflects the strength of several Winsor values: interdisciplinary cooperation, communal effort within the class, and a response to the students' love of playacting.

Class I established early the tradition of giving a "singing play" in the spring, and for many years it was *At the End of the Rainbow,* written by Berta Elsmith, a music teacher from 1916 to 1921.* Stories such as *Rumpelstiltskin* and *Cinderella* were standbys, but in 1962 Class I staged *The Mikado,* and for the next ten years their musical was almost always a somewhat modified

* Berta Elsmith also wrote other "song plays," including *Rumpelstiltskin* and *Jeanette-Isabella*, and adapted others (Humperdinck's *Hansel and Gretel* and Bach chorales, for example).

The cast of the 1984 production of H.M.S. Pinafore *performed by Class I, the Class of 1991.*

Gilbert and Sullivan operetta. Everyone loved to act! From time to time Class V gave their own productions, and Class III divided into thirds for smaller productions so each girl could have a speaking part in the year before she got her role in the Shakespeare Play. Under the energetic guidance of teachers and parent volunteers, the students themselves built sets and made costumes; they learned to do makeup, publicity, lights, and ropes; they served as stage managers, business managers, and ushers, and they designed and printed their own advertising posters, tickets, and programs. And afterward, all participated in the bittersweet "striking of the set," during which all sets, props, and costumes had to be taken apart and stored.

The positive learning experiences of dramatic productions, athletic games, and student government are invaluable. Studies show that when schools omit art and music from the curriculum, academic achievement is adversely affected. The enhanced skills that Winsor girls received from participating in the newspaper, the literary magazine, the Science Club, the Glee Club, the Dance Club—in fact every club—rounded out their Winsor education in ways difficult to calculate. By the late 1990s, the same spirit that lay behind Mary Winsor's original Current Events Club was evident in student-initiated clubs such as Amnesty International, Women's Issues Club, Human Relations Forum, A.L.A.I. (African, Latina, Asian, Indian), GBSA (Gay, Bisexual, Straight Alliance), Debating, and Model United Nations. In 2010 The Winsor School Mock Trial team became the first girls' school team to win the state championship—a significant achievement for a club started by the students themselves only six years before.

~ GENEROUS-MINDED WOMEN ~

At the end of her Winsor years, every graduate automatically becomes a member of the School's largest club, the Winsor Alumnae Association. (The girls may well have inherited the "committee gene" from their female elders.) Through its publications and meetings Winsor women have maintained contact with their classmates as well as with the ongoing life of the School. From its earliest days as Miss Winsor's School in the Back Bay, the School has benefited from alumnae who have returned to share their life experiences with the student body or lead a fund-raising effort or serve on the Corporation or Board of Trustees. This continuous involvement of former students, parents, and teachers has expanded the sense of what a community can be when alumnae return to tell the students about their activities in the city, the nation, and the world. As each speaker takes the podium on the Winsor stage, she invariably remarks that she has a vivid recollection of her school-girl self in the audience at such events and notes the odd thrill of now being on the stage. When she entertains questions at the end of her talk, she gains a perspective on the sophistication of the current Winsor student, something that consistently impresses non-alumnae speakers.

Highlighting some of those Winsor graduates who returned to address the School on Graduates' Days provides a cross section of successful and creative alumnae from the earliest days.* A chronological overview paints a picture of a female population stretching further and deeper into all professions and taking a leadership role at a surprisingly early time.

Theresa Helburn 1903 had gone to Bryn Mawr after graduating from Winsor; there she proved her passion for theater. The Jewish Women's Archive says, "She graduated in 1908 with many senior prizes, having organized, directed, and acted in all the school plays."[47] Her broad interest in drama led her to help found the Theatre Guild in New York City in 1918.

Emily Storer 1905 worked initially at Boston's first settlement house, the Ellis Memorial Settlement in downtown Boston,[48] and later at the Pine Mountain School in Appalachia, where "she found a people who knew little more of civilization than they did 100 years ago."[49]

Other early alumnae achieved distinction by stretching themselves at a time when women still could not vote and were discouraged from speaking in public (that is, where men were present). Martha May Eliot 1909 majored in classical literature at Radcliffe while simultaneously taking pre-med courses. Since Harvard Medical School did not accept women until 1945, she

---

* There have been thousands of alumnae, and not all can be mentioned; the naming of some who came back to speak provides a framework for this chapter, but their stories cannot all be told in detail.

went to Johns Hopkins and received her M.D. with honors in 1918.* She and her sister, Abigail Adams Eliot 1910 (whose nursery school was described in chapter 6) were the daughters of Christopher Rhodes Eliot, the Unitarian minister and social worker at Bulfinch Place Church, a mission church of the Benevolent Fraternity in Boston's West End.†

Carina Hanks Michelson 1910 was a labor organizer and manager of sit-down strikes in the "ten-cent" stores of New York City. Mary Coolidge Winsor 1910 taught philosophy at Vassar. A number of graduates were attracted to nursing and to volunteering in hospitals. Margaret Vickery 1906 graduated from the Boston School of Social Work in 1911, taught at the Calhoun School from 1916 to 1918, afterward taking her bachelor's degree in nursing and teaching at the School of Nursing of the Children's Hospital. Dorothy Hale 1905, Sylvia Bowditch 1929, and Dorothea Newman 1929 all joined the Frontier Nursing Service in the Appalachian Mountains of Kentucky.

The large assembly hall in the new building made formal assemblies of the whole student body more feasible, and weekly gatherings often featured returning graduates. Some of the first speakers had participated in the war effort. World War I had been a turning point for women in the United States, and their usefulness both at home and abroad created momentum for the final passage of the Women's Suffrage Amendment in 1920. Both students and alumnae were deeply involved in the war effort, and the *Lamp* printed stories and editorials about the war as well as long letters (often anonymous) from graduates assisting the war effort abroad. In January 1916 Helen Homans 1902 gave "a thrilling account of her experiences as a nurse in France." The month before, on Graduates' Day, the students had heard about a new Boston school for social workers from Margaret Curtis 1901, and Rosamund Eliot 1913, a Radcliffe student at the time, told them of the importance of college. In the following years they heard from Elizabeth Grey 1905, a member of the Red Cross, Mabel Harte 1915, who was working on infantile paralysis at Children's Hospital, and Julia Lyman 1917, at Massachusetts General Hospital in the X-ray Department. In 1924 Frances Webster 1912 "spoke about her visit to the League of Nations in Geneva, which had made her enthusiastic for the participation of the U.S."

---

* From the early 1920s to 1935, she served in various positions in the pediatric department of Yale Medical School. From 1924 to 1934 she also served as director of the Division of Child and Maternal Health of the federal Children's Bureau. From 1934 to 1949 she was the Children's Bureau's assistant chief. She then served for two years as the assistant director general of the World Health Organization in Geneva. On her return to the United States, she was appointed chief of the Children's Bureau, a position she held until 1957, when she accepted a professorship in child and maternal health at the Harvard School of Public Health. She retired in 1960. American Public Health Association, "Martha May Eliot Biography," www.apha.org/membergroups/sections/aphasections/mch/benefits/mmebio.htm.

† Their brother, Frederick May Eliot, was a liberal minister who served as president of the American Unitarian Association from 1937 to 1958; their great-great-grandfather was Louisa May Alcott's maternal grandfather, and T. S. Eliot was a cousin.

Caroline Farrar Ware 1916 began her distinguished career as a cultural historian early, receiving a $10,000 prize for her doctoral dissertation, "The Industrial Revolution in the New England Cotton Industry," which was later published as *The Early New England Cotton Manufacture: A Study in Industrial Beginnings.* Among her other important works are *Greenwich Village, 1920–1930: A Comment on American Civilization in the Post-War Years* and *Pauli Murray and Caroline Ware: Forty Years of Letters in Black and White;* they represent Ware's thesis that historians should be open to cultural influences in history when studying patterns of social growth and change. She eventually worked for the government in the newly important area of consumer protection.

These women were just the beginning of a long procession of Winsor alumnae who brought their stories to the Winsor podium: Sarah Merry Gamble 1916, an international advocate for birth control early in the 1920s; Helenka

"One year we had sewing. We made enormous white smocks that completely covered our clothes and white caps, which restrained our hair. We wore these outfits the following year when we had cooking. During our lesson on bread making, I forgot to put the yeast in mine. Peggy, our lively classmate, used my dough as a football. What fun we had. Alas, the cooking teacher returned just as Peggy threw the dough to the ceiling, where it stuck. I got a 'zero' that day" (Katharine Fowler-Billings 1921 in her book Stepping-Stones: The Reminiscences of a Woman Geologist in the Twentieth Century, *1996).*

Adamowska Pantaleoni 1917, who established the fund for UNICEF in this country; and Katherine Woodward Holmes 1917, a pioneer in pediatric psychiatry. These women had graduated before they were allowed to vote, and the mere listing of their contributions to society does not reveal the struggles they faced as women seeking to do more than their predecessors had done.

The geologist Katharine Fowler-Billings 1921 told the girls that when she was not allowed to accompany her geologist husband on an exploration in Africa, she applied for her own independent project and did the earliest exploration for iron ore deposits in Sierra Leone in 1933. Her fascinating book about the adventure is *The Gold Missus: A Woman Prospector in Sierra Leone.*

Elizabeth Bradley Janeway 1927, a social worker, accompanied her husband, Dr. Charles Janeway, in his world travels to spread information about pediatric practice; she spoke to the student body on UNICEF in Africa. Her classmate Cornelia Balch Wheeler 1927 was a six-term Cambridge city councilor who was tirelessly devoted to civic projects, including an investigation in 1965 into the refusal by Harvard to allow a female to be class marshal.

In the 1930s graduate speakers provided perspective on national and international issues as well as on art history. The girls heard from Alice Shurcliff 1933, a labor economist with the United States government, who eventually became involved in research at the Energy Laboratory at MIT.[50] Priscilla Sprague Krancer 1938 came to speak about the United Nations Relief and Rehabilitation Administration. The reviewer in the *Lamp* felt she underestimated her audience: "It was interesting to note that Mrs. Krancer approached us on this last point as if we'd never thought about it before. She just doesn't know about the Student Federalists." But the comment on the speech by the banker Anita Sturgis 1916 expressed appreciation for the "privilege of hearing a graduate of Winsor speak on her chosen profession." Eleanor Sayre 1934, an authority on the prints of Francisco Goya and one of the first female curators at the Museum of Fine Arts, Boston, was an expert on the art scene.

In the years following World War II the returning speakers continued to reflect a wide variety of adult experiences. Lydia Weston Kesich 1946, a professor of Russian at Vassar College, spoke to the girls on Russian literature and read excerpts from Tolstoy. She told of getting hooked on the works of Tolstoy and Dostoevsky when she was still a student at Winsor and eventually earning her doctorate from Columbia University. Edith Arnold Sisson 1947 charmed her listeners more than once, speaking from her perspective as an educator, naturalist, author, and farmer. Her interests led to her writing *Nature with Children of All Ages* and *Animals in the Family: Tales of Our Household Menagerie.*

Betsy Wakefield Doermann 1949 spoke on her experience at the Harvard-Radcliffe Program in Business Administration, a management training course for Radcliffe women at a time when the Harvard Business School admitted men only. The program grew to include courses taught by Business School professors, but women were not admitted to the men's MBA program until 1962.[51]

Alumnae speakers consistently inspired their Winsor audiences with a wide range of career possibilities—in academics, the arts, social action, science, medicine, and politics. Marion Dusser de Barenne Kilson 1954, a professor of sociology at Simmons College, had done extensive anthropological research in West Africa and authored several papers, such as "West African Society and the Atlantic Slave Trade, 1441–1865."[52] Moira Wylie 1956, an actress then appearing onstage in Boston in *A Man for All Seasons*, spoke on women in Shakespeare. The Science Club presented a panel of graduates in 1960 that included Constance Gibbs Oliver 1949, a physiotherapist who worked at Boston's Children's Hospital, Rosamund Wheeler Thorp 1953, a nurse and health-care administrator, and Daphne Stillman Holmquist 1954, who began her scientific research career working on cancer tumors and immunology. Clara Mack Wainwright 1955, a Boston-based fabric artist, was the founder of Boston's First Night celebration. Olivia Hood Parker 1959 had not expected to become an artist of any kind, but she became a respected photographer whose work has been acquired by Boston's Museum of Fine Arts, the Art Institute of Chicago, and Museum of Modern Art. She has said that her creativity was nurtured at Winsor, especially by her science teacher Helen Hamilton.

When Virginia Wing retired in 1988, a lectureship in her name was established by Bradford Washburn, the father of a former student, with the aim of attracting the most extraordinary people "on the cutting edge" of their fields to speak at assembly programs.

Laurie H. Glimcher, M.D., 1968 spoke in 2007. She is the Irene Heinz Given Professor of Immunology at the Harvard School of Public Health and professor of medicine at Harvard Medical School. She heads the Immunology Program at Harvard Medical School and the Division of Biological Sciences program at the Harvard School of Public Health.

Adrienne Torf 1973 spoke in 2001. A composer and keyboard artist, she released *Brooklyn from the Roof,* her first solo album of original music for piano and synthesizers in 1986. The *Boston Globe* selected it as one of the year's ten best albums, stating "*Brooklyn From The Roof* is a gem of an album. . . . [It] shows [Torf] to be a commanding talent, by turns romantic, introspective and witty."

Anne Manson 1979 gave the Virginia Wing Lecture in 2006. She is one of only three women to have been appointed music director of a leading American symphony orchestra, having served in that capacity for the Kansas City Symphony from 1999 to 2003.

Kristin Bennett 1985, a nationally recognized expert in materials sciences and a leader in nanotechnology, earned her B.S. from Trinity College in mechanical engineering and her Ph.D. from the University of California at Berkeley in geology.

Elizabeth Samet 1987 was the Virginia Wing Lecturer in the fall of 2008. She spoke of her experience as a professor of English at the West Point Military Academy. Her acclaimed book *Soldier's Heart: Reading Literature through Peace and War at West Point* connects her Winsor education in English literature and writing to her career in teaching future soldiers.

Kerilynn Crockett 1991 founded and directed MY TOWN (Multicultural Youth Tour Of What's Now) to provide youth-led walking tours of the South End, hoping to "add their family and neighborhood stories to their larger understanding of the city's growth and change."

The most recent alumna to be a guest for the Virginia Wing Lectureship was Kristine Guleserian, M.D., 1986, a pediatric cardiothoracic surgeon, who asked that every student be given a walnut as she entered the assembly hall for her address. Her listeners learned that the heart of a newborn baby is the size of a walnut. "Your education never ends," she said. "I learn every day I go to work."

The challenge for educators in all eras has been to prepare young people for a future that cannot be anticipated; for female students in the last century, this has been particularly difficult since the possibilities for women have widened so unexpectedly—indeed, even men are finding themselves in jobs that did not exist at all when they were in school. Winsor was able to present the increasing career options in the wider world by inviting back alumnae whose unpredicted paths could inspire younger women.

There is always a featured speaker—though not an alumna—at the final assembly of the year, Graduation Day. Originally called simply Last Day (which can have an ominous sound unless you are a student or a teacher), the name soon changed but it has remained, essentially, an all-School assembly with invited guests. The day's rituals go back to the beginnings of the School, preserving practically intact most of the elements of the original Last Days. It progresses as all assemblies do: all students and teachers are present, the students enter in the order of their classes (from youngest to oldest), two by two, the entire school sings together, and a program of readings and speeches follows. The songs at graduation are traditional, but the readings are chosen by Class VIII, as are the main speaker and the senior valedictory speaker.* Afterward there is a small feast, cookies and punch on the lawn, just as recess has followed all assemblies through the year. There are small additions or subtractions from time to time. The singing of "The Lamp of Learning" and "Jerusalem" has become a permanent tradition, and Carolyn Peter added the

---

* The senior speaker is selected not by class rank but for her speaking prowess. Winsor has persistently avoided the practice of ranking students.

hymn "Lift Every Voice and Sing" in 1998. When the gymnasium was being renovated in 1992–93, she initiated the practice of holding Graduation in a huge tent in the courtyard, in response to the seniors' plea that the ceremony be held on campus.

Cherished traditions help secure the community in its past, and when they are threatened the citizens sometimes revolt. As Alfred North Whitehead said, "The art of progress is to preserve order amid change and to preserve change amid order." The perennial challenge for a school is to change judiciously and to maintain a consistent identity. A community must anticipate the consequences of a change and continually pay heed to the essential character of an institution. The very fact of having traditions is part of a school's strength, and Winsor girls through the years have enjoyed observing the old rituals and adding new ones.

An overview of Winsor School traditions will serve as a retrospective on the past customs and time-honored events that keep the community anchored in its history. Many of them have already been described: the Shakespeare Play, the Class I musical play, the Summer Experience Assemblies, the *Lamp* and yearbook, and Graduates' Days. There are the continuing academic traditions of poetry reading, the Hemenway Prize speeches, Prize (or Awards) Day,* the annual anxiety of taking some sort of standardized tests, and the rite of passage known as Expos. These traditions are both ceremonial and academic; some annual occurrences are such a natural part of the year that one may be unaware of their longevity. There is record of one of the Scholar's Day assemblies in the ballroom at 96 Beacon Street in the 1906 *Scrapbook*. "Miss Winsor rings her bell and we all read the psalm, our voices go way, way down and give the effect almost of men's voices."[53] Since then that original bell has become part of opening day assembly.

In 1910 the record books began to list—in detail—every single occasion and the students, teachers, alumnae, or distinguished guests who participated. One interesting fact from the past stands out: certain girls were chosen to read their Long Themes aloud to the School, and, according to the reports, their classmates enjoyed them. Assemblies perpetuated many traditions in addition to the Summer Experience talks: the annual winter and spring concerts by all the various musical groups, the plays by individual classes, and student government days, when officers addressed the School or announced the next year's candidates.

There are also tangible reminders, such as the antique brass lamp, the Class VI banner, the ring, the clock on the cupola (gift of the Class of 1915), and newer symbols like the wildcat mascot and the "Under the Lights" shirt-design contest.

The handmade lamp was a gift of the Class of 1910, the last class to gradu-

---

* Some early graduation programs were so long that an intermission was necessary.

ate from Miss Winsor's on Beacon Street. It symbolized the "light of knowledge" shining in Miss Winsor's Back Bay School and then moving to the Riverway. More than anything else, it connects the incorporated School to its simple origins. Along with the lamp came a red and white banner inscribed with "Lux Veritatis," a motto that was regularly printed at the beginning of each issue of the *Lamp*. A photograph taken after the senior play shows Valeria Knapp, future Director of the School, and Harriet Amory 1916 holding the lamp, the banner, and a large white shield.*

At Miss Winsor's School in 1904 one of the girls had designed a school pin. "The shield represents courage and strength and truth, the white enamel signifies all that is clean and pure, while most prominent is the [gold] *Lamp* of learning; the other qualities are in the background, but without them the lamp would be useless." The pin is an example of a tradition that did not survive.

In their senior play, Lux Veritatis, *written by Sarah Bradley 1916, Valeria Knapp 1916 (right) and Harriet Amory 1916 hold the banner that was brought from Miss Winsor's School to the new School in 1910.*

Each spring the community sees the hand-sewn banners that each sophomore class has made and presented to the senior class. The banner ceremony during the last week of school changes slightly as successive classes add their special touch. The banner always has a theme, which in a creative way honors the seniors. A selection of the banners since 1931 is displayed at each reunion. Two other celebratory events for the seniors—banquets given in the spring by Classes V and VII—have occurred for decades. By the time Graduation Day comes, the senior class is thoroughly bonded.

The senior class rings are presented during the Class VII spring by an individual senior to an individual junior—an event whose time and place are always a surprise to the eager recipients. In 1926, when the idea of a class

* Sarah Bradley 1916 wrote that year's original play, *Lux Veritatis.*

ring was first being discussed in what were apparently heated homeroom debates, the *Lamp* editorialized: "Doesn't it seem a trifle lacking in that elusive quality defined as 'school spirit' not to want a school ring, as an eternal, lasting bond between ourselves and all other classes of Winsor, those that have gone before and those that will come after?"[54] By the end of that academic year, the class heard the final report about the ring: "The Committee went to Arts and Crafts to get an individual ring, and finally chose a plain gold one, with a W in the center. The school is to discuss the ring and vote as to whether we are to keep it."[55] The discussion must have led to the design we know today, a small engraved lamp replaced the W.

Some traditions have come and gone—students no longer do Indian clubs or Maypoles or marching drills, but Spirit Week leading up to the "Under the Lights" pep rally in October is the modern equivalent of those bygone sporting events. Nor does the entire School celebrate Mary Winsor's birthday on Halloween as it did for many years even after she retired. Another discontinued old practice: after the opening assembly on the first day of school, everyone went outside and cheered the new members of each class in turn. The animated and personal features of the old-fashioned rituals have not changed, however, and new celebrations are born from the same impulse to share, include, and connect.

In the seventy-fifth anniversary year, 1961, the traditional banner made by the sophomore class for the seniors used a butterfly image to symbolize the School's growth from its origins in 1886.

In 2010 a committee of teachers and trustees formulated a new mission statement: "Winsor prepares young women to pursue their aspirations and contribute to the world." The Winsor community—like that of any good school—is a reciprocal one, enriched by the varieties of age and experience. "We are all teachers," said Carolyn Peter. We are also all learners. The success of Winsor graduates comes from the intense joy of the life of the mind for learning what the world is and what it was and imagining what one can do to make it better

APPENDIX: BIOGRAPHIES OF THE DIRECTORS OF THE WINSOR SCHOOL

MARY PICKARD WINSOR, 1860–1950

Mary Pickard Winsor was born in Salem, Massachusetts, the second of seven children. Her father, Frederick, was a doctor; her mother, Ann Ware Winsor, was a teacher and head of her own small primary school. Mary grew up in Winchester and attended her mother's school and others like it. After one year at Smith College, at age nineteen she left to take over her mother's school in Winchester. While running that school for twenty boys and girls, she was asked to start a six-month school on Beacon Hill. By 1900 Miss Winsor's School had grown to a student body of 99; in 1908 it was over 200.

Mary Winsor became the first Director of The Winsor School on the Riverway, which opened in 1910 with 225 students. She continued her mission of providing for young women the highest academic preparation possible for whatever their futures might hold.

Mary Winsor was a vivid presence in the School, at once revered and somewhat intimidating. She had begun to lose her hearing as a young woman, and the loss became progressively worse over her lifetime, but nothing stood in the way of her complete involvement in the School. She was as devoted to her graduates as they were to her.

She retired in March 1922, turning the directorship over to Katharine Lord. "I do not like to go," she wrote to the Trustees. "My relation to the School has been so happy . . . that our parting will be hard." She died September 1, 1950, at her home in Newton.

KATHARINE LORD, 1880–1959

Katharine Lord, the second Director of The Winsor School, was born in Plymouth, Massachusetts, the oldest of six children. She was valedictorian of her class at Plymouth High School and, after attending the Baldwin School in Pennsylvania, received her A.B. in 1901 from Bryn Mawr College, where she had been president of the Student Association. She completed a year of graduate work at Radcliffe College.

Katharine Lord came to Winsor in 1914 as assistant director, having been a reader at Wellesley College and Bryn Mawr and a teacher at the Baldwin School and the Wheeler School in Providence, Rhode Island. She became the Director of The Winsor School in the winter of 1922. She initiated Winsor's participation in the Eight-Year Curriculum Experiment, the New Plan.

Katharine Lord served as president of the Head Mistresses Association of the East and of the Independent School Association of Boston. She received an honorary degree from Tufts College in 1939 in recognition of her work in upholding standards in secondary education.

She was an avid traveler all her life and often delighted Winsor audiences with illustrated talks about her exotic trips. She lived in Plymouth after her retirement in 1939, where she was active in the community. When she died in February 1959, Valeria Knapp said in tribute, "Miss Lord enjoyed life to the full. . . . I have never known any one more quick to appreciate the first rate and more firm in ruling out the second rate. . . . Education under Miss Lord's leadership was an exciting adventure as well as a responsible profession."

Frances Dorwin Dugan, 1891–1967

Frances Dorwin Dugan, the third Director of The Winsor School, was born in Decatur, Indiana, the oldest of four girls. She attended high school in Decatur and Ferry Hall in Lake Forest, Illinois, and graduated from Vassar College in 1912.

She came to Winsor in 1918 as an English teacher, becoming assistant director in 1922 and associate director in 1926. A gifted classroom teacher, she was involved in the Eight-Year Curriculum Experiment known as the New Plan at Winsor.

Frances Dugan assumed the role of Director in 1939 upon Katharine Lord's retirement. She placed a strong emphasis on building and retaining an excellent teaching staff. During her tenure the School increased from 269 to 302 students, and she sought to broaden the social and cultural base of the School.

She guided the School through the troubled years of World War II, preserving a feeling of normalcy and maintaining the physical plant. Mary Winsor said of her: "She is a born educator. . . . For her pupils she has such a rare gift of sympathy and understanding that her skill and energy are more than matched by her patience."

Upon her retirement in 1951 she returned to Decatur to live with her widowed mother. She continued to summer in Rockport, Massachusetts, where she shared a house in Folly Cove with her successor, Valeria Knapp. Frances Dugan died in Decatur in December 1967.

Valeria Addams Knapp, 1898–1984

Valeria Addams Knapp, the fourth Director of Winsor, the only alumna to hold that position, was born in Menomonie, Wisconsin. She entered Winsor in 1912 as a member of Class V and graduated in 1916. After Winsor she went to Vassar, graduating in 1920, Phi Beta Kappa and president of her class for life.

After graduate work at Columbia Teachers College, she returned to Winsor in 1922, teaching history and math and serving as Class I homeroom teacher and, eventually, as head of the Lower School. In 1937 she became the headmistress of Concord Academy, until she returned to Winsor in 1940 as associate director.

Valeria Knapp became the Director of Winsor in 1951. During her tenure she initiated or oversaw renovations and additions to the School, including the Franklin Dexter Wing, a reexamination of the curriculum, and a change in form of student government; she continued improvement of faculty and staff salaries, established the Annual Fund, and invited a foreign student's enrollment each year in the senior class.

She was active in a number of professional organizations and served as president of the Head Mistresses Association of the East and of the Independent School Association of Boston.

She retired in 1963 and continued to live at the College Club on Commonwealth Avenue, her home since 1925, of which she was the president. She shared a house in Rockport with her predecessor, Frances Dugan, where she could indulge her love of long-distance swimming.

After her death in 1984, her successor, Virginia Wing, called her a person who "used her superb mind to demonstrate daily that problems can be solved if you approach them with a sense of adventure and a conviction that change is possible."

Virginia Wing

Virginia Wing was born in Massachusetts but spent considerable time during her early years in Denver, Colorado, where she was a student at the Kent School. She earned her A.B. degree from Smith College in 1945 with a major in philosophy and a minor in English. She was the president of Student Government and of the Athletic Association.

Before coming to Winsor in 1952 as associate director and college advisor, she taught English at the Kent School and was associate director of Admission at Smith. She succeeded Valeria Knapp as Director of The Winsor School in 1963 and retired in 1988.

Virginia Wing's steady good sense guided the School through the turbulent 1960s and 1970s, providing wise leadership in several key events, especially the decision not to merge with the Noble and Greenough School in Dedham but to remain a girls' school in the city of Boston. Beyond Winsor, she took part in a number of educational organizations, serving as a member of the Smith Board of Counselors and president of the National Association of Principals of Schools for Girls and the Head Mistresses Association of the East.

Virginia Wing had the ability to clarify the School's needs in such a way that innovations could happen without the Winsor community's departing from the traditional values that had made it so strong. She endorsed senior projects and Jan Term; she encouraged the building of the science wing; she urged faculty input in curriculum change, and she reminded all constituencies of the fact that Winsor would not discriminate in its entrance policies and would need to increase scholarship funds in order to be more inclusive.

Virginia Wing always cared about the faculty. She had a gift for identifying wonderful teachers and fought for salary increases and benefits for them. "We must speak out about the worth of excellent teaching and of a school which cares about the growth of each individual," she told the Board in 1974.

In her retirement she has continued to serve as a trustee of many area schools and returns frequently to Winsor for special events.

Carolyn McClintock Peter

Carolyn McClintock Peter grew up in Columbus, Ohio, the second of three sisters. She earned her A.B. in English at Wellesley College and an M.A.T. from Brown University. At the time of her appointment as Winsor's sixth Director in 1988, she was an experienced English teacher and school leader who had worked primarily in girls' schools, including the Columbia School in Rochester, New York, and Lincoln School in Providence, Rhode Island. At the latter, in addition to teaching English, she served as head of the English Department and as head of the Upper School.

During her sixteen years at Winsor and after she retired, she served as a trustee of the National Association of Independent Schools and of the Association of Independent Schools of New England and of numerous independent schools, including Roxbury Latin School and Belmont Hill School. She was president of the Head Mistresses Association of the East, the fourth Director of Winsor to serve in that capacity. She became a founder and later chair of the Board of Trustees of Beacon Academy.

Carolyn Peter was committed to issues of difference and diversity, and she fostered many initiatives to confront racism and classism throughout the School. She was also committed to Winsor's historic excellence and worked closely with colleagues to maintain and strengthen the School's curriculum and cocurricular programs. The number of students increased from 364 to 421 during her tenure, and she guided the School through many improvements to the campus, including the renovation of the gymnasium, the additions to the library, the creation of new classrooms, and, of course, the impressive building named for her.

A regionally and nationally recognized school leader, Carolyn Peter has continued her active involvement with Winsor and other institutions. She lives in Brookline with her husband, Georges Peter, M.D., and has two children and two grandchildren.

Rachel Friis Stettler

Rachel Friis Stettler is Winsor's seventh Director. She assumed the role in 2004, drawn by a deep belief in the value of girls' education and the dynamic nature of urban schools.

She grew up near New York City, the daughter of a school superintendent. She attended the Wheatley High School on Long Island and earned a merit scholarship to study at Juilliard Preparatory Music School. She went on to receive an A.B. in politics from Princeton University and an M.A. from Parsons School of Design. Awarded a Klingenstein Fellowship, she pursued postgraduate work in educational leadership at Columbia University.

She began her career at Montclair Kimberley Academy in New Jersey, where she was the first woman to join its history department. She went on to teach English, urban studies, and humanities there and to serve as college counselor and admission director. Before coming to Winsor, Rachel Stettler was the principal of Fieldston, the middle and upper divisions of the Ethical Culture Fieldston School in New York City. She also served as the founding director of CITYterm at the Masters' School, a groundbreaking, experience-based semester program for high school juniors.

She has led Winsor through a comprehensive campus-planning process and spurred significant investment in core areas, from academic technology to student support to faculty development, and she has inspired the forward-thinking strategic work that continues to shape teaching and learning at Winsor in the twenty-first century. In addresses and assembly talks, she articulates her sense that Winsor's students bring their whole selves to school. An avid amateur cellist, she performs at Winsor concerts and with Boston-area ensembles and orchestras. In college she was among the pioneering athletes to play women's ice hockey in post–Title IX days, and she has coached varsity swimming and lacrosse.

In considering Winsor's future, Rachel Stettler has said, "What matters is the kind of women our students will become and that their futures are open to boundless possibility."

She is married to a Princeton classmate, David Stettler, who also heads a Boston-area independent school, the Fessenden School, on whose campus they reside. They have two sons.

NOTES

Chapter 1

The chapter subtitle is from Gretchen Waldo 1903, "Lamp of Learning Song." The first epigraph is from Dorothy Appleton Weld 1895, "Looking Back—44 Years," *Winsor Bulletin,* January 1936, Winsor Archives. The second epigraph is from Susan Hallowell Brooks 1901, "Reminiscences." She goes on to say: "In stormy weather we could take 'the Little Green Car' which ran from North Station to Charles Street, right on Beacon, skirting the Public Garden, left on Arlington etc. The little car was pulled on tracks by two horses whose driver stood on the front platform, totally unprotected from the weather. The floor of the car was covered with straw for rainy weather." Manuscript in Winsor Archives.

1   Charles Hamlin to R. Clipston Sturgis, January 1910, Winsor Archives.

2   F. Washington Jarvis, *Schola Illustris* (Boston: David R. Godine, 1995).

3   Thomas H. O'Connor, *Bibles, Brahmins, and Bosses: A Short History of Boston*, 3rd ed. (Boston: Trustees of the Public Library, 1991); Robert Middlekauff, *Ancients and Axioms: Secondary Education in Eighteenth-Century New England* (New Haven: Yale University Press, 1963).

4   Lawrence A. Cremin, *American Education: The Metropolitan Experience, 1876–1980* (New York: Harper and Row, 1988).

5   "The school shall always be maintained as an unsectarian institution." Bylaws, Article XX, Winsor Archives.

6   New England Anti-Slavery Society, *Annual Report and Proceedings* (Boston: Garrison and Knapp, 1833).

7   James O. Horton, "King: Out Front in March for Equality Leader Symbolizes 350-Year Struggle for Black Equality," *Orlando Sentinel,* January 19, 1986.

8   Mary Antin, *The Promised Land* (Boston: Houghton Mifflin, 1912).

9   Oscar Handlin, *Boston's Immigrants, 1790–1865: A Study in Acculturation* (Cambridge: Belknap Press of Harvard University Press, 1941).

10 Cremin, *American Education.*

11 Mary Pickard Winsor's Fiftieth Anniversary Address to the School is printed in the 1936 *Alumnae Bulletin,* Winsor Archives. Hereafter Mary Winsor's address will be referred to as MPWFAA.

12 Ibid.

13 Ibid.

Chapter 2

The first epigraph comes from Eleanor Childs Dodge 1920, Valedictory Speech, *Winsor Lamp,* Graduation Issue, 1920. The second is from Sarah W. Hallowell, speech given at graduation, June 1920.

1   Commission on the Population Growth and the American Future, "Population Growth," in *Population and the American Future* (New York: New American Library, 1972), 9–21.

2   MPWFAA.

3   Ibid.

4   From services held in the Unitarian Church at Winchester: "In Memory of Frederick Winsor, March 10, 1889" (Cambridge: privately printed, 1889), at New York Public Library.

5   Quoted in Hubert C. Fortmiller Jr., *Find the Promise: Middlesex School, 1901–2001* (Concord, Mass.: Middlesex School, 2003). Ann Ware Winsor died in 1907.

6   June Gale, "Generation unto Generation," Winsor Archives.

7   MPWFAA.

8   *Encyclopedia Britannica,* 2009 ed., s.v. "Sarah Fuller," www.britannica.com/EBchecked/topic/221907/Sarah-Fuller.

9   MPWFAA.

10 Claude M. Fuess, "Boston Schools before Winsor," *Winsor Bulletin,* October 1961.

11 These enrollment books are in the Winsor Archives.

12 William Carroll Hill, "Memoirs of the Deceased Members of the New England Historic Genealogical Society," *New England Historical and Genealogical Register* 103 (Boston: Newbury Street Press, 1949).

13 Nina A. Kohn, "Cambridge Law School for Women: The Evolution and Legacy of the Nation's First Law School Exclusively for Women," *Michigan Journal of Gender & Law* 12 (2006).

14 "History of the Winsor School," *Graduate Club Register,* 1910.

15 Ibid.

16 Florence N. Levy, ed., *American Art Directory,* vol. 14 (Washington, D.C.: American Federation of Arts, 1917), s.v. "Loud, May Hallowell," p. 324; http://members.cox.net/academia2/cassatt6e.html#hallowell.

17 Harriet Eliza Paine, *Girls and Women* (Boston: Houghton, Mifflin, 1890). This book can be read online at http://onlinebooks.library.upenn.edu/webbin/book/search?author=harriet+paine&amode=words&title=&tmode=word. The book was published under the pseudonym E. Chester.

18 Leslie White Hopkinson, *Greek Leaders,* ed. William Scott Ferguson (Boston: Houghton Mifflin, 1918).

19 Ibid.

20 "Ella Lyman Cabot," in "Memoirs of Deceased Members of the New England Historic Genealogic Society," *New England Historical and Genealogical Register* 89 (January 1935).

21 Ella Lyman Cabot, *Everyday Ethics* (New York: Henry Holt, 1906).

22 Nancy F. Cott, ed., *No Small Courage: A History of Women in the United States* (New York: Oxford University Press, 2000).

23 Ella Lyman Cabot, *Ethics for Children: A Guide for Teachers and Parents* (Boston: Houghton Mifflin, 1910).

Chapter 3

The subtitle is from MPWFAA: "Too much praise cannot be given its originators for the far-sightedness, the energy, with which they organized and financed [the School]." The first epigraph is from the Report to the Corporation, December 1941. The second is from the Report to the Corporation, December 1964.

1   American Association of University Women, St. Lawrence County, N.Y., branch, *Woman of Courage* profile, www.northnet.org/stlawrenceaauw/college.htm.

2   "John Simmons and the Presidents of Simmons College," www.simmons.edu /library/archives/exhibits/368.php.

3   This story is recounted in Jennifer Price, *Flight Maps: Adventures with Nature in Modern America* (New York: Basic Books, 1999), chap. 2, "When Women Were Women, Men Were Men, and Birds Were Hats"; Jennifer Price, "Hats Off to Audubon," December 2004, http://magazine.audubon.org/features0412/hats.html.

4   Julia A. Sprague, *History of the New England Women's Club from 1868 to 1893* (Boston: Lee and Shepard, 1894).

5   Price, *Flight Maps.*

6   The Hemenway girls were Hope 1905, Charlotte 1907, Hetty 1910, and Mary 1911.

7   The Bradley girls were Amy 1912, Mary 1913, Sarah Merry 1916, and Edith 1921.

8   The article appeared in the *Journal of Home Economics* 4.1 (February 1912).

9   Ibid.

10 Moses Purnell Handy, official catalogue to the World's Columbian Exposition, 1893.

11 John W. C. Carlson, "A Couple of Old Landmarkers," address delivered to the Chicago Literary Club, November 21, 1999, www.chilit.org/Papers%20by%20 author/Carlson%20-%20Landmarkers.HTM. The present R. M. Bradley & Company real estate firm in Boston was started by Richards M. Bradley.

12 See http://oasis.lib.harvard.edu/oasis/deliver/~sch00096.

13 "State of the Arts, 1929–1934," www.nh.gov/nharts/artsandartists/pdf /stateofthearts4.pdf.

14 Susan Hallowell Brooks 1901, "Reminiscences," Winsor Archives.

15 Nora Saltonstall, *"Out Here at the Front": The World War I Letters of Nora Salton-stall*, ed. Judith Graham (Boston: Northeastern University Press, 2004).

16 See chapter 6 for more about these women.

17 Agnes Irwin is quoted in MPW to Charles S. Hamlin, August 1907, Winsor Archives.

18 "Miss Agnes Irwin Dead; First Dean of Radcliffe College Succumbs at 73," *New York Times,* December 6, 1914.

19 Rosemary Skinner Keller, Rosemary Radford Ruether, and Marie Cantlon, eds., *Encyclopedia of Women and Religion in North America*, vol. 2 (Bloomington: Indiana University Press, 2006).

20 Joseph Lee, *Constructive and Preventive Philanthropy* (New York: Macmillan, 1902).

21 Daniel McLean, Amy R. Hurd, and Nancy Brattain Rogers, *Kraus' Recreation and Leisure in Modern Society,* 8th ed. (Sudbury, Mass.: Jones and Bartlett, 2008).

22 "Charles S. Hamlin Papers, 1869–1968," http://hdl.loc.gov/loc.mss/eadmss .ms009205.

23 Huybertie Pruyn Hamlin, *An Albany Girlhood,* ed. Alice P. Kenney (Albany: Washington Park Press, 1990).

24 Pamela W. Fox, "Francis Blake and Charles Wells Hubbard: The 'Eccentric Suburban' and the Quiet Idealist," *WellesleyWeston Online,* May 18, 2010, www.wellesleywestonmagazine.com/summer10/weston_history.htm.

25 MPW to Mrs. R. M. Saltonstall, n.d. [1935], Winsor Achives.

26 Ibid.

27 John N. Ingham, *Biographical Dictionary of American Business Leaders,* vol. 4 (Westport, Conn.: Greenwood Press, 1983), s.v. "Winsor, Robert."

28 Pamela W. Fox, "A 'Quiet and Natural' Place," *WellesleyWeston Online,* February 18, 2009, http://www.wellesleywestonmagazine.com/spring09 /quietandnaturalplace.htm.

29 Ibid.

30 Robert Winsor to MPW, December 4, 1919, Winsor Archives.

31 Carolyn McClintock Peter (hereafter CMP), Report to the Corporation, April 1996, Winsor Archives.

Chapter 4

The quotation in the subtitle comes from the song "Jerusalem" (words by William Blake, music by Sir Hubert Parry), which has been sung at every Winsor graduation since 1928. The last line is "In England's green and pleasant land." The first epigraph is from Mrs. Charles S. Hamlin, "The Building of the Winsor School," Winsor Archives. The second epigraph is from the reminiscence of Elizabeth Saltonstall 1918, *Winsor Bulletin,* 1977.

1 MPWFAA.

2 Ibid.

3 Ibid.

4 Frances Parkinson Keyes, *Roses in December* (Garden City, N.Y.: Doubleday, 1960).

5 MPW to Charles S. Hamlin, n.d. [1909], Winsor Archives.

6 Shelby Cull, "Below Boston's Hills" (Travels in Geology series), *Geotimes,* February 2006, www.geotimes.org/feb06/Travels0206.html.

7 Russell G. Fessenden to Mrs. Robert W. Lovett (wife of an Incorporator), April 25, 1906, Winsor Archives.

8 Hamlin, "The Building of the Winsor School."

9 Ibid.

10 MPW to Charles S. Hamlin, n.d., Winsor Archives.

11 MPW to Mrs. Robert W. Lovett, n.d., Winsor Archives.

12 Charles W. Hubbard to Charles S. Hamlin, April 29, 1908, Winsor Archives. A portion of this letter was inserted in the circular the committee created to attract Boston parents.

13 William A. Newman and Wilfred E. Holton, *Boston's Back Bay: The Story of America's Greatest Nineteenth-Century Landfill Project* (Boston: Northeastern University Press, 2006).

14 Ibid.

15 R. Clipston Sturgis to Charles W. Hubbard, n.d., Winsor Archives.

16　Hamlin, "The Building of the Winsor School."

17　Ibid.

18　This source cannot be confirmed.

19　Hamlin, "The Building of the Winsor School."

20　Ibid.

21　Ibid.

22　Katharine Lord (hereafter KL), Report to the Corporation, 1922–23, Winsor Archives. She added, "For new land the graduates are now working and Mr. Weed has told you the proposal."

23　Ibid.

24　KL, Report to the Corporation, 1923–24, Winsor Archives.

25　"The Finish for Old Longwood," *Boston Globe*, November 17, 1923.

26　The Fitch girls were Catherine 1960, Priscilla 1962, Barbara 1966, and Frances 1968.

27　MPWFAA.

28　Dedication to Mary Mahoney in 1982 yearbook.

29　Winsor Catalogue, 1918–19, Winsor Archives.

30　Charles W. Hubbard to R. Clipston Sturgis, November 10, 1910, Winsor Archives.

Chapter 5

The subtitle comes from Mary Pickard Winsor's speech at the 1910 dedication of the new school. The first epigraph is from Valeria Addams Knapp (VAK), Report to the Corporation, December 1952, and the second is from Virginia Wing (VW), Report to the Corporation, April 1969, both in Winsor Archives.

1　Long Range Curriculum Planning Committee (LRCPC), Report to the Faculty, June 2004, Winsor Archives.

2　Ibid.

3　The complete report can be found at http://tmh.floonet.net/books/commoften/mainrpt.html.

4　Katherine P. English, "The Boston or Long Theme," *Winsor Graduate Bulletin,* 1955.

5　Frances Dorwin Dugan (FDD), Report to the Corporation, December 1929, Winsor Archives.

6　Ibid.

7　KL, Report to the Corporation, April 1932, Winsor Archives.

8　See KL, Reports to the Corporation, 1932 and 1933, Winsor Archives.

9　KL, Report to the Corporation, April 1934, Winsor Archives.

10　Paul Diederich, *Thirty Schools Tell Their Story* (New York: Harper & Brothers, 1943).

11　KL, Report to the Corporation, April 1933, Winsor Archives.

12　Ibid.

13　KL, Report to the Corporation, December 1936, Winsor Archives.

14　Handlin, *Boston's Immigrants.*

15　Middlekauff, *Ancients and Axioms.*

16　Handlin, *Boston's Immigrants.*

17　FDD, Report to the Corporation, December 1940, Winsor Archives.

18 VAK, Report to the Corporation, May 1955, Winsor Archives.

19 FDD, Report to the Corporation, April 1942, Winsor Archives.

20 Ibid.

21 *General Education in School and College: A Committee Report by Members of the Faculties of Andover, Exeter, Lawrenceville, Harvard, Princeton, and Yale* (Cambridge: Harvard University Press, 1952).

22 "Mathematics in School and College," *American Mathematical Monthly* 60.6 (1953).

23 VAK, Report to the Corporation, April 1952, Winsor Archives.

24 Ibid.

25 "The habits of heart and mind" is a concept first articulated by the Coalition of Essential Schools in 1984.

26 FDD, Report to the Corporation, April 1951, Winsor Archives.

27 VAK, Report to the Corporation, April 1952, Winsor Archives.

28 *Winsor Graduate Bulletin,* June 1951, Winsor Archives.

29 VAK, Report to the Corporation, December 1958, Winsor Archives.

30 Private conversation between Virginia Wing and the author.

31 James B. Conant, *Shaping Educational Policy* (New York: McGraw-Hill, 1964).

32 George B. Thomas, *Elements of Calculus and Analytic Geometry* (Reading, Mass.: Addison Wesley, 1959).

33 VW, Report to the Corporation, April 1968, Winsor Archives.

34 Ibid.

35 Science Research Associates (SRA) began publishing instructional materials in the early 1960s. It is now Direct Instruction System for Teaching Arithmetic and Reading (DISTAR). See http://www.sraonline.com.

36 VW, Report to the Corporation, April 1967, Winsor Archives.

37 Report of Long Range Planning Committee, November 1969, Winsor Archives.

38 VW, Report to the Corporation, April 1982, Winsor Archives.

39 Ibid.

40 VW, Report to the Corporation, April 1988, Winsor Archives.

41 Self-Study, 1990, Winsor Archives.

42 CMP, Report to the Corporation, April 1989, Winsor Archives.

43 Report of the Visiting Committee, 1990, Winsor Archives.

44 Winsor School course catalogue, 1987–88, Winsor Archives.

45 Ibid.

46 Report of the Visiting Committee, 1990.

47 CMP, Report to the Corporation, April 1991, Winsor Archives.

48 *How Schools Shortchange Girls: The AAUW Report: A Study of Major Findings on Girls and Education* (Washington, D.C.: AAUW Educational Foundation, 1992).

49 GUTSE was started by the Baldwin School in Baltimore and exists as a forum for spreading information about environmental projects.

50 CMP, Report to the Corporation, April 1990, Winsor Archives.

51 Ibid.

52 The Multicultural Awareness Project was the work of the Multicultural Concerns Committee (MCC) and the Center for Research on Developmental Education and Urban Literacy (CRDEUL), General College, University of Minnesota–Twin Cities; see www.cehd.umn.edu/CRDEUL/pdf/map_it.pdf.

53 CMP, Report to the Corporation, April 1994, Winsor Archives.

54 CMP, Report to the Corporation, April 1996, Winsor Archives.

55 CMP, Report to the Corporations, April 1997, Winsor Archives.

56 Self-Study, 2000, Winsor Archives.

57 From the May 2000 Mission Statement, Winsor Archives.

Chapter 6

The subtitle comes from the 2000 Mission Statement. The first epigraph is from the correspondence of Charles Hamlin, 1908. The second epigraph is from the *Lamp,* February 1924. The third epigraph is from VW, Report to the Corporation, April 1970, all in Winsor Archives.

1   Claire Gaudiani, *The Greater Good: How Philanthropy Drives the American Economy and Can Save Capitalism* (New York: Times/Henry Holt, 2003).

2   FDD, Report to the Corporation, April 1944, Winsor Archives.

3   MPWFAA.

4   KL, Report to the Corporation, April 1932, Winsor Archives.

5   Ibid.

6   Janet Sabine 1921, letter dated September 21, 1921, Winsor Archives.

7   VW, Report to the Corporation, December 1970, Winsor Archives.

8   VW, Report to the Corporation, April 1972, Winsor Archives.

9   VW, Report to the Corporation, April 1964, Winsor Archives.

10 Boyd Rhetta, speech made to the School, 1916, Winsor Archives.

11 "In Aid of Colored Men," *New York Times,* January 21, 1896.

12 Elisabeth Lasch-Quinn, *Black Neighbors: Race and the Limits of Reform in the American Settlement House Movement, 1890–1945* (Chapel Hill: University of North Carolina Press, 1993).

13 Hampton Institute, *What Hampton Graduates Are Doing in Land-Buying, in Home-Making, in Business, in Teaching, in Agriculture, in Establishing Schools, in the Trades, in Church and Missionary Work, in the Professions, 1868–1904* (Hampton, Va.: Hampton Institute Press, 1904).

14 *Scrapbook,* 1906, Winsor Archives.

15 *Winsor Lamp,* February 1916, Winsor Archives.

16 Rhetta, speech made to the School, 1916.

17 Winsor Graduate Club, *The Overseas War Record of the Winsor School, 1914–1919* (Boston: privately printed, 1919).

18 MPWFAA.

19 *Winsor Lamp,* February 1916, Winsor Archives.

20 Winsor Graduate Club, *The Overseas War Record of the Winsor School.*

21 *Winsor Graduate Bulletin,* 1944, Winsor Archives.

22 "Standing Committee of Massachusetts Association Opposed to Further Extension of Suffrage to Women" (1898), Harvard University, Collection Development Department, Widener Library, http://pds.lib.harvard.edu/pds/view/2575235?n=1, sequence 2.

23 Ernest Bernbaum, ed., *Anti-Suffrage Essays by Massachusetts Women* (Boston: Forum Publications, 1916).

24 Mrs. Herbert Lyman, "The Anti-Suffrage Ideal," ibid.

25 *Graduate Club Register,* 1915, Winsor Archives.

26 Jane Addams, speaking in London, May 12, 1915, quoted in Margaret C. Robinson, "Suffrage a Menace to Social Reform," in Bernbaum, *Anti-Suffrage Essays.*

27 David Hackett Fischer, *Liberty and Freedom* (New York: Oxford, 2005).

28 Pamphlet, Winsor Archives.

29 *Winsor Lamp,* Graduation Issue, 1918, Winsor Archives.

30 Ibid.

31 Paula Robbins, "Abigail Adams Eliot," www25.uua.org/uuhs/duub/articles /abigailadamseliot.html.

32 Ibid.

33 Friedrich Fröbel, *Education by Development* (New York: D. Appleton, 1895) and *The Education of Man* (New York: D. Appleton, 1887).

34 Dorothy Canfield Fisher, *Montessori for Parents* (first published as *A Montessori Mother*) (1912; repr., Cambridge, Mass.: Robert Bentley, 1965).

35 See Francesca Morgan 1986, *Women and Patriotism in Jim Crow America* (Chapel Hill: University of North Carolina Press, 2005).

36 *Winsor Lamp,* February 1916, Winsor Archives.

37 "First School Camp for Girl-Scout Leaders Established in Longwood," *Boston Daily Globe,* July 8, 1917.

38 FDD, Report to the Corporation, April 1941, Winsor Archives.

39 FDD, Report to the Corporation, April 1942, Winsor Archives.

40 VW to Edward Yeomans, May 27, 1966, Winsor Archives.

41 Rebecca Palmer Kirk 1972, personal essay, Winsor Archives.

42 VW, Report to the Corporation, April 1966, Winsor Archives.

43 Ibid.

44 John G. Palfrey and C. F. Weed (parents), "Playground Endowment Fund Statement," November 27, 1923, Winsor Archives.

45 KL, Report to the Corporation, April 1935, Winsor Archives.

46 Ibid.

47 Nicholas Danforth, "The Evolution of Annual Giving at Winsor," *Newsletter,* Fall 1966, Winsor Archives.

48 CMP, Report to the Corporation, April 2004, Winsor Archives.

Chapter 7

The subtitle comes from VW, Report to the Corporation, December 1971, Winsor Archives: "This is the strength of an independent school: to meet a child where she is, to work with her so that she becomes the kind of person and the kind of student who will go on learning all of her life." The first epigraph is from FDD, Report to the Corporation, December 1949, and the second is from VW, Report to the Corporation, December 1968, both in Winsor Archives.

1 KL, Report to the Corporation, April 1934, Winsor Archives.

2 KL, Report to the Corporation, December 1937, Winsor Archives.

3 FDD, Report to the Corporation, December 1939, Winsor Archives.

4 FDD, Report to the Corporation, April 1940, Winsor Archives.

5 FDD, Report to the Corporation, April 1942, Winsor Archives.

6 Ibid.

7 VAK, Report to the Corporation, December 1959, Winsor Archives.

8 VAK, Report to the Corporation, December 1957, Winsor Archives.

9   KL, Report to the Corporation, April 1937, Winsor Archives.

10 KL, Report to the Corporation, dated merely 1922–23, Winsor Archives.

11 FDD, Report to the Corporation, April 1941, Winsor Archives.

12 Some are named in the faculty list: Susan Morse 1929, Lydia Evans 1931, Mary Brigham 1933, Eleanor Shaw 1933, Virginia Morss 1936, Margaret (Peggy) Rice 1936, Charlotte Hutchins 1936.

13 KL, Report to the Corporation, April 1933, Winsor Archives.

14 FDD, Report to the Corporation, December 1949, Winsor Archives.

15 Dorothy Davis, "History Revisited: An Interview with Eleanor Roosevelt II," *Education Update Online,* June 2004, www.educationupdate.com/archives/2004 /june/html/spot_history.html.

16 Keyes, *Roses in December.*

17 Alexandra Sterling Cross Moffat 1946, *Winsor Bulletin,* Winter–Spring 2004, Winsor Archives. (All subsequent quotations from this issue are indicated by B-WS.)

18 Lorena "Scottie" Brigham Faerber 1960, B-WS.

19 Ann Hornor Cutter 1945, B-WS.

20 Virginia Wing, quoted in B-WS.

21 Hope Green Arns 1962, B-WS.

22 Vivian Steir Rabin 1977, quoted in B-WS.

23 Emily Perlman Abedon 1986, B-WS.

24 FDD, Report to the Corporation, December 1940, Winsor Archives.

25 Katharine Lawrence 1947, B-WS.

26 Joan L. Griscom 1948, B-WS.

27 Medh Mahony Sichko 1974, B-WS.

28 Debra Watt Fraser 1952, B-WS.

29 Ibid.

30 Cyril Simmons taught math from 1941 to 1943, eventually leaving after marriage to one of the science apprentices, Katherine MacDonald.

31 Deborah Brown Green 1957, letter to *Winsor Bulletin,* Spring 2004, Winsor Archives.

32 Barbara Beatley Anthony 1946, B-WS.

33 Virginia Wing, in her eulogy for Harriet Littlefield, Winsor Archives.

34 Ruth Chute Knapp 1960, B-WS.

35 Caroline Haussermann, undated reminiscences, Winsor Archives.

36 Eiblis Goldings 1981 B-WS.

37 "In Memoriam," http://www.wellesley.edu/PublicAffairs/Illuminator /illuminator399.html#2.

38 Margaret W. Rossiter, *Women Scientists in America: Before Affirmative Action, 1940–1972* (Baltimore: Johns Hopkins University Press, 1995).

39 VW, Report to the Corporation, April 1987, Winsor Archives.

40 See www.lincoln.edu.ar.

41 See Christine Ammer, *Unsung: A History of Women in American Music* (Westport, Conn.: Greenwood Press, 1980).

42 See "Oral History Interview with Elizabeth Saltonstall," November 18, 1981, www.aaa.si.edu/collections/oralhistories/oralhistory/salton81.htm.

43 *A Handbook of American Private Schools* (Boston: Porter Sargent, 1922).

44 VW, Report to the Corporation, December 1976, Winsor Archives.

45 "Edith Park (Edy) Truesdell (1888–1986)," www.askart.com/askart/t/edith_park_truesdell/edith_park_truesdell.aspx. Edith Truesdell had a studio in Brookline and also taught at the Park School.

46 See "David Park," www.sfmoma.org/artists/560, and "David Park," http://fredericsterngallery.com/artists/david-park.

47 "In Memoriam," *Winsor Notations* (newsletter), Spring 1989, Winsor Archives.

48 "Featured Artist: Joanne Kao," *Making the Art Seen,* May 19, 2009, http://as16online.blogspot.com/2009/05/featured-artist-joanna-l-kao.html.

49 *Winsor Bulletin,* May 1949, Winsor Archives.

50 The other founders were Eduarda Boehm and Anne Townsend; see "Camp Merestead," www.hopehist.com/MERESTEAD.html.

51 Carol Haydn-Evans, "Obituary: Margaret Boyd," December 13, 1993, www.independent.co.uk/news/people/obituary-margaret-boyd-1467168.html.

52 Adam Krauss, "Natalie Park, 89, Star of Lacrosse Field, Art Teacher," *Boston Globe,* October 23, 2002, C12.

53 Charles Trout, *Boston, the Great Depression, and the New Deal* (New York: Oxford University Press, 1977). Professor Trout's wife, Katherine Taylor Trout, taught at Winsor from 1964 to 1967, and again from 1976 to 1984.

54 KL, Report to the Corporation, December 1937, Winsor Archives. Frederick J. Deane was president of the Executive Committee from 1936 to 1941.

55 KL, Report to the Corporation, April 1932, Winsor Archives.

56 FDD, Report to the Corporation, December 1950, Winsor Archives.

57 VAK, Report to the Corporation, December 1954, Winsor Archives.

58 VAK, Report to the Corporation, December 1958, Winsor Archives.

59 Now called the Smith College Campus School, it was founded in 1926 and is still a lab school for grades K–8.

60 VW, Report to the Corporation, December 1967, Winsor Archives.

61 Helen Brown 1962, BW-S.

Chapter 8

The first epigraph is from Richard P. Flood, with drawings by Laura Putnam, *The Story of the Noble and Greenough School* (Privately printed, 1966). "Nobles" was founded in 1866 in the Back Bay and occupied 97 and then 100 Beacon Street before moving to Dedham in 1922. The second epigraph is from the *Winsor Lamp,* December 1946. (Some things never change: when the assembly "runs over," teachers lament lost time but students feel otherwise.) The third epigraph is from VW, Report to the Corporation, December 1968.

1 See *The Book-Plates of Dorothy Sturgis Harding,* with text by C. Howard Walker (Boston: Graphic Arts Co., 1920), http://catalog.hathitrust.org /Record /009042149.

2 MPW to Graduate Club, November 22, 1915, Graduate Club Register, 1915, Winsor Archives.

3 Karen Manners Smith, "New Paths to Power," in *No Small Courage: A History of Women in the United States,* ed. Nancy F. Cott (New York: Oxford University Press, 2000).

4   Ibid.

5   *Winsor Lamp,* Graduation Issue, 1929, Winsor Archives.

6   MPW in *Graduate Club Register,* 1910.

7   MPWFAA.

8   Keyes, *Roses in December.*

9   *Winsor Bulletin,* Spring 1951, Winsor Archives.

10 Keyes, *Roses in December.*

11 Ibid.

12 Susan Hallowell, *Graduate Club Register,* 1915, Winsor Archives.

13 *Winsor Lamp*, December 1915.

14 Sharon M. Harris, ed., *Blue Pencils and Hidden Hands: Women Editing Periodicals, 1830–1910* (Boston: Northeastern University Press, 2004).

15 Hetty Hemenway, "Four Days," *Atlantic Monthly* 119 (1917) (published as a novella later that year by Little, Brown), and "Their War," *Atlantic Monthly* 121 (1918).

16 Linda H. Davis, *Onward and Upward: A Biography of Katharine S. White* (New York: Harper & Row, 1987). Katharine White had written *Onward and Upward in the Garden* in 1958.

17 Dorothy Foster Gilman, *The Bloom of Youth* (Boston: Small, Maynard, 1916).

18 See the online finding aid for her papers in the Schlesinger Library, http://oasis .lib.harvard.edu/oasis/deliver/~sch00699.

19 Helen Morton 1916, *Highlights: 80 Years Worth Living* (Falmouth, Me.: Kennebec River Press, 1990).

20 Keyes, *Roses in December.*

21 Nancy Hale, *A New England Girlhood* (Boston: Little, Brown, 1958).

22 Elizabeth Saltonstall 1918, "Through the Looking Glass" *Winsor Bulletin,* 1977, Winsor Archives.

23 *Winsor Lamp,* June 1917, Winsor Archives.

24 Winsor Catalogue, 1913–14, Winsor Archives.

25 Mary Hill Coolidge 1917, "Through the Looking Glass," *Winsor Bulletin,* 1977, Winsor Archives.

26 Ibid.

27 *Class Book,* 1922, Winsor Archives.

28 KL, Report to the Corporation, 1923–24, Winsor Archives.

29 *Winsor Lamp,* February 1935, Winsor Archives.

30 Hannah Hoyt 2008, "Winsor's Lost and Forgotten Tradition: Fifes and Drums," *Panel,* December 7, 2007 (the *Panel* is a paper Winsor girls publish jointly with boys from Belmont Hill School). The Eastern Independent League began to include competitions between girls' teams in 1985: www.lca.edu/uploaded/PDFs /Athletics/EIL_History.pdf.

31 "Education and Title IX," www.now.org/issues/title_ix/index.html.

32 Quoted in Tara Parker Pope, "As Girls Become Women, Sports Pay Dividends," http://well.blogs.nytimes.com/2010/02/15/as-girls-become-women-sports-pay-dividends/#more-24259.

33 Jane H. Hunter, *How Young Ladies Became Girls: The Victorian Origins of American Girlhood* (New Haven: Yale University Press, 2002).

34 *Winsor Scrapbook,* editorial, 1913, Winsor Archives.

35 The School City is more fully described in Wilson L. Gill, *The Gill System of Moral and Civic Training* (New Paltz, N.Y.: Patriotic League, 1901). The other system is outlined in a booklet entitled *Democratic Government of Schools,* by John T. Ray, principal of the John Crerar Grammar School (Chicago, 1899).

36 Dorothy Thomas, "Susan Brandeis Gilbert," *Jewish Women: A Comprehensive Historical Encyclopedia* (2005), Jewish Women's Archive, http://jwa.org/encyclopedia/article/gilbert-susan-brandeis.

37 Amy Butler, "Elizabeth Brandeis Raushenbush," *Jewish Women: A Comprehensive Historical Encyclopedia* (2005), Jewish Women's Archive, http://jwa.org/encyclopedia/article/raushenbush-elizabeth-brandeis.

38 VAK, Report to the Corporation, April 1956, Winsor Archives.

39 Ibid.

40 VW, Report to the Corporation, December 1972, Winsor Archives.

41 Ibid.

42 *Winsor Newsletter,* June 1974, Winsor Archives.

43 Medieval pageant folder, Winsor Archives.

44 See chap. 7 for more on Florence Cunningham.

45 Rose Dresser to "Elizabeth(?)," n.d., Winsor Archives.

46 *Winsor Lamp,* Graduation Issue, 1932, Winsor Archives.

47 Glenda Frank, "Theresa Helburn," *Jewish Women: A Comprehensive Historical Encyclopedia* (2005), Jewish Women's Archive, http://jwa.org/encyclopedia/article/helburn-theresa.

48 See Ellis Memorial & Eldredge House, "History," www.ellismemorial.org/history.

49 *Winsor Lamp,* April 1927, Winsor Archives.

50 Alice W. Shurcliff, "Local Economic Impact of Nuclear Power Plants," http://hdl.handle.net/1721.1/27276.

51 "Program in Business Administration. Records of the Harvard-Radcliffe Program in Business Administration, 1936–1977 (Inclusive), 1936–1963 (Bulk): A Finding Aid," http://oasis.lib.harvard.edu/oasis/deliver/~sch01121.

52 The full article is available at http://journeytohistory.com/History110/Readings2.html.

53 *Scrapbook,* 1906, Winsor Archives.

54 *Winsor Lamp,* February 1926, Winsor Archives.

55 *Winsor Lamp,* Graduation Issue, 1926, Winsor Archives.

BIBLIOGRAPHY

Alcott, Louisa May. *Diana and Persis,* ed. Sarah Elbert. New York: Arno, 1978.

Ammers, Christine. *Unsung: A History of Women in American Music.* Westport, Conn.: Greenwood Press, 1980.

Antin, Mary. *The Promised Land.* Boston: Houghton, Mifflin, 1912.

Axtell, James. *The School upon a Hill: Education and Society in Colonial New England.* New York: W. W. Norton, 1976.

Benfey, Christopher. *The Great Wave: Gilded Age Misfits, Japanese Eccentrics, and the Opening of Old Japan.* New York: Random House, 2003.

*Billings, Katharine Stevens (Fowler). *The Gold Missus: A Woman Prospector in Sierra Leone.* New York: W. W. Norton, 1938.

Bundy, Carol. *The Nature of Sacrifice: A Biography of Charles Russell Lowell, Jr., 1835–64.* New York: Farrar, Straus and Giroux, 2005.

*Cabot, Ella Lyman. *Ethics for Children: A Guide for Teachers and Parents.* Boston: Houghton Mifflin, 1910.

———. *Everyday Ethics.* New York: Henry Holt, 1906.

*Coolidge, Mary Perkins. *Once I Was Very Young.* 1960. Reprint. Portsmouth, N.H.: Peter E. Randall, 2000.

Cott, Nancy F., ed., *No Small Courage: A History of Women in the United States.* New York: Oxford University Press, 2000.

Cremin, Lawrence A. *American Education: The Metropolitan Experience, 1876–1980.* New York: Harper & Row, 1988.

Davis, Allen F. *Spearheads for Reform: The Social Settlements and the Progressive Movement, 1890–1914.* New York: Oxford University Press, 1967.

Davis, Linda H. *Onward and Upward: A Biography of Katharine S. White.* New York: Harper & Row, 1987.

DeBare, Ilana. *Where Girls Come First.* New York: Tarcher/Penguin, 2004.

Ehrenreich, Barbara, and Deirdre English. *For Her Own Good: 150 Years of the Experts' Advice to Women.* Garden City, N.Y.: Anchor, 1978.

Fisher, Dorothy Canfield. *Montessori for Parents.* 1912. Reprint. Cambridge, Mass.: Robert Bentley, 1965.

———. *The Squirrel-Cage.* New York: Henry Holt, 1912.

Flood, Richard T., with drawings by *Laura Putnam. *The Story of Noble and Greenough School, 1866–1966.* Privately printed, 1966.

Fortmiller, Hubert C., Jr. *Find the Promise: Middlesex School, 1901–2001.* Concord, Mass.: Middlesex School, 2003.

Fröbel, Friedrich. *Education by Development.* New York: D. Appleton, 1895.

———. *The Education of Man.* New York: D. Appleton, 1887.

Frothingham, Eugenia Brooks. *The Finding of Norah.* Boston: Houghton Mifflin, 1918.

*Indicates a Winsor graduate or faculty member.

Gaudini, Claire. *The Greater Good: How Philanthropy Drives the American Economy and Can Save Capitalism.* New York: Times/Henry Holt, 2003.

Gilman, Dorothy Foster. *The Bloom of Youth.* Boston: Small, Maynard, 1916.

Graham, Elinor Mish. *The Story of Hetty Hemenway Richard: A Journey Worth the Taking.* [New York]: Privately printed, 1964.

Green, Martin. *The Problem of Boston.* New York: W. W. Norton, 1966.

Halberstam, David. *The Fifties.* New York: Villard Books, 1993.

*Hale, Nancy. *A New England Girlhood.* Boston: Little, Brown, 1958.

Handlin, Oscar. *Boston's Immigrants, 1790–1865: A Study in Acculturation.* Cambridge, Mass.: Belknap Press of Harvard University Press, 1941.

Harris, Sharon, ed. *Blue Pencils and Hidden Hands: Women Editing Periodicals, 1830–1910.* Boston: Northeastern University Press, 2004.

Hentoff, Nat. *Boston Boy.* New York: Alfred A. Knopf, 1986.

Herbst, Jurgen. *The Once and Future School: Three Hundred and Fifty Years of American Secondary Education.* New York: Routledge, 1996.

*Homans, Abigail Adams. *Education by Uncles.* Boston: Houghton Mifflin, 1966.

Howells, William Dean. *The Rise of Silas Lapham.* Boston: Houghton Mifflin, 1884.

Hunter, Jane H. *How Young Ladies Became Girls: The Victorian Origins of American Girlhood.* New Haven, Conn.: Yale University Press, 2002.

Jarvis, F. Washington. *Schola Illustris.* Boston: David R. Godine, 1995.

*Keyes, Frances Parkinson. *Roses in December.* Garden City, N.Y.: Doubleday, 1960.

Kreiger, Alex, David A. Cobb, and Amy Turner, eds. *Mapping Boston.* Cambridge, Mass.: MIT Press 1999.

Lasch-Quinn, Elisabeth. *Black Neighbors: Race and the Limits of Reform in the American Settlement House Movement, 1890–1945.* Chapel Hill: University of North Carolina Press, 1993.

Lee, Joseph, and Jacob Riis. *Constructive and Preventive Philanthropy.* New York: Macmillan, 1902.

Lemons, J. Stanley. *The Woman Citizen: Social Feminism in the 1920s.* Champaign: University of Illinois Press, 1973.

Lukas, J. Anthony. *Common Ground: A Turbulent Decade in the Lives of Three American Families.* New York: Alfred A. Knopf, 1985.

Mattingly, Carol. *Appropriate[ing] Dress: Women's Rhetorical Style in Nineteenth-Century America.* Carbondale: University of Southern Illinois Press, 2002.

McLean, Daniel, et al. *Kraus' Recreation and Leisure in Modern Society,* 8th ed. Sudbury, Mass.: Jones and Bartlett, 2008.

Merrill, Marlene Deahl. *Growing Up in Boston's Gilded Age.* New Haven, Conn.: Yale University Press, 1990.

Meyer, Howard N., ed. *The Magnificent Activist: The Writing of Thomas Wentworth Higginson, 1823–1911.* Cambridge, Mass.: Da Capo Press, 2000.

Middlekauff, Robert. *Ancients and Axioms: Secondary Education in Eighteenth-Century New England.* New Haven, Conn.: Yale University Press, 1963.

Miller, Perry. *The New England Mind: The Seventeenth Century.* Boston: Beacon Press, 1939.

*Morgan, Francesca. *Women and Patriotism in Jim Crow America.* Chapel Hill: University of North Carolina Press, 2005.

Morgenroth, Lynda. *Boston Firsts: 40 Feats of Innovation and Invention That Happened First in Boston and Helped Make America Great.* Boston: Beacon Press, 2006.

*Morton, Helen. *Highlights: 80 Years Worth Living.* Falmouth, Me.: Kennebec River Press, 1990.

Newman, William A., and Wilfred E. Holton. *Boston's Back Bay: The Story of America's Greatest Nineteenth-Century Landfill Project.* Boston: Northeastern University Press, 2006.

O'Connor, Thomas H. *Bibles, Brahmins, and Bosses: A Short History of Boston,* 3rd ed. Boston: Trustees of the Public Library, 1991.

*Paine, Harriet E. (Harriet Eliza). *Girls and Women.* Boston: Houghton, Mifflin, 1890.

Pease, Jane H., and William H. Pease. *Ladies, Women, and Wenches: Choice and Constraint in Antebellum Charleston and Boston.* Chapel Hill: University of North Carolina Press, 1990.

*Rotch, Lydia. *Hilltop Farm.* Privately printed, 1929.

Rousmaniere, John P. "Cultural Hybrid in the Slums: The College Woman and the Settlement House, 1889–1894." *American Quarterly* 22 (Spring 1970): 45–66.

*Saltonstall, Nora. *"Out Here at the Front": The World War I Letters of Nora Saltonstall,* ed. Judith Graham. Boston: Northeastern University Press, 2004.

Sarna, J. D., E. Smith, and S.-M. Kosofsky, eds. *The Jews of Boston.* New Haven, Conn.: Yale University Press, 2005.

Schlesinger, Arthur M., Jr. *The Age of Jackson.* Boston: Little, Brown, 1945.

Selleck, George A. *Quakers in Boston, 1656–1964: Three Centuries of Friends in Boston and Cambridge.* Cambridge, Mass.: Friends Meeting at Cambridge, 1976.

Sizer, Theodore R. *The Age of the Academies.* New York: Columbia University Press, 1964.

Small, Walter Herbert. *Early New England Schools.* Boston: Ginn, 1914.

Solomon, Barbara Miller. *In the Company of Educated Women.* New Haven: Yale University Press, 1985.

Sprague, Julia A. *History of the New England Women's Club from 1868 to 1893.* Boston: Lee and Shepard, 1894.

Thayer, Helen Rand. "Aim in College Settlement Work Is toward Sharing Good Things." Unidentified newspaper clipping, 1910, Denison House files, Schlesinger Library, Radcliffe Institute.

Trout, Charles. *Boston, the Great Depression, and the New Deal.* New York: Oxford University Press, 1977.

Weidensaul, Scott. *Of a Feather: A Brief History of American Birding.* New York: Harcourt, 2007.

*White, Katharine S. *Onward and Upward in the Garden.* Boston: Beacon Press, 1958.

Whitehill, Walter Muir, and Lawrence W. Kennedy. *Boston: A Topographical History,* 3rd ed. Cambridge, Mass.: Harvard University Press, 2000.

Woods, Robert A., ed. *Americans in Process: A Settlement Study.* Boston: Houghton, Mifflin, 1902.

———. *The City Wilderness: A Settlement Study.* Boston: Houghton, Mifflin, 1898.

Woods, Robert A., and Albert J. Kennedy, eds. *Handbook of Settlements.* New York: Arno, 1911.

Zaitzevsky, Cynthia. *Frederick Law Olmsted and the Boston Park System.* Cambridge, Mass.: Harvard University Press, 1982.

INDEX

~ INDEX ~